THE EFFECTIVE TEACHER SERIES

THE LEGAL CONTEXT OF TEACHING

NEVILLE HARRIS

WITH PENELOPE PEARCE AND SUSAN JOHNSTONE

LONGMAN
London and New York

Longman Group UK Limited
Longman House, Burnt Mill, Harlow,
Essex CM20 2JE, England
and Associated Companies throughout the world.

*Published in the United States of America
by Longman Inc., New York*

First published 1992

British Library Cataloguing in Publication Data

Harris, N.S. (Neville S.) *1954–*
    The legal context of teaching. - (The Effective teacher series).
    1. England. Schools. Teaching. Law
    Title II. Pearce, Penelope III. Johnstone, Susan IV. Series
    344.20478

Library of Congress Cataloging-in-Publication Data

Harris, Neville S., 1954-
    The legal context of teaching / Neville Harris with Penelope Pearce and Susan
Johnstone.
    p. cm. — (The Effective teacher series)
    Includes bibliographical references and index.
    ISBN 0-582-03956-8
    1. Teachers—Legal status, laws, etc.—Great Britain.
    2. Educational law and legislation—Great Britain. I. Pearce, Penelope. II. Johnstone,
Susan. III. Title. IV. Series.
    KD3636.H37 1991
    344.41'078--dc20
    [344.10478]
                                        90-21978
    CIP

Set in 10/11 point Times
Printed in Malaysia
by Vinlin Press Sdn. Bhd.,
Sri Petaling, Kuala Lumpur

13.99

This book is to be re*

The Legal Context Of Teaching

THE EFFECTIVE TEACHER SERIES

General editor: Elizabeth Perrott

CONTENTS

EDITOR'S PREFACE

This new series was inspired by my book on the practice of teaching (*Effective Teaching: a practical guide to improving your teaching*, Longman, 1982), written for trainee teachers wishing to improve their teaching skills as well as for in-service teachers, especially those engaged in the supervision of trainees. The books in this series have been written with the same readership in mind. However, the busy classroom teacher will find that these books also serve their needs as changes in the nature and pattern of education make the inservice training of experienced teachers more essential than in the past.

The rationale behind the series is that professional courses for teachers require the coverage of a wide variety of subjects in a relatively short time. So the aim of the series is the production of 'easy to read', practical guides to provide the necessary subject background, supported by references to guide and encourage further reading, together with questions and/or exercises devised to assist application and evaluation.

As specialists in their selected fields, the authors have been chosen for their ability to relate their subjects to the needs of teachers and to stimulate discussion of contemporary issues in education.

The series aims to cover subjects ranging from the theory of education to the teaching of mathematics and from primary school teaching and educational psychology to effective teaching with information technology. It will look at aspects of education as diverse as education and cultural diversity and pupil welfare and counselling. Although some subjects, such as the legal context of teaching and the teaching of history are specific to England and Wales, the majority of subjects such as assessment in education, the effective teaching of statistics and comparative education, are international in scope.

Elizabeth Perrott

AUTHORS' PREFACE

There is a legal framework to the provision of all public services, and education now has one of the most all-embracing and complex of them all. The Education Reform Act 1988 and the legislation linked to it have undoubtedly raised teachers' awareness of the legal environment to their professional practice. Teachers will be most acutely aware that the reforms wrought by this legislation, and by previous Conservative legislation of the 1980s, are effecting comprehensive structural changes to educational provision in England and Wales. They are also playing a part in the changes to the nature of teaching as a profession. Many of the legislative reforms have proved contentious, and often controversial – increased 'parent power', the National Curriculum with its prescribed content and assessment arrangements, 'opting-out', financial delegation (LMS), Christian collective worship, the abolition of corporal punishment, and so on. This book aims, therefore, not simply to present a factual statement of the main areas of law affecting teachers, but also to raise critical awareness of some of the problems to which the law gives rise in practice and of the key policy issues underlying the legal changes.

Education law is now a very broad subject, incorporating various specialist areas of law – possibly too much for any one individual to cover authoritatively. Thus, whilst much of the book was written by Neville Harris (Chapters 1–4 and 6–8), chapters on two specialist areas, confidentiality/access to information (Chapter 5) and employment law (Chapter 9), have been contributed by Penelope Pearce and Susan Johnstone respectively.

Neville Harris
Penelope Pearce
Susan Johnstone   July 1991

CHAPTER 1

The legal environment

THE NEW CLIMATE OF REGULATION IN EDUCATION

A meeting is taking place at a comprehensive school between Tony, head of religious education, and Kate, equal opportunities co-ordinator:

Tony: It says clearly in the 1988 Act that collective worship must be 'wholly or mainly of a broadly Christian character'.

Kate: Exactly – *'wholly or mainly'*. Surely this means that other faiths can be catered for as well? Also, it says in the Act that in any school term *'most'* acts of worship must be Christian in character, but not *every* one needs to be.

Tony: Well, it says in the Circular that *'the majority'* of acts have to be Christian.

Kate: What does *'the majority'* mean – 51 per cent or 99 per cent? Anyway, you're getting hung up on this word 'Christian'. The Act says that worship must reflect the 'broad traditions' of Christianity but should not be 'distinctive of any particular religious denomination'.

Tony: You're right, but what about the part that talks about the ways in which the 'broad traditions of Christian belief' are to be reflected in the act of worship. It says that this should depend on the family backgrounds of the pupils. Most of our kids have Church of England parents. The Circular says that the faith of the family is relevant here.

Kate: We're back to that word 'most' again!

Tony: Yes, and let me refer you to another one – 'many'. The Act says that the head can ask the local statutory advisory committee on RE to lift or modify the Christian collective worship requirements for us. The Circular says that this might happen where 'many' pupils in a class or group belong to a faith or religion other than a Christian one. It could be lifted for the whole school or just these pupils. I'm not sure that we have 'many' non-C of E kids. But anyway, don't forget that parents may withdraw their children from assembly on religious grounds.

Kate: Hm . . . a lot of this sounds rather divisive . . .

Tony: . . . and complex.

Kate: Yes, and I'm still not sure exactly what 'worship' means.

Tony: The Act doesn't define it. (*He then reaches for the* Shorter Oxford English Dictionary, *opens it, peruses it briefly and continues.*) It says here that to worship means 'To honour or revere as a supernatural being or power or as a holy thing'.

Kate: Oh my God!

Tony: Exactly, Kate.

Debates like the above fictitious one have doubtless been conducted, perhaps with not always quite the same level of intensity, up and down the country ever since the Education Reform Act (ERA) 1988 was enacted (in July 1988). (The requirements about Christian collective worship came into force on 1 August 1989.) Teachers like Tony and Kate are increasingly having to grapple with the complexities of statute law. For most teachers, this is a largely unprecedented task. But the case for teachers acquainting themselves with the legal context of teaching is now completely irrefutable. The process of familiarisation should ideally begin during initial training, when a critical and practical approach can be taken. It should continue as part of in-service education and training, when specific aspects of the legal environment, and changes in the law, can be focused upon. Unfortunately, neither such training, nor books like this one can provide all the answers to the legal questions raised daily by events in schools. But in the application of law it is just as important to identify the questions as it is to know the answers.

The volume of law relevant to education has increased dramatically over the past few years, as a result of the ERA 1988 and the fifty-plus sets of Regulations and Orders made in pursuance of parts of this legislation. These reforms, and indeed those before them in the 1980s, have had an enormous impact on the administration and practice of education in England and Wales. (Separate reforms have occurred in Scotland.) The legislation has made the education system as heavily regulated as any other concerned with the welfare of citizens – old or young. Successive Acts of Parliament promoted by the Conservative governments of the 1980s and culminating in the 1988 Act have instituted a new regime for the provision of education, reshaping all the key areas, such as school government, the financial management of schools, school admissions and the curriculum. Under banners such as 'accountability' and 'quality', the Conservatives have incrementally shifted power away from local education authorities (LEAs) and into the hands of school governing bodies and, indirectly, parents.

The new climate of regulation and consumerism in education is affecting not only the traditional target of legal reform in education – administration – but also the day-to-day life of every schoolteacher in the state sector. For this reason, practising and trainee teachers need to join the ranks of those already engaged in a quest for knowledge and understanding of the new legal environment – such as school governors and head teachers. But these goals can prove somewhat elusive. The law is detailed, complex, subject to rapid and piecemeal amendment and diverse in its sources, as will be shown later. Indeed, there might, perhaps, be a tendency among some classroom teachers to leave to others, especially senior management, the difficult and time-consuming job of familiarisation with the law. Even the latter group might be dissuaded from this task by an awareness that even where the law is certain (and it frequently is not), its correct application may not be. As Lord Justice Stephenson said in one case, 'It is quite clear what the duty of an education authority and of its teachers is; the difficulty is to apply the law correctly to the facts of any particular case'.[1]

The above statement is contained in a judgment in a case concerned with the alleged negligence of a teacher. This is an area of education law which has attracted some attention from legal writers over the years.[2] Allegations of negligence arising out of the tragedies during school trips to Land's End and the Austrian Alps, and the *Van Oppen* case[3] arising out of a crippling injury to a pupil during a game of rugby, have served to raise awareness of the legal context of teaching in a most forcible fashion.

Even long-established areas of the law, like negligence, are constantly developing. Indeed, it is important to realise that the pace of legal change is increasingly rapid. At the turn of the 1980s, much of the 1944 Education Act was still in place. Now, even provisions like those dealing with school attendance are being amended to reflect changes in policy. Legislation of wider application, such as the Data Protection Act 1984 and recent Employment Acts, have also changed the legal context of teaching. For those entering the teaching profession, and those with some years' service, coping with the new legal environment is, to say the least, challenging. It is, of course, part of the overall climate of change which is putting teachers under so much pressure at the present time.

The new recruit to the profession will be affected by many of the new laws even before s/he enters the classroom as a salaried teacher for the first time. The ERA 1988, like previous legislation, enables the Secretary of State to lay down rules on who may or may not teach in the state sector. Regulations – (currently the Education (Teachers) Regulations 1989) – set out the requirements concerning qualified teacher status, the employment of unqualified teachers (for example, under the new 'licensed teacher' scheme), probationary periods and so on. Teachers' pay and conditions are laid down via ministerial Order made under the Teachers' Pay and Conditions Act. In 1987 Parliament ended the previous system of collective bargaining on these matters. (A pay review body will soon be introduced, however – see chapter 9.) Recent legislation, the ERA 1988, has altered the arrangements for financial management of schools, giving delegated budgets to school governing bodies. Along with this budget has come a power of appointment of staff. (In schools without delegated budgets, the changes with regard to staff appointments made by the Education (No.2) Act 1986, continue to apply.) A further part of the legal context to the appointment of our new recruit is the fact that legislation may well have created the employment opportunity for the teacher concerned in the first place. The newly-appointed teacher will probably have been selected because his/her subject specialism or specialist skills are needed by the school in furtherance of its obligations concerning the curriculum – expertise in a National Curriculum foundation subject (or subjects) or religious education (the ERA 1988), or ability to teach children with particular learning difficulties (Education Act 1981).

The importance for teachers of gaining an understanding of the legal context of teaching may appear self-evident, because the law has a major bearing on how schools are run and on what takes place in institutions. A teacher who seeks a change in a particular practice in a school needs to understand the hierarchy of legal authority within the education system. More particularly, the teacher needs to know who is legally responsible for, or able to exert control over, the various aspects of school life which are relevant, as most are, to his or her role. The teacher should also be aware of the appropriate forum for decision making; often nowadays it is the school governors' meeting, but in some cases the law permits decisions to be delegated to the head teacher or a sub-committee of the governors.

Sometimes, educators must bow to parental pressure. One reason for becoming appraised of the law is to know when parents' views must prevail. Parents now have a battery of rights in education; many of the key rights are procedural rather than substantive, such as rights to be consulted and rights of appeal, but all are becoming increasingly important. A parent can demand to see the schemes of work being followed in his or her child's class, can insist on inspecting the child's school record and can ask for it to be amended if s/he regards it as inaccurate and the school agrees, can withdraw his/her child from religious education and collective worship, can refuse to pay for his/her child's participation in a school trip and most other types of provision, can complain via a local statutory complaints procedure about any curricular matter and in some cases can appeal in respect of disciplinary measures taken against his/her child. In due course parents will acquire further rights in respect of their child's assessment under the National Curriculum. Parents whose children have special educational needs have many further rights (under the Education Act 1981). There are, however, many gaps in this network of parental rights, as will be shown in due course.

How can teachers cope with the new climate of regulation? To start with, it is essential to ascertain the true nature and extent of the classroom teacher's personal autonomy within the new legal framework. Some teachers may regard themselves as straitjacketed by, for example, the requirements concerning the National Curriculum and, indeed, the curriculum in general. This is discussed in Chapter 6. Of course, most professions have to work in a closely regulated environment, including medics, lawyers, accountants and social workers. As in these professions, teachers will find that much will still be left in practice to the personal judgement and commitment of individuals. Indeed, teachers may in reality enjoy more professional freedom than other groups. Furthermore, the possibility of teachers being the subject of legal proceedings is also smaller. Paranoia may well have swept the teaching profession following each of the tragic incidents relating to pupils referred to above, prompting many teachers to avoid outings and more dangerous physical pursuits for pupils; but doctors and nurses face the risk of causing injury to patients every minute of each day of their professional lives, and everyday decisions by social workers can be of critical significance *vis-à-vis* the health and welfare of children. This is not to underplay the importance of the legal context of teaching, but rather to encourage teachers to accept that it is possible to function professionally in a more regulated environment than has prevailed hitherto.

But it is important to avoid falling into the trap of taking too simplistic a view of the new rights and responsibilities in education. Such rights and responsibilities should rarely be regarded as unequivocal. Whilst there is undoubtedly an impetus towards achieving a clearer definition of what is expected from the education service – for example, in relation to the curriculum[4] – the government itself acknowledges the lack of clarity. For example, the DES Circular outlining the rules on charging for education emphasises that an objective behind the new rules was clarification of the law; equally, it acknowledges that 'a definitive interpretation is a matter for the courts and its application is dependent on the circumstances of each individual case'.[5] No wonder that in view of the uncertainty surrounding the new rules on charging many school trips were 'lost in thick legal fog'.[6] There is also the danger that teachers may be misled into believing that the law offers more certainty but also more discretion than is actually the case. Take, for example, the new regulations governing the keeping, transfer and disclosure of school records – the Education (School Records) Regulations 1989. The government has advised schools that the Regulations do not prescribe how records should be kept or what they should contain. But the guidance goes on to state that each pupil record 'must include material on the pupil's academic achievements, other skills and abilities and progress in school', to be updated once a year.[7] Apparent contradiction of this kind is distinctly unhelpful.

One way in which, it is hoped, new teachers may be helped to cope with this new era of regulation is by reading this book! It is not intended to offer a detailed guide to the law – the mass of legal rules which have deluged and transformed the education system over recent years cannot be covered in their entirety in a work of this nature. What *is* offered, however, is a critical overview, aimed to stimulate awareness and discussion of the law as it affects the teacher. There is some selectivity, but all the key areas are covered. Uncertainty or complexity in the law is not disguised for the sake of straightforward comprehension, although simplicity and clarity have been aimed for wherever possible. As many areas of education law deal with politically controversial issues, such as schools opting out of local authority control and becoming grant-maintained, the policy context cannot be, and is not, ignored.

THE NATURE AND SOURCES OF REGULATION

In the 1980s four major Education Acts were passed. Acts of Parliament, otherwise known as statutes, are the principal instruments of education reform, establishing a new legal framework for provision. During the twentieth century there has been phenomenal growth in the volume and range of social legislation covering diverse fields – not only education but also social security, housing, health services and the protection of children. Most governmental activity in these fields, whether central or local, is carried out within a statutory framework.[8] So extensive have the government's economic and social reforms, including those to the education system, been during the 1980s, that it comes as little surprise that the volume of new laws per annum during the Thatcher years doubled that passed by the last Labour government – for example, 2,984 pages a year between 1984 and 1986, compared with 1,401 between 1977 and 1979.[9]

Acts of Parliament begin as bills, which have to progress through the various stages of debate and possible amendment in both Houses (Commons and Lords) before they can pass on for the Royal Assent. The notion of 'Parliamentary sovereignty', which has been a feature of the British constitution for the past 300 years, implies that it is Parliament's will that is embodied in each statute. Such may be the constitutional position; but the reality is usually that 'Parliament merely legitimates what the government has proposed'.[10] However, although most bills are government measures, individual MPs or members of the Lords can influence the final form of an Act as it passes through Parliament as a bill; in some cases they will propose amendments which, if accepted by a majority (or if unopposed) can be incorporated into the legislation. The provisions relating to Christian collective worship in the ERA 1988 were the result of a House of Lords' amendment. MPs may also promote private members' bills, although they generally have little chance of enactment without government backing. A number of attempts to abolish corporal punishment in state schools were made under private members' bills, before the government's Education (No.2) Act 1986 outlawed it.

A statute in its enacted form will consist of a number of sections and, in the case of a more substantial Act, several schedules (at the end of the Act, after the last section). Often a section of the Act is divided into sub-sections and perhaps paragraphs and sub-paragraphs within the sub-section. For example, section 2, sub-section (1), paragraph (a) (cited as section 2(1)(a)) of the ERA 1988 is set out as follows:

2 – (1) The curriculum for every maintained school shall comprise a basic

curriculum which includes –
(a) provision for religious education for all registered pupils at the school;

The precise meaning of the words in a statute is not always clear from the words themselves. At various points, either at the end of a part of an Act, or in an interpretation section near the end of an Act, certain words or phrases appearing in the statute will be defined. If we want to know what is meant by 'maintained school' in section 2(1)(a) above, we could refer to the definition in section 25(1) of the Act. But for some purposes that definition will be different. When the phrase 'maintained school' is used in section 6 of the Act, its meaning is not the one in section 25(1) but the different one given in section 6(7). Such complexity sometimes is unavoidable, but at other times may result from poor draftsmanship – judges and commentators frequently complain about this.[11] If the statute offers no definition to aid construction, the meaning may have to be determined by the courts, should the matter be brought before them (see below).

Social legislation like the ERA 1988 frequently contains provisions granting legislative powers to the appropriate Secretary of State. Any legislation made under such a power is known as delegated or secondary legislation. It differs from primary legislation – statutes – in two important respects. First, although it may have to be laid before, and in some cases approved by, Parliament – if the statutory provision granting the power so requires – it does not have to pass through an elaborate procedure before becoming law. Ministers may make or amend statutory instruments (orders or regulations) quickly. For example, the Education (School Premises) Regulations 1981 were amended in 1989 by the Education (School Premises) (Amendment) Regulations. The 1981 Regulations seek to ensure that school premises offer appropriate facilities for the pupils who will use them. The Amendment Regulations have extended the scope of the 1981 Regulations to grant-maintained schools; that is, those which have been allowed to opt out of local authority control. The Amendment Regulations were made on 25 July 1989, under section 10 of the EA 1944 which also empowered the making of the 1981 Regulations; they were laid before Parliament three days later, and came into force on 1 September 1989. The process leading to enactment of a bill by contrast takes many months to complete.

The second important difference between a statutory instrument and a statute is that the legality of the former but not of the latter may be questioned by a court. The unchallengeability of a statute is a facet of the doctrine of Parliamentary sovereignty, referred to earlier. (It should be noted that if there is a conflict between the EC Treaty and a statute, the courts have said that the former should prevail.[12]) The validity of a statutory instrument may, however, only be questioned on a number of specific grounds which relate either to the procedure by which it was made or to the scope of the enabling power in the parent statute.

An increasing proportion of education law now takes the form of delegated legislation, which, it should be stressed, is equally as binding as statutes. Over 40 statutory instruments relevant to schools were issued in 1989. It is convenient for ministers to be able to change the detail of a particular scheme quickly and without having to steer an amendment bill through Parliament. Furthermore, much delegated legislation is of a technical nature and is uncontroversial – so there would be little interest in Parliament (which, in any event, keeps a watchful eye over such legislation via its Joint Select Committee on Statutory Instruments) and no need to expend valuable parliamentary time on the provision in question. Nevertheless, many of the legislative powers granted by Parliament nowadays are quite far-reaching – including, in some cases, a power to, in effect, amend the law as laid down in an Act. Constitutional lawyers have expressed concern at this practice, which is regarded as conferring too much legislative power on the Executive.

The ERA 1988 contains a large number of legislative powers, far more than any previous Education Act. Section 218, for example, contains about 20 such powers. A particularly striking example of a far-reaching power appears in section 3 of the 1988 Act, which deals with the National Curriculum. Sub-sections (1) and (2) lay down the core and other foundation subjects to be taught; sub-section (3) defines the four 'key stages' through which pupils will pass, for which various 'attainment targets' and 'programmes of study' may be imposed. Not only may the Secretary of State by order prescribe those attainment targets and programmes of study (section 4(2) – see Chapter 6), he may also, again by order, amend sub-sections (1) and (2) themselves, and thus change the National Curriculum subjects (section 3(4)(a)). It may seem worrying to some that central government may in law have such control over the content of education to be provided in schools. However, the power in section 3(4)(a) is one of only three legislative powers, out of the hundred or more granted by the Act, where Parliament must approve the order (section 232(3)). Other powers, such as the power to require special schools maintained by LEAs to have delegated budgets (section 43(1)), may be exercised without such affirmation.

Some of the statutory instruments issued under the ERA 1988 have taken the form of commencement orders. These orders are used to bring parts or sections of an Act into force on a stipulated date. Where a major scheme of reform, such as that in the ERA 1988, is concerned, it is considered useful for the government to be able to phase in the changes, allowing for a period of preparation and adjustment among those affected by them. Nine commencement orders have been made under the 1988 Act. For example, the sections setting out the rules on charging parents for educational provision, sections 106–111, 117 and 118, were brought into effect on 1 April 1989, by the Education Reform Act (Commencement No.2) Order 1988.

Legislation of the European Communities can similarly be divided into primary and secondary types. The former comprises the treaties. The latter comprises regulations, decisions and directives, although only the first two of these create law which is directly applicable in the UK, in the sense that Parliament's approval is not required. Generally directives specify an object to be achieved whilst leaving member states to decide individually on the most appropriate form and means of doing so; however, occasionally a directive will be directly applicable.[13] Although education so far has been left largely untouched by EC law, one might expect that it and, more especially, training will increasingly fall within its ambit as European integration progresses. One of the directives which have been acted upon[14] is Council directive 89/48, passed on 21 December 1988, which aims to make it easier for teachers to practice in member states other than their own. The government acted quickly on what offered, because of the possibility of recruiting more teachers from EC countries, a useful additional remedy to the teacher shortage in Britain. The Education (Teachers) Regulations 1989 provide that from 1 September 1989 any person who was a recognised teacher in a member state after three years' higher education and training there would be eligible for qualified teacher status in England and Wales.

The UK's obligations under EC law must be distinguished from those which it has under the European Convention on Human Rights (1950), which is part of international law. Unlike EC law, which is enforced via the European Court of Justice in Luxembourg against nations or individuals/companies, the European Convention on Human Rights is enforced only against governments, initially by application to the European Commission on Human Rights and subsequently, if the case is not resolved or filtered out, by the European Court of Human Rights in Strasbourg. Several important cases concerned with such matters as corporal punishment and comprehensive schools have been brought against the UK government. However, pursuit of redress under the European Convention demands patience. It can often take many years before all stages of a case are concluded. Moreover, the court has no sanctions it can impose for breaches of the Convention.

Returning to the law in England and Wales, a further important source is case law, or what lawyers refer to as *stare decisis* or judicial precedent. This may be defined as the decisive points of law and argument enunciated in judgments and applied in subsequent cases; they can have binding force if they represent the crux of the decision (the *ratio decidendi* or that which decides the case), or otherwise persuasive force (if *obiter dicta* – remarks other than the *ratio*), depending on the position, in the hierarchy of the courts, of the courts which tried the earlier decided case and the case being decided. A decision by a lower level court, such as a county court or magistrates' court, is never binding on other courts trying later cases. A decision by the High Court is binding on such courts but not on itself. At the upper level, a decision of the Court of Appeal is binding on all lower courts but not always on itself. A decision of the highest domestic court of all, the House of Lords, is binding on all other courts, but since 1966 this court has been free to depart from its own previous decisions where it considers it 'right to do so'.[15] The system of precedent, which, incidentally, is self-imposed on the courts, is not as rigid as the above may suggest. Judges often avoid applying a particular precedent by distinguishing, in a material respect, the facts on which the earlier case was decided from those in the case before them.

In some cases these judicial pronouncements relate to the meaning or construction of a statutory provision; in other cases they offer a further refinement of the 'common law', which is based on precedent or, rather, precedents established over the centuries. Areas of the law like torts (forms of civil wrong) and contract impose obligations which derive from the common law, although in modern times statute law has made an important contribution to these fields. For example, negligence is a tort at common law; as we shall see, it imposes a duty of care on, amongst others, teachers. But so far as premises (including, incidentally, school premises) are concerned, the duty of care owed by occupiers towards visitors is laid down in the Occupiers' Liability Act 1957.

In the field of education law, the courts have clarified the rights and obligations imposed by the Education Acts, in cases which have become important precedents. Perhaps the best example is the decision of the House of Lords in *Secretary of State for Education and Science v Tameside MBC* (1976) which established the meaning of 'unreasonably' for the purposes of section 68 of the Education Act 1944, which empowers intervention by the Secretary of State where an LEA or governors are acting or proposing to act in this way. The removal of uncertainty by the courts is especially important given the wide discretion which rests with LEAs and governors, often the result of less than fully · prescriptive duties. Although the courts have generally demonstrated an unwillingness to interfere with the exercise of this discretion, they have, in defining the correct scope of particular duties, limited its extent. For example, the courts have decided that the Education Act 1981 imposes responsibilities on LEAs towards, *inter alia*, pupils with dyslexia and those in need of speech therapy.[16]

Important education cases are usually reported in the education or national press. For example, the recent decision of the House of Lords in the case brought by the Equal Opportunities Commission against Birmingham LEA's arrangements for single-sex schooling[17] was widely referred to, as was the successful first challenge to the Secretary of State's approval of grant-maintained status for Beechen Cliff School in Bath.[18] The full text of the judgment in the case will only be published if the case is reported in the law reports (such as the *All England Law Reports*, the *Weekly Law Reports*, the *Local Government Reports* or *Family Law Reports*), although transcripts can sometimes be obtained, especially of cases heard in the Court of Appeal. *The Law of Education* (ed. P. Leill and J.B. Saunders, published by Butterworth) is a loose-leaf encyclopaedia which contains, amongst other things, summaries of cases likely to be of interest to education administrators, teachers and local government lawyers.

The combination of this diversity of sources and the scale and pace of reform to the law makes it virtually impossible for any teacher to have a comprehensive and up-to-date knowledge of the law of education. Parts of reference books aiming to bring these diverse sources into one work will undoubtedly be out of date within months if not weeks of publication. Nevertheless, these works are still useful, and should be consulted. Teachers should, in any event, have access to some of the primary legal sources at schools. The law now requires that each school has a copy of statutory instruments, departmental circulars and administrative memoranda relevant to the curriculum under the ERA 1988, available for consultation by parents and others 'at all reasonable times' on request.[19]

Departmental (DES or Welsh Office) circulars have been issued in great profusion since the enactment of the ERA 1988.[20] Nearly 30 circulars relevant to schools were issued in 1989 alone. In fact, the practice of disseminating departmental guidance on the implementation of new laws, policies and financial and administrative arrangements long pre-dates the 1988 Act. DES/Welsh Office Circulars could not be regarded as legally binding. Moreover, it seems that an LEA which departs from the guidance contained in a circular or adopts an interpretation of a legal provision's requirements which contradicts that offered in a circular will not automatically be acting *ultra vires* (outside its authority or power). Circulars are 'no more than advice from the Minister as to a course which, in general, he suggests the education authority should follow'.[21]

ENFORCEMENT OF RIGHTS AND DUTIES

The jurisdiction and organisation of the civil courts in England and Wales is currently under review and changes are expected in the near future. It would, therefore, be undesirable to offer the reader anything more than a brief description of the courts concerned and their hierarchical structure. It is also necessary to consider the role of the criminal courts and the forums which exist outside the courts system for the resolution of legal disputes, such as tribunals.

Persons and organisations generally institute civil proceedings because they have suffered physically and/or financially as a result of another's actions and have been unable to obtain satisfaction from the person or organisation they hold responsible. The remedy sought will generally be compensation (in the form of damages), but in some cases proceedings are pursued with a view to obtaining a declaration of the rights of the parties or an order that a person desists from a particular course of action (an injunction). There are various forms of civil proceedings, some of which are specific to a particular type of dispute – for example, possession proceedings under the Rent Act 1977 or Housing Act 1988 for the recovery of rented premises by a landlord, or judicial review proceedings under Order 53 of the Rules of the Supreme Court in respect of alleged public law breaches by public authorities such as LEAs (see below). The proposed reforms being considered at the present time will aim to make the court system more efficient, but also more accessible to the litigant. The one major step previously taken towards accessibility was the introduction of the arbitration (or 'small claims') procedure in the county court, designed to enable claims of up to a set amount (£500, but to be increased to £1,000) to be pursued without legal representation.

Most civil proceedings must be commenced in either a county court or the High Court. (The magistrates' court also has civil jurisdiction; for example, in child care cases.) Reforms are due, under the Courts and Legal Services Act (1990). At present High Court proceedings, which are more expensive and formal, are required for claims for damages in excess of £5,000 or in respect of libel and slander, unless the parties agree otherwise. In the case of *Van Oppen v Bedford Charity Trustees*, referred to earlier (see also pp. 3 and 163 below), a boy aged 16 and a half sustained a spinal injury while playing rugby at school and sued the school trustees under various heads of negligence. His total claim came to £55,000, so the case was pursued in the High Court. (Many such cases are settled out of court, by the payment of a sum with or without admission of liability.) When his case was dismissed, Simon Van Oppen decided to appeal under one of the heads. Civil appeals lie (with leave) to the Court of Appeal (Civil Division) and subsequently, with leave, and providing the case raises a point of law of general public importance, to the House of Lords.

One rather special form of civil procedure is 'application for judicial review'. An increasing number of education disputes are being resolved via judicial review proceedings, which take place in the High Court. The Queen's Bench Division of the Court has a power, dating back over several centuries, to review the actions of government ministers and departments, local authorities and certain other bodies exercising 'public law' functions. The distinction between 'public' and 'private law' is not always easy to draw, as the courts have acknowledged in a number of cases over the past decade; some commentators regard it as extremely artificial. Why, for example, should an LEA's duty to maintain school premises so that injury to a child is avoided give a right to that child in private law,[22] whereas a decision to close a school is a matter of public law challengeable only via judicial review under Order 53 of the Rules of the Supreme Court? It would take at least one whole chapter to explain adequately the rationale behind this. It is sometimes explained, in rather simplistic terms, that in private law the LEA is treated as an individual causing harm to another individual who may claim a private law remedy such as damages. In public law, the LEA has also harmed an individual but at the same time is deemed to have failed in its broader public duty.

A better understanding of the distinction is possible once the role of the courts in judicial review proceedings is appreciated. When reviewing a decision or action the court does not have the power of an appellate court. It cannot substitute its decision for that of the minister. This point was re-emphasised in the case of *R v Secretary of State for Education and Science ex parte Avon County Council* (1990), where the Secretary of State's decision to allow Beechen Cliff school to opt out of local authority control and become grant-maintained was challenged. (This case is referred to on page 28 below.) When powers and duties rest with public authorities it is often for them to decide how and when they should be exercised. But the courts are concerned to see that such power is exercised lawfully. This means that, for example, an LEA must act within the scope or remit of its power. So, when an LEA used its power to remove certain governors it had appointed to schools in its area its decision was quashed by the High Court. The LEA had dismissed the governors because they had failed to support its plans for the future of the schools. This was an abuse of power as well as a 'usurpation of the governors' independent function'.[23]

The court will consider whether the public authority took into account relevant factors and ignored irrelevant ones when reaching its decision. In the case above involving the dismissal of governors, the LEA's decision was activated by political rather than educational motives. The court will also consider whether the statute authorised the action, as in the case where the Greater London Council (as was) levied a supplementary rate to subsidise its 'Fare's Fair' public transport policy – which the court held it had had no power to do.[24] Action beyond the remit of a public body's powers is said to be *ultra vires*. One way in which a body will be acting *ultra vires* is if it acts 'unreasonably', taken to mean, *inter alia*, 'acting in a way in which no reasonable authority would have acted'.[25]

A further ground for intervention by the courts would be breach of the rules of 'natural justice'. One rule is concerned with potential bias on the part of the decision maker. It enables the court to quash a decision if it is of the opinion that reasonable people might suspect that the decision maker would be biased as a result of his/her relationship to a person or thing that is the subject of the decision. This rule is, in fact, incorporated into the rules on attendance and voting at governors' meetings contained in the Education (School Government) Regulations 1989 (see pages 54–55 below). The other rule of natural justice guarantees the right to be heard, which is taken to be wide enough in many cases to confer a right to be consulted. For example, in *R v Brent LBC ex parte Gunning* (1985) the LEA had taken a decision to make proposals for the amalgamation and closure of secondary schools. When circulating draft proposals it had failed to consult parents. Mr Justice Hodgson said that parents had a 'legitimate expectation' to be consulted over the plans, and quashed the LEA's decision.

A further basis for judicial review would be that the authority made an error of law – in, for example, misconstruing its duties or powers. For example, the Chief Constable of Gwent made an error of law in disqualifying a police officer from serving on a school governing body on the ground of possible conflict of interest. The House of Lords held that contrary to what the Chief Constable believed to be the case, Police Regulations would *not* be infringed by a constable holding such a governorship.[26] Another example occurred in the case of *R v Secretary of State for Education and Science ex parte Keating* (1986). An LEA had been permitted to close its only single-sex boys' school whilst continuing to maintain two single-sex girls' schools. The authority had failed to fulfil its duty under the Sex Discrimination Act 1975 to ensure that there were equal opportunities, in this case over access to single-sex schooling, for both sexes. Mr Justice Woolf (as he then was) summed up the supervisory role of the courts here thus:

If there is a case, of which I find this to be one, where . . . it appears that the [Secretary of State or LEA] has gone wrong in his [or its] application of the relevant statutory provisions, it is important that the court intervenes so that the member of the public who makes the complaint can be satisfied that the courts will ensure the Secretary of State [or LEA] properly exercises the very important statutory duties which are entrusted to him [or it].[27]

Finally it may be noted that the courts will also require public authorities to give adequate reasons for their decisions.[28]

The courts are willing to review decisions if the now well-established grounds are made out. But they are well aware that they should not usurp powers vested by constitutional convention or statute in ministers and others. To quote Mr Justice Woolf again, this time from a different case, the courts seek to 'avoid a possible conflict between the minister's view of what is adequate, necessary and expedient and that of the court'.[29] But as we saw earlier, the court will interfere if there is illegality: 'It is not for any court of law to substitute its own decision for [the Secretary of State's]; but it is for a court of law to determine whether it has been established that in reaching his decision . . . he had directed himself properly in law.'[30]

The court's judicial review jurisdiction is increasingly being invoked in what has become, not surprisingly in view of the radical reforms of the past decade, a particularly disputatious era in the politics of education. To prevent the courts being deluged by claims by persons aggrieved by all sorts of decisions by public bodies, there are various requirements which act as a sieve. First, an applicant must have a sufficient interest (called *locus standi*) in the decision (for example, as a parent, teacher, governor or community charge payer). Second, the applicant must obtain leave of the court (a requirement designed to filter out frivolous or fruitless applications which would waste the court's time and hinder public bodies). Third, the applicant must act without delay (usually having to apply within three months of notice of the decision which is the subject of the complaint).

Although a statutory remedy is often available as a means of challenging a decision, it will not preclude all intervention by the High Court under judicial review. For example, in *Meade v Haringey LBC* (1979), the Court of Appeal held that despite the Secretary of State's power, in section 99 of the 1944 Act, to give directions to LEA or governors he believes are acting in default of their duty, the court could intervene if an LEA or governors acted *ultra vires* (see above).

It must be stressed that many aspects of civil procedure are in the process of changing at the present time. For example, the Children Act 1989 is instituting important reforms, enabling first instance courts at all levels, magistrates, county and High Court, to administer the orders provided for by that Act. Under the Courts and Legal Services Act 1990, the County Court's jurisdiction is to be extended.

There remains a significant volume of dispute resolution activity which is conducted outside the courts system. For example, appeals by parents over the allocation of school places are heard by school admission appeal committees, constituted under the Education Act 1980. A teacher who claimed to have been unfairly dismissed would be able to pursue a case before an industrial tribunal. A complaint of maladministration could be investigated by a local commissioner for administration (or 'local ombudsman'), in the case of an LEA, or the Parliamentary Commissioner for Administration ('the Ombudsman'), where the complaint is about the DES.

Brief mention of the criminal courts is also necessary. Where there is to be a prosecution, a criminal case is first brought before the magistrates' or juvenile court. The latter deals with young offenders; that is, those aged between 10 and 17 years. Under the age of 10 (8 in Scotland) a child is presumed to be *doli incapax* (incapable of doing wrong); between the ages of 10 and 13 s/he may be deemed capable of forming criminal intent if the court considers that s/he is of 'mischievous discretion' (meaning basically that s/he is mature enough to appreciate the wrongfulness of his/her action), but can neither be the subject of criminal sanctions nor (unless there is evidence of harm, actual or likely, to the child) of a care order.[31]

Where a serious, or 'indictable', offence is alleged to have been committed, the case will be transferred to the Crown Court for trial provided the magistrates are satisfied that there is a prime facia case against the accused. The case will be tried before a jury (unless, of course, the defendant decides to plead guilty). Teachers and students (aged 18 or over and thus eligible for jury duty) may be summoned to serve on a jury, but could ask the court to excuse them if their attendance would cause difficulties for them. The less serious offences will be tried by the magistrates themselves; an example relevant to education would be the prosecution of parents for the non-attendance at school of their children. Certain offences may be tried either by the magistrates or Crown Court (sometimes known as 'either way' offences – for example, threats to kill). Criminal appeals are heard by the Divisional Court, Court of Appeal (Criminal Division) and (subject to the same pre-conditions as apply to civil appeals – above), the House of Lords.

Finally, as mentioned above (page 9), the European Court of Justice has jurisdiction over matters of EC law; and the European Court of Human Rights may deal with alleged breaches of the European Convention on Human Rights (if, *inter alia*, the European Commission on Human Rights says that the matter may be referred to the Court).

Questions

1. What is the distinction between primary and secondary legislation?
2. What role is played by the courts in the development of education law?
3. What is the scope and purpose of judicial review procedure in the High Court?

Notes

1 *Porter v City of Bradford Metropolitan Council* (1985) 14 Jan. (unreported, apart from *Lexis*).
2 See, for example, Barrell G 1970 *Legal Cases for Teachers*, Methuen.
3 *Van Oppen v Clerk to the Bedford Charity Trustees* (1989).
4 See, for example, DES 1989 *National Curriculum from Policy to Practice*, HMSO, para.2.4.
5 DES 1989 Circular 2/89, para.3.
6 *Times Educational Supplement*, 14 April 1989.
7 DES Circular 17/89, para.5.
8 Miers D R and Page A C 1982 *Legislation*, Butterworths, p. 15.
9 *The Times*, 22 Oct. 1987.
10 Stein P (1982) *Legal Institutions The Development of Dispute Resolution*, Butterworths.
11 Professor Wade, for example, has referred to legislation as being 'excessive in quantity and deficient in quality': Wade HWR 1980 *Constitutional Fundamentals*, Stevens, p. 22.
12 *McCarthy's Ltd v Smith* (1979); the conflict or inconsistency must be clear: *Factortame v Secretary of State for Transport* (1989).
13 See *Van Duyn v The Home Office (No.2)* (1975).

14 For examples of EC directives relating to education, see Poole K 1987 *Education Law*, Sweet & Maxwell, p. 46.
15 *Practice Statement (Judicial Precedent)* [1966] 1 WLR 1234. More generally on precedent, see further Zander M 1989 *The Law-Making Process*, 3rd edn, Weidenfeld & Nicolson, ch. 3.
16 *R v Hampshire Education Authority ex parte J* (1985) (dyslexia); *R v Lancashire County Council ex parte CM* (1989) (speech therapy).
17 *Equal Opportunities Commission v Birmingham City Council* (1989) 1 All ER 769.
18 *R v Secretary of State for Education and Science ex parte Avon County Council* (1990).
19 Education (School Curriculum and Related Information) Regulations 1989 SI 1989 No. 954, reg.6.
20 The 1988 Act was granted the Royal Assent on 29 July 1988.
21 Per Woolf J in *R v ILEA ex parte Bradby* (1980) 30 Jan. (unreported).
22 E.g. *Ching v Surrey County Council* (1910); *Refell v Surrey County Council* (1964).
23 *R v Governors of Haberdashers' Aske's Schools ex parte ILEA (Brunyate v ILEA)* (1989) (HL), per Lord Bridge at 421.
24 *R v GLC ex parte London Borough of Bromley* (1982).
25 *Associated Provincial Picture Houses Ltd v Wednesbury Corporation* (1948) (CA); *Secretary of State for Education and Science v Tameside Metropolitan Borough Council* (1976) (CA) & (HL).
26 *R v Chief Constable of Gwent* (1989).
27 *R v Secretary of State for Education and Science ex parte Chance (1982)*.
28 See, for example, *R v Surrey County Council ex parte H* (1985).
29 *R v Secretary of State for the Environment ex parte Ward* (1984) at p. 566.
30 *Tameside Metropolitan Borough Council, op. cit.*, n.25 at p. 695, per Lord Diplock.
31 Children Act 1989, sections 31(2) and 90(2).

CHAPTER 2

Provision of education

INTRODUCTION

Until the radical reforms of the 1980s, the legal framework for the provision of education in England and Wales laid down in the Education Act 1944 had remained virtually unchanged. Although the reforms of the past decade have not changed the basic structure of the education system – we still have a Secretary of State, LEAs, governors, and the same categories of schools as before (with some notable additions) – there has been a shift in power in two directions, resulting in two distinct forms of control. First, central government, traditionally said to be a partner with local government in the management of the education system, has acquired increased powers at the expense of LEAs. Control of the curriculum, discussed in Chapter 6, offers a clear example of this centralisation of power, of central control. Second, school governing bodies have been reshaped and given overall control over the management of their schools and their resources, again largely at the expense of LEAs. This is a facet of what has been described as a *'laissez-faire* model of control'.[1]

Under the pattern of provision laid down by the 1944 Act, the amount of control able to be exercised by LEAs and governing bodies did, in fact, vary as between the different types of schools – governors of voluntary aided schools, for example, having a degree of autonomy not enjoyed by other governors (see below). Once local financial management (usually referred to as 'local management of schools' or 'LMS') is fully operational in schools to which it applies, such variation will be much less evident, even if the differences in character between denominational and non-denominational schools will remain. However, there are now 'grant-maintained' schools and 'city tech nology colleges' which are independent of LEA control.

The progressive diminution of their powers has led to questions about the future role of LEAs. It has been emphasised that they will continue to have an important strategic role to play.[2] Indeed, although pressure to reduce poll tax bills may yet persuade ministers to reduce or remove local administration of education at present the law continues to place a considerable number of duties on LEAs to ensure that appropriate educational provision is made in their area. Moreover, although governors and the Secretary of State are now the dominant parties, LEAs must be consulted over a large number of matters. Inevitably, conflicts between the parties will intensify, and the disputatious era which has already been entered will ensure a steady flow of education cases before the courts.

In the remainder of the chapter we shall, in fact, be concerned principally with the *nature* of the duties resting with the various parties over the provision of education, rather than with the locus of power. Whilst many of the legal provisions discussed in this chapter are concerned with matters somewhat remote from the day-to-day practice of teaching, they are important as part of the broad legal context to educational provision in which a teacher operates. Of particular relevance are the legal consequences of teacher or equipment shortages and the different types of schools in which teachers may be employed.

THE DUTY OF LEAs TO ENSURE THE PROVISION OF SCHOOLS

The 1944 Act requires there to be LEAs (section 6, as amended) – the county councils, district councils in former metropolitan counties, and the inner and outer London boroughs (ERA 1988, sections 162 and 163). Each LEA is required to have an education committee, which must include persons with experience of education and local education conditions and which will make the major policy and budgetary decisions, and a chief education officer, who has overall responsibility for the administration of the service.

The duties of LEAs in ensuring the provision of education may be divided into two categories: the absolute and specific duties and those which may be (and have been) described as 'target duties' – laying down goals but leaving LEAs with varying degrees of discretion as to how those goals may be achieved. It will be seen that the target duties are the more difficult of the two categories to enforce in the courts or via complaint to the Secretary of State.

Among the absolute duties is that laid down in section 7 of the 1944 Act, requiring the statutory system of public education in England and Wales to be organised into 'three progressive stages' – primary, secondary and further education. The same section then proceeds to lay down a target duty; LEAs must, so far as their powers allow, 'contribute towards the spiritual, moral, mental and physical development of the community by securing that efficient education throughout those stages shall be available to meet the needs of the population of their area'. (Similarly, section 1 of the ERA 1988 spells out broad aims with regard to curricular provision in schools, as discussed in Chapter 6.) There is a necessary amount of discretion built into this broad duty – LEAs must be free to assess the needs of their local population, whilst ensuring that 'efficient education' (not defined in the 1944 Act) is available.

A similar division between absolute and target duties occurs in section 8 of the 1944 Act. This section has been subject to considerable judicial scrutiny over the past twenty years, most recently in connection with teacher shortages. Section 8(1) states that LEAs must ensure that there are available in their area 'sufficient schools' for primary and secondary education (see below). (There is also a duty, under section 41, to secure the provision of adequate facilities for further education – see below.) After defining primary and secondary education, the sub-section states that LEAs must ensure that the schools in question are sufficient in 'number, character and equipment to afford for all pupils opportunities for education offering such variety of instruction as may be desirable in view of their different ages, abilities and aptitudes, and of the different periods for which they may remain at school'.

This paragraph was once described with unashamed hyperbole as a 'glorious passage, which should be hung up in the meeting room of every education committee' and one which 'should be learned by every citizen'.[3] This part of the section 8 duty is clearly a target duty, a fact which has implications for the enforcement of the duty. In the case of *R v Inner London Education Authority ex parte Ali and Murshid* (1990) a number of issues relating to section 8 and its enforcement were considered. The case arose out of the failure by the ILEA to ensure the provision of sufficient teachers in the borough of Tower Hamlets. Around 300 children of primary school age, mostly from the local Bangladeshi community, were without school places as a result of the shortage of teachers. Despite various national and London-based measures taken by the government, such as the introduction of the licensed and articled teacher schemes, the provision of additional incentive allowances and a new allowance for London teachers, and despite the efforts of the local education authority to recruit teaching staff, the problem in Tower Hamlets continued. Mr Ali, whose son had been without a school place for over twelve months, and Mr Murshid, who was chair of a charity involved in the welfare of the Bangladeshi community, asked the Secretary of State to use his power in section 99 of the 1944 Act (discussed further below) to declare the LEA to be in default of its duty and to issue directions to it. The Secretary of State refused, arguing that the LEA was doing all it could to rectify the situation. Mr Ali and Mr Murshid subsequently applied for judicial review, on the ground that its failure to provide sufficient teachers had put the LEA in breach of its duty under section 8(1).

It was clear from an earlier case, *R v Liverpool City Council ex parte Ferguson* (1985), that the duty to provide 'sufficient schools' – schools 'sufficient in number, character and equipment' – included a duty to provide teachers and other essential personnel. But the court, after considering whether the statutory remedy in section 99 was exclusive in cases alleging breach of section 8, and concluding that it was not,[4] held that the LEA was not in breach of its duty. The court in *Ali* reinforced the prevalent view that section 8(1) lays down a minimum duty and leaves LEAs with a broad discretion as to what should be provided. LEAs are required to act within the reasonable bounds allowed by this discretion, referred to by Woolf LJ as the 'tolerance provided by the section'. This discretion has been regarded as wide enough, for example, to enable LEAs to choose between selective or non-selective schools,[5] and, in *Ali*, to deny some children a school place for a 'limited period of time' (unspecified) – provided the authority is doing all that it reasonably can to remedy the situation. The courts have accepted that the discretion, which is 'at the margins of the duty' in section 8(1),[6] enables LEAs to have regard for a variety of legitimate considerations, including financial constraints and (now) teacher shortages, when carrying out their responsibilities under section 8(1).[7] Thus, when central government forced local authorities to make major economies which resulted in shortages of school textbooks and other equipment, section 8(1) proved of little value to parents mounting challenges.[8]

The problem, though, is that the precise extent of this 'target duty' is unclear. Whilst section 8(1) would seem to require LEAs to provide school places for all children who need them, Woolf LJ was keen to emphasise in *Ali* that this duty is far from 'absolute'. Indeed, Dent once referred to 'the ideal of section 8' which 'no one could pretend it is easy to achieve'.[9]

Of course, if an LEA, in exercising the discretion conferred by section 8, acts unreasonably or outside the remit of its powers (*ultra vires*), it would be acting illegally. One such example occurred in the case of *R v Liverpool City Council ex parte Ferguson* (1985), where the local authority issued redundancy notices to all of its teachers after setting a rate which was inadequate to meet its projected level of net revenue expenditure. Part of the illegality of this action was that the authority was in breach of section 8. Moreover, the authority's decision had not been taken for educational reasons. In *Meade v Haringey LBC* (1979) the LEA decided to close its schools during a caretakers' strike. After the schools had been closed for three weeks, a parent took the matter to court, seeking a declaration that the authority was in breach of its duty under section 8. The authority admitted to being sympathetic to the union's grievances, but claimed to be acting not from a political motive but rather an educational one – in that the maintenance of good industrial relations would help the authority to continue providing an education service for the children. The trial judge refused to grant an order and the matter came before the Court of Appeal. Eveleigh LJ said that parents would be entitled to relief where an authority's decision was taken 'without just and reasonable cause'. The argument that this was a 'simple failure' of the section 8 duty and as such was not justiciable, because the court should not usurp the power of the Secretary of State (in section 99 of the Act) to give directions to an LEA in default of its duty,[10] was rejected. Eveleigh LJ said that there was not a 'simple failure' to provide education, but rather a positive decision to 'stop production bringing the system to a halt'. Lord Denning emphasised that if the LEA had acted honestly, reasonably and with due regard for relevant considerations, the court would not interfere. So if the decision had been taken for purely political reasons, there might have been an illegality on that ground. Action which flew in the face of the statute and which aimed to 'frustrate or hinder the policy and objects of the Act' could be challenged in the courts, as could an act or omission which was so unreasonable that no reasonable authority would have decided upon it.[11]

The above cases illustrate the contentious nature of local decision making over educational provision. They also demonstrate how the educational issues become obscured by the questions of legality with which the cases become concerned. (This will also be exemplified by the cases on school closures, discussed below.) On the duty to provide 'sufficient schools', it may be observed that the comment by Wringe,[12] that 'there is not strictly a right to education in Great Britain' is reinforced by the decision in *Ali*.

Finally, it may be noted that the duty to provide 'sufficient schools' includes a duty to secure that there are sufficient schools for making special educational provision for pupils who have special educational needs.[13]

THE THREE PROGRESSIVE STAGES

There may be a critical educational divide between primary and secondary education; but in *law* the distinction is based solely on age. Both are defined (in section 8(1)(a) and (b)) as full-time education suitable to the requirements of pupils of the ages involved. Primary education is education suitable for pupils aged up to 10 years six months, and for older pupils 'whom it is expedient to educate together with junior pupils who have not attained that age'. The classification of some schools or departments as 'infants' and others as 'juniors' is not a legal requirement. Secondary education is that suitable for pupils aged at least 12 and not more than 18 years and for junior pupils aged at least 10 years six months 'whom it is expedient to educate together with senior pupils'.

The developments in vocational education at the secondary stage, and the trend towards tertiary provision post-16, make the division between the later stages of secondary education and further education more difficult to define. In law, further education (FE) has been redefined under the ERA 1988, which in fact has imposed more clear-cut responsibilities on LEAs with regard to FE provision. Section 41 of the 1944 Act (as substituted by section 120(2) of the ERA 1988) defines FE as full- or part-time education provided for persons above compulsory school age, including vocational, social, physical and recreational training, plus any organised leisure-time occupation provided in connection with such education or training. In effect, FE may not be provided in a school; the law says that education of a kind given in schools is not FE if the institution providing it does not provide part-time senior education or post-school education (full or part-time education for the 19-plus age group) 'to a significant extent'. LEAs must ensure there are adequate facilities for FE in their area, and in fulfilling this duty must have regard for the requirements of persons above compulsory school age who have learning difficulties (usually referred to as 'special educational needs'). For this purpose 'learning difficulty' is defined as a significantly greater difficulty in learning than that experienced by the majority of persons of a particular age; or a disability which prevents or hinders a child from using FE facilities of a kind generally provided by the LEA.

The 1944 Act identifies various classes of school:

1. primary schools, providing primary education;
2. nursery schools (when primary education is provided in a school for 2- to 5-year-olds it is a 'nursery school'; LEAs may maintain such schools, although provision of nursery education is not compulsory);
3. secondary schools, providing secondary education;
4. special schools – which are organised to make special educational provision for pupils with special educational needs and which must be approved by the Secretary of State.[14]

Primary or secondary education may also be provided in 'middle schools', for which provision was first made by the Education Act 1964, section 1. The idea appears to have been that a pupil's transition from primary to secondary schooling might be eased by having an intermediate stage. Officially, these schools will be classed as either primary or secondary, depending on the stage which a majority of the pupils have reached. Provision of middle schools requires the approval of the Secretary of State.[15]

SCHOOLS – THE MIXED ECONOMY

Until comparatively recently, the chief areas of contention in relation to the types of school in our education system were centred on selective as against comprehensive schools and public versus private provision. The debates about grammar and comprehensive schools, which raged in the 1960s and early 1970s, have virtually petered out, and the existence of an apparently buoyant private sector appears to have become tolerated by even the most vociferous opponents of 'privilege'. Now, new areas of contention have emerged – over voluntary aided status and, more particularly, over grant-maintained schools and city technology colleges, which some see as representing a new elitism in education.[16]

Around three-quarters of pupils in state schools in England and Wales attend *county schools*. At the secondary stage, most of these schools are comprehensives, providing for the whole ability range, although the legal duty to establish comprehensive schools, imposed following the 1974–79 Labour government's Education Act 1976, was swiftly abolished by the in-coming Conservative government's Education Act 1979. County schools are maintained wholly by LEAs. Their premises belong to the local authority, although the Education (No.2) Act 1986 gave governing bodies control over the use of the premises outside school hours.

Traditionally, the Church played a significant role in the provision of education in Britain, and this has continued with the *voluntary school*. Voluntary schools are basically denominational schools, of which about two-thirds are Church of England and the remaining third Roman Catholic, although there is a small residue of schools of other denominations, for example Jewish.

In simple terms, a voluntary school will be *controlled* if the Secretary of State is not satisfied that the governors are able and willing to meet certain costs (with the help of a grant from the DES). Even before the 1986 and 1988 legislation there were relatively few differences between county and voluntary controlled schools, apart from the obvious one relating to the latter category's religious character. The maintenance and running costs of controlled schools had to be met by the LEA.[17] Admissions and the secular curriculum were controlled by the LEA, although the governors did enjoy certain additional powers, for example in relation to control of the use of school premises – ownership of which rested with the foundation (the body which established the school). However, the 1986 and 1988 Acts, in extending the powers of governing bodies, have removed most of the differences. In 1988 there were almost 3,000 voluntary controlled schools, all Church of England, with a total of 411,000 pupils on roll.

Voluntary *aided* status confers a considerable amount of independence, although again the legislative changes of the past few years have made aided schools less marked in this respect. Aided status may be conferred if the Secretary of State is satisfied that the governors are able to meet certain maintenance costs (set out in section 15(3) of the 1944 Act) with the help of an 85 per cent contribution from the Secretary of State. Aided schools must be conducted in accordance with the terms of the trust deed for the school, although the deed can be modified by the Secretary of State if its terms are inconsistent with those of the school's instrument or articles of government. Of voluntary aided schools in England and Wales in 1988, 2,076 were Church of England and 2,400 Roman Catholic, providing education to 378,000 and 657,000 pupils respectively. Very similar to aided schools are *special agreement* schools, for which provision was first made in the Education Act 1936. A special agreement gives the LEA an obligation to pay a contribution grant towards the cost of building or enlarging a voluntary school. There are only about 100 of these schools, all of which are secondary schools.

Aided status has been favoured by a number of religious denominations because in aided schools the governing body, on which foundation governors are in the majority, are able to control the school with relatively little outside interference whilst at the same time enjoying the advantage of having to make only a small contribution to the upkeep of the school. Although other governing bodies are acquiring equivalent independence under LMS (see below), voluntary aided status will continue to be favoured by denominational groups whose particular religious traditions these schools help preserve. Some foundations and parent groups will seek also to capitalise on the opportunity for enhancing their independence whilst retaining the existing character of an aided school by applying for grant-maintained (GM) status for it (see below). One of the first schools to vote for, and be granted, GM status was the voluntary aided St Francis of Xavier RC secondary school in Liverpool.

At the present time there are a number of independent (fee-charging) denominational schools which lack funds and would dearly like voluntary aided status. In March 1991 an attempt was made by an all-party group of peers (Baroness Cox, Lord Young and Lord Grimmond) to amend the law in order to give these schools both the opportunity of acquiring grant-maintained status and, as an alternative, of improving their prospects of obtaining voluntary aided status. The Education (Amendment) Bill failed to progress beyond its second reading, but it gave rise to a lengthy debate in the House of Lords about the principles involved.[18] Acknowledging the fact that nearly all voluntary aided schools are Christian, Baroness Cox, moving the second reading, argued that there was a denial of the human rights of the parents who had been instrumental in setting up many of the independent denominational schools in not conferring state funding on them; the European Convention on Human Rights provides that the state must respect the right of parents to ensure that their children's education 'is in conformity with their own religious and philosophical convictions'. The chief reason given by the Secretary of State for denying voluntary aided status to independent denominational schools is, according to Baroness Cox, the existence of surplus places in local state schools. One of the proposed amendments to the law included in the Bill was that voluntary aided status could not be denied for this reason alone. The Baroness argued that it was 'anomalous to continue to put public money into subsidising empty places in schools which parents do not want and to refuse to support highly successful schools which parents do want'. (For further discussion of this issue, see Poulter,[19] Cumper[20] and Anderson.[21])

Grant-maintained schools

Maclure has commented that no provision in the ERA 1988 'aroused stronger feelings than those on grant-maintained schools'.[22] LEAs, teachers, educationalists and politicians outside the Conservative party were, each for their own particular reasons, vehemently opposed to the creation of a new category of school which would lie outside local authority control. But when grant-maintained (GM) status was first introduced many of these opponents, while objecting to the principle of state schools being allowed to opt out of LEA control, saw little prospect of a wholesale shift in that direction. GM status was viewed by them almost as a gimmick which, like the city technology college before it, would barely alter the educational landscape of England and Wales. When little more than a handful of schools opted out in the first year of GM status their predictions appeared to have been accurate. But their concern began to increase when it became clear that in 1991–92 GM schools were going to be given preferential treatment so far as capital allowances for schools were concerned. By the spring of 1991, when Government plans for reform of local government and its financing were being launched, there was talk of the Government planning to take most state sector schools out of local authority control, by legislating for the conferment of GM status on them. Should this occur, it will rank with the National Curriculum as one of the most fundamental reforms to the education system of England and Wales this century. The plans for colleges of further education and sixth form colleges to be taken out of local authority control, announced on 21 March 1991, have added further fuel to the speculation about whether the concept of a *locally* administered education service, based on the Butler reforms in the Education Act 1944, has any future.

By June 1991 around 80 schools, including one primary school, had been granted GM status. If GM status is to be *imposed* on schools by the Secretary of State amendment of sections 60–72 of the ERA 1988 will be necessary. Transitional arrangements would have to be made, and the Secretary of State would presumably be given control of the time-table for implementation of this reform.

So much for the future, but what about the present? The current legal position is defined in Chapter IV of, and Schedule 5 to, the ERA 1988. Grant-maintained (GM) schools are maintained by central government rather than LEAs; the Secretary of State has a duty to 'make payments in respect of the expenses of maintaining' any school on which GM status has been conferred.[23] At present there is a no provision for the creation of a new GM school other than by the acquisition of GM status by an existing school. Such status is acquired via approval of the Secretary of State, which is only possible if there has been parental endorsement of the change to GM status. Such endorsement must come from a secret postal ballot of parents with children registered at the school (see below).

The two elements of parental choice and freedom from LEA control formed the basis of the rationale for the creation of this new category of school. The government's official statements tended to emphasise the former rather than the latter. For example, the Consultation Paper issued in 1987 said that there would be 'a new and powerful dimension to the ability of parents to exercise choice within the publicly provided sector of education'.[24] Critics have been quick to point out the divisiveness which would flow from opting-out.[25] But the government preferred to emphasise the desirable 'diversity' which would result, arguing that this in turn would 'enhance the prospect of improving educational standards in all schools'. The implication was that LEAs could not be relied upon to meet the expectations of certain groups of parents, who were concerned about the policies of extremist councils and falling standards in schools. Not only would standards in GM schools be more in line with parental expectations, but the establishment of these schools would also provide 'a stimulus for higher standards at all schools' by setting a standard with which other schools would have to compete. The element of competition is, in fact, the key to many of the ERA reforms – open enrolment and LMS are, amongst other things, designed to encourage schools to compete for 'customers', and, in the process, raise their standards to attract custom.

However, whilst opting out will doubtless play its part in the subjection of the education system to market forces, in the short term it has, as predicted,[26] been seized upon by parents and governors as a means of avoiding unpopular LEA plans for future of a particular school. Of the first 20 schools to acquire GM status, 17 had chosen to opt out because of threat of closure, amalgamation or reorganisation; of the next eleven to opt out, between 1 April and 1 September 1990, the main reason for seeking greater independence via GM status was to safeguard their future.[27] In fact, section 73 of the 1988 Act contains important provisions designed to encourage consideration of opting out where closure, change of character and so on are planned for the school. For example, if an LEA has published plans to change a school, any application for GM status is treated as a statutory objection to the proposals for the purposes of the Education Act 1980. If an application for GM status is made while the LEA's proposals are before the Secretary of State, both will be considered on their merits, but a decision about GM status will be made first (but see below).

It has, in fact, been made comparatively easy for schools to be taken out of LEA control via opting out. The balloting procedure is weighted in favour of opting out, and once the necessary majority has been obtained and the governors have published their proposals (which they must do within six months of the ballot) in the appropriate manner,[28] it is merely a matter of the Secretary of State being satisfied that opting out is 'appropriate' – although he must consult first and must consider any objections raised to the governors' proposals. He must not consider the appropriateness of allowing a school to opt out in isolation from the effect that such opting out would have on any school reorganisation plans the LEA might have submitted to him, but has a wide discretion.[29] He may approve or reject the governors' proposals (perhaps asking them to submit further proposals), or approve them with modifications.

A ballot for the acquisition of GM status must be called either (1) if there is a written request from a sufficient number of parents (a figure represented by the total number of pupils at the school divided by five) or (2) if the governors have resolved twice (within an interval of between four and six weeks between resolutions) to hold a ballot.[30] In the case of (1), the ballot must be held within two months after the 29th day after the written request. Where (2) is relevant, it must be held within three months of the second resolution. There are various requirements about informing parents of their right to vote; the arrangements for voting; and the consequences of GM status. The ballot must be conducted by the Electoral Reform Society.[31] There was heated debate both inside and outside Parliament over what should be the required majority for opting out. The main objection to the original proposal in the bill that a simple majority of votes cast should determine the issue was that a small group of activists might be able to instigate a reform which perhaps a majority of parents did not favour sufficiently to take the trouble to vote for. After various options were considered and voted on by Parliament, the government pushed through a final amendment which is now in the Act. The position is that a simple majority of those voting must vote in favour if the school is to opt out; however, if less than 50 per cent of eligible persons vote, there must be a second ballot, within 14 days of the first, decided by a simple majority of those voting, irrespective of how small a percentage of eligible voters actually vote.[32] One further criticism has not been assuaged. It relates to the eligibility to vote. It seems unfair, and indeed undemocratic, to allow parents whose children may be leaving the school before it would actually become GM to vote on its status, especially when parents of an imminent intake of pupils, who clearly have a stake in the matter, are unenfranchised.

Teachers at the school will also have a keen interest in any opting-out proposals. Yet they are denied a vote on the matter, with the exception of teachers serving as members of the school's governing body, who are entitled to vote in a governors' first or second resolution on the question of opting out. The case of *R v Governors of Small Heath School ex parte Birmingham City Council* (1989) held that a teacher governor would have no pecuniary interest in such a decision, because the financial position of the teacher would be unlikely to change following opting out. In any event, the Education (School Government) Regulations 1989 (Sch, para.2(4)), now permit teacher governors to vote on a change to GM status.

As to the effect of a change to GM status, we can conveniently ignore the detailed provisions concerned with property, apart from perhaps noting that property rights (apart from those in property held on trust) and liabilities are transferred to the governors, whereas existing loan obligations and premature retirement payments to former staff remain the LEA's responsibility.[33] We can concentrate on certain basic questions which might concern both experienced and newly qualified teachers alike.

Are all schools eligible for GM status?

Before 1 November 1990 the position was that all county and voluntary secondary schools were eligible to be considered for GM status; but primary schools had to have at least 300 pupils to be so eligible. Now, under regulations (the Education (Eligibility of Primary Schools for Grant-maintained Status) Order 1990 SI No. 2031) introduced by the Secretary of State, *all* county and voluntary schools (apart from those due to close) are eligible. Nursery schools and special schools remain ineligible, as do county and voluntary schools which have been granted permission to close and voluntary schools whose governors have given notice of their intention to discontinue the school (s. 52(5)).

As a teacher, would I have to continue at the school if it opted out, and would the governors have to continue employing me?

A teacher who wished to disassociate him or herself from GM schools and who resigned when the school acquired its new status would have no rights. Section 75(8) of the ERA 1988 states that any employee of the LEA could not treat the change of employer as a 'substantial change to his working conditions' such as would entitle him or her to regard his or her contract of employment as terminated by the employer. The teacher would, of course, be free to terminate his or her contract (after proper notice) and seek employment elsewhere. In practice, many LEAs have agreed to redeploy any teachers working in a school which becomes GM.

The governors would have no legal right to sack the teacher simply because of the change of status. A teacher's contract of employment would from the date of incorporation be with the governors, with no interruption to the continuity of employment and no diminution of job security. The teacher's pay and conditions would continue to be determined by the relevant Teachers' Pay and Conditions Document which was in force at the time. As the educational character of the school is expected to remain unchanged for at least five years after incorporation (although this restriction may be lifted), and given the expectation that GM schools will prove popular with parents and be over-subscribed, it is extremely unlikely that the teacher need fear redundancy consequent on the school's acquisition of GM status.

Will the school be better off financially once it becomes GM?

All the way along, the government has been keen to stress that the acquisition of GM status should have a financially neutral effect on the school,[34] by virtue of the fact that the annual maintenance grant for the school would be based on the amount the school would have received from the LEA (for example, as the school's budget share under a delegation scheme), increased only to the extent necessary to cover the additional expenditure the GM school would have to incur on administrative costs and on certain services centrally provided to other categories of school. There has, however, been a suspicion that GM schools will be better resourced than those which remain in LEA control, even if it is not at the charge-payers' expense (the government having given an assurance that the conversion to GM status will not change the financial position of local charge-payers[35]). The Secretary of State has a discretion to make provision for the payment of capital grants and special purpose grants to GM schools. Regulations have been made detailing the purposes for which these grants may be paid and the conditions which may be attached.[36] The Circular implies that there will be parity between GM and LEA-maintained schools in terms of central government support for capital projects.[37] Moreover, the purposes for which special purpose grants may currently be paid to GM schools are somewhat limited, intended to provide the equivalent of education support grant, in-service training and certain other costs which would otherwise be met by the LEA (or central government via the LEA). Nevertheless, the Secretary of State could extend the scope of these special purpose grants; and there is the 'possibility of more favoured treatment of grant-maintained schools in consideration of bids for capital grants'[38] and of extending the scope of these grants as well. It has now become clear that many GM schools can expect higher capital allocations than LEA schools – an extra £10.5m is being allocated for 1991–92. In 1988 Maclure commented that 'if grant-maintained status were not to prove attractive on present terms, it would be relatively easy at a future date to increase the financial incentives'.[39] This is precisely what has happened.

Will LEAs have any involvement in GM schools?

LEAs will have continuing responsibilities under the Education Act 1981 towards pupils with special educational needs and under the

Education Act 1944 in respect of the enforcement of school attendance and the provision of free transport in certain cases. Pupils in GM schools must receive no less favourable treatment with regard to such provision as pupils in LEA-maintained schools (ERA 1988, s.100(1)). School meals, milk and cleaning will become the responsibility of the governing body.

(N.B. The government of GM schools is discussed in Chapter 3.)

City technology colleges and colleges for the technology of the arts

The creation of city technology colleges and colleges for the technology of the arts (referred to collectively hereafter as CTCs) represents a radical experiment in educational provision in this country. Unlike GM schools, which are funded entirely by the state, the intention with CTCs is to attract private capital to create the 'centres of excellence' capable of producing the skilled workers and managers desperately needed by industry. Private capital has not been provided in anywhere near sufficient amounts, and a major criticism of the CTCs is that they are sustained as elitist institutions (officially classed as 'independent' schools) soaking up huge amounts of public money while neighbouring state schools continue to be starved of resources by comparison.

The government has defended the CTC policy, which so far has yielded less than half-a-dozen of the 20 or so 'urban' colleges which it originally planned, by arguing that they will not aim to cream off the more academically able children in their area but rather will cater, as the ERA 1988 says, for pupils with 'different abilities' who will be selected on the basis of their motivation to succeed. Critics, including a large number of LEAs, regard CTCs as divisive and a cynical attempt to divert attention away from the poorly resourced LEA sector whilst promoting the New Right free market ideology which has pervaded so much of Conservative social policy since 1979.

The teacher who works in a CTC will notice not only the better facilities that exist and the more commercial ethos; s/he will also find a curriculum which is unencumbered by the ERA 1988 requirements concerning the National Curriculum, collective worship and religious education. CTCs are simply required to have a 'broad curriculum', with an emphasis on science and technology, or (in the case of city colleges for the technology of the arts) technology in its application to the performing and creative arts. A teacher employed by a CTC will not be able to re-live the days when s/he might have had the option of using corporal punishment; the government has sensibly excluded its use in these schools as in the LEA sector.[40] Finally, s/he may well be better remunerated than if s/he had remained in the state sector, although s/he may work longer hours. In *Bostock v Kay* (1989) it was held that teacher governors voting on whether to support the establishment of a CTC in place of their school, which involved voting to discontinue the school, had a direct pecuniary interest in the outcome of the vote and should take no part in it. This case was distinguished in the *Small Heath* case discussed earlier; the court there held that a change to GM status was far less fundamental than the creation of a CTC in place of a school.

The independent sector

The remainder of the mixed economy of schools in England is made up by the independent sector, of which CTCs in fact form a highly specialised sub-division. Around 600,000 pupils currently attend independent schools in Britain, about 7 per cent of the school population, and the number is growing.[41]

Independent schools are those providing full-time education to at least five children of compulsory school age and which are not LEA-maintained, grant-maintained or a special school not maintained by an LEA.[42] They are largely free from state control, although they must be registered by the Registrar of Independent Schools and may be inspected by Her Majesty's Inspectorate of Schools. The Registrar must be kept informed of changes in location and senior management of the school. Some smaller residential independent schools are now classed as 'children's homes' for the purposes of the Children Act 1989 which regulates their activities. Independent schools receive no direct funding from the state, but are able to benefit financially from charitable status – although some are run as businesses with a view to profit.

Around 34,000 children attending independent schools have their fees heavily subsidised by the government under the 'assisted places' scheme, which was introduced under the Education Act 1980 to provide help to pupils whose parents would be unable to pay. Under the scheme in force in 1990–91, if 'relevant' parental income was £8,200 or below, the fees for the child's education in 1990–91 would be covered in full. If income is higher than this prescribed figure, a sliding scale of contribution operates. The scheme covers tuition fees but not boarding charges. School uniform and transport costs may be covered, as 'incidental expenses'. The scheme applies only in schools which have entered into a 'participation agreement' with the Secretary of State – nearly 300 schools at present. Critics of the scheme argue that it involves unnecessary expense – the average assisted place contribution from the government in 1989 was £2,264 – because these children could attend state schools. In defence, it may be argued that it does relieve the LEA of the burden of educating children whose parents are nevertheless paying the community charge. The main criticism which has been raised is, however, that the scheme represents state support, both financial and ideological, for the elitist private sector.

Most independent schools appear to achieve high academic standards; many are well supported by parents and places are often over-subscribed. Salaries paid to teachers in many independent schools are no higher than in the state sector, but in general these schools are better resourced and thus equipped. Nevertheless, there is no requirement for these schools to follow the National Curriculum, with its rigorous assessment requirements, nor to have their work 'audited' in the public domain. Some commentators having contrasted the independent and state sectors suggest that regardless of the right of parents to register their dissatisfaction by withdrawing their child, there ought to be more control of independent schools. In fact, the Secretary of State does have a power to declare an independent school's provision to be 'objectionable' on the grounds of the unsuitability of premises, accommodation, teachers or proprietor of the school, or because the instruction given is inefficient or unsuitable.[43] The courts have held that the Secretary of State would be entitled to serve and enforce a notice of objection on a school which, whilst legitimately preparing a pupil to take his/her place in the sectional group to which s/he belongs, is failing to equip the pupil for life in the wider community.[44] The notice of objection must specify a period of time, of at least one month, in which the complaint may be referred to the Independent Schools Tribunal.

SCHOOL CHANGES

The statutory requirements

There is probably nothing more unsettling to the professional life of a teacher than a major change to the institution in which he or she works. Demographic changes, such as fluctuating birth rates, and urban drift, coupled with the pressure exerted on local authorities by central government to reduce unit costs and improve efficiency, have resulted in important and numerous local structural changes in educational provision. Amalgamations and closures have featured prominently; many have been keenly resisted – by teachers, through their trade unions, and by governing bodies and parents. In deciding whether to back rationalisation plans, central government has been treading the thin line between, on the one hand, supporting initiatives aimed at reducing overall costs without compromising standards, whilst, on the other, giving credence to the notion of parental choice which is so central to Conservative education policy.

Central and local government, as well as parent and teacher objectors, have to conduct their negotiations and battles within the legal framework. The legal procedures, which are outlined below, seem to be designed to ensure that there is an element of public participation, as a result of proper consultation with those likely to be affected by changes to provision, whilst the real power is left with the Secretary of State.

The statutory procedures for establishing, making a significant change to the character of, and closing a county or voluntary school are contained in sections 12 and 13 of the Education Act 1980. Changes to GM schools are covered by sections 89, 92 and 93 of the ERA 1988. It would be inappropriate to provide a detailed exposition of the procedures here, and a summary will suffice.

First, certain terms require elucidation. A 'change of character' involves change to the age range or gender composition of the pupil population for which education is to be provided at the school or a change to selection by ability or aptitude (see section 16(2) of the 1980 Act). The question of what degree or type of change is 'significant' is left to the Secretary of State. An 'amalgamation' (a term not found in the legislation) of two schools would be treated as two closures and the establishment of one school.

Turning to the procedures, it may be noted that the provisions which will now be referred to apply to all proposals for significant changes to, establishment of, and closures to, county, voluntary and grant-maintained schools, except where stated otherwise.

Section 73(1) of the ERA 1988 states that consultation with the governing body (or bodies) of any school(s) which could be eligible for GM status must occur before the LEA formulates its proposals. The purpose of this requirement has been explained as being to give the governors an opportunity to consider whether the parents should be asked whether they would favour applying for GM status for the school.[45] The LEA must then complete the formulation of its proposals and publish them, in the manner prescribed.[46] Details are to appear in a newspaper distributed in the area and must be posted in at least one conspicuous place. They must be sent to the Secretary of State. At this stage the published proposals must contain sufficient, accurate details to enable persons affected to understand their effect,[47] and must in particular state the (new) admissions total for the school and the date of implementation of the proposals.[48]

If a written objection is submitted to the LEA by 10 or more local government electors within two months of publication, or if an application is made for GM status (see above), the objection(s) must be sent to the Secretary of State for consideration by him. Where such objections have been made, the LEA's proposals require approval by the Secretary of State – an exception to the general rule, although the Secretary of State can, in any event, insist that the final decision on relevant school changes rests with him rather than the LEA if he gives notice to that effect to the authority concerned.[49] Certain proposals *always* require Secretary of State approval – those to cease maintaining a voluntary school or to change the status of the school from voluntary to county or to establish a voluntary school.[50]

The Secretary of State can either approve the proposals outright or with modifications, or reject them. Even in a case where Secretary of State approval is not required, the LEA must submit the proposals to him. Within four months of doing so they must decide whether to implement them and must communicate their decision to the Secretary of State. Assuming they have decided to implement the proposals, they must do so in accordance with their pre-determined timetable. It would appear to be the case that if they wish to modify the proposals before implementation, they need the Secretary of State's agreement.[51] Note that where a school is to be established or significantly altered, the premises require Secretary of State approval under section 14 of the Education Act 1980 (or section 90 of the ERA 1988 in the case of a GM school).

Certain special provisions may also be noted here. In a voluntary or GM school the governors may themselves resolve to discontinue the school (section 14(1) Education Act 1944 and section 92 ERA 1988). In the case of GM schools, the Secretary of State expects the discontinuance of such a school to be exceptional and unlikely to occur within the first 10 years after the establishment of the school.[52] The Secretary of State has the power under section 93 of the ERA 1988 to initiate the closure of a GM school (or, to be more accurate, to cease maintaining such a school) if he considers that it has certain 'irredeemable' deficiencies.

Challenging decisions in the courts

Challenges by parents, teachers or governors to the merits of the decision would not be possible in the courts. The courts could only interfere on the grounds of procedural unfairness or illegality of the *ultra vires* type referred to above (pp. 13 – 15). Examples of successful challenges appear below. Falling rolls in many areas have led to full- scale reorganisations and closures which, especially where village schools are concerned, have aroused great passion within the local community, leading to 'save our school' campaigns. It is clear that parental wishes must be taken into account when such decisions are taken. Apart from the right to lodge objections, parents may also cite section 76 of the Education Act 1944 which requires LEAs to secure that children are educated in accordance with the wishes of their parents. However, such wishes need only be adhered to where to do so would be compatible with the provision of efficient instruction and the *efficient use of resources*, offering little hope for a successful challenge to a school closure or reorganisation occasioned by a need to rationalise provision in the interests of efficiency and economy. Moreover, parental wishes are only one of a number of factors to be taken into account when decisions are taken by LEAs.[53] The limitations to section 76 as a basis for challenging changes to educational provision were highlighted in the 1960s when there were a number of largely unsuccessful attempts by parents and governors to stave off the introduction of comprehensive schools.[54] Nevertheless, there is another possibility: to argue that the LEA or Secretary of State has unlawfully failed to give consideration to all the issues, as happened in the first challenge to the decision by the Secretary of State to approve GM status for Beechen Cliff school and re organisation of other secondary schools in Bath.[55]

What must sometimes be frustrating for parents, teachers and governors fighting school closures or amalgamations is not only the very limited opportunity afforded by the statutory machinery to present their arguments[56] but also the narrow scope for judicial intervention. Most of the legal challenges by parents and others have been based on inadequate consultation.[57] (Note now the statutory duty to consult governing bodies over closures, and so on, contained in ERA 1988, section 73(1), above.) Parents and others may be said to have a 'legitimate expectation' that adequate consultation will take place,[58] although the duty to consult is not absolute – the authority is only required to do all that is reasonable to inform interested parties and hear representations.[59] Other procedural bases for challenge have been shown to be a failure of an education committee to fix the date for closure (leaving the matter to the chairman) and the failure of an education authority to consider a report concerned with the closure of a school.[60]

THE SECRETARY OF STATE

The essentially *local* provision of education represents an important continuity in the evolution of the education system of England and Wales, despite the centralising reforms contained in the Education Reform Act 1988. What has happened, of course, is that many powers previously enjoyed by LEAs have been transferred to governing bodies. Even so, overall responsibility for ensuring that there is sufficient educational provision, including provision in respect of children with special educational needs, still rests with LEAs.

During the late 1960s and 1970s central government began to push LEAs towards national policies, as the lack of consensus among LEAs, and even polarity (for example, over comprehensive schools), appeared to hinder progress and reform. Nevertheless, the argument that local needs required locally-tailored provision, proved powerful enough to prevent any wholesale attempt by central government to dominate the system. Central government continued to oversee the conduct of the education system, with powers to intervene (known as 'default powers') only in the most extreme of cases. The legal framework created by the 1944 Act for this role remains intact, even though overshadowed in recent years by the controls over local authorities' spending – education being the largest budget item for local government – and by the numerous central powers created by the 1988 Act.

The Secretary of State has two important legal powers under the 1944 Act, which are exercisable on his own initiative or following complaint by an individual. First, section 68 empowers him, where he is of the opinion that an LEA or governors are acting or proposing to act 'unreasonably', to give 'such directions as to the exercise of . . . the performance of [a] duty [under the Act] as appear to him to be expedient'. The courts have held that if section 68 directions are issued to an LEA the authority would be statutorily bound to comply with them and could be forced to do so by an order of *mandamus* (a court order requiring a body with a statutory duty to carry out that duty).[61] The other default power is in section 99 of the Act. It also enables the Secretary of State to issue directions to an LEA or governors, in this case if he is of the opinion that they 'have failed to discharge any duty imposed upon them by or for the purposes of this Act'. Section 99 specifically states that the directions which it authorises are enforceable by *mandamus*. The scope of the default powers has been extended to cover GM schools, and LEA-maintained special schools and FE establishments.[62] It may be noted that default powers of this nature are not uncommon; section 84 of the Children Act 1989 contains a similar power, exercisable where a local authority has failed in its duty towards children under that Act.

The courts (and the DES[63]) have viewed the default powers as intended to enable the Secretary of State to comply with the broad duty conferred on him by section 1(1) of the 1944 Act, to:

promote the education of the people of England and Wales and the progressive development of institutions devoted to that purpose, and to secure the effective execution by local authorities, under his control and direction, of national policy for providing a varied and comprehensive educational service in every area.

Traditionally there has been a marked unwillingness on the part of the Secretary of State to use the default powers. The DES has referred to their use as being a 'last resort'.[64] This is borne out by the fact that although several hundred complaints are lodged each year, generally referring to section 68 'unreasonableness', the Secretary of State has intervened in a mere handful of cases.[65] The refusal to intervene in the dispute in Dewsbury between the LEA and parents who wanted their children to attend a school where most of the pupils were white demonstrated central government's desire not to interfere in local disputes. In response to a Select Committee's call for greater default powers for those cases where the curriculum was threatened,[66] the government said it was unwilling to extend the existing powers because to do so would be contrary to the notion of partnership which the 1944 Act intended[67] (significantly weakened since, by the ERA 1988). The reluctance to make use of the default powers in the past may also have been due to the fact that the DES has tended to be 'engagingly modest in its estimation of its own power'.[68] But recent years have witnessed a rapid move away from a consensus approach to education policy making, towards one based on central autonomy; the Secretary of State and DES have acquired and are asserting greater control over the education system. So the current unwillingness may well stem from the courts' confirmation that the Act places admin istration in the hands of LEAs and only contemplates intervention by the Secretary of State in extreme cases. In the leading case, *Secretary of State for Education and Science v Tameside Metropolitan Borough Council* (1976), the House of Lords concluded that, given the considerable degree of autonomy given to LEAs by, in particular, section 8(1) of the 1944 Act – which 'leaves [LEAs] a broad discretion to choose what in their judgment are the means best suited to their areas for providing . . . instruction'[69] – the power in section 68 could only be exercised if an authority had acted in a way that 'no reasonable authority would engage in'.[70] A similar approach has been taken to the scope for intervention under section 99.[71]

In the current era of consumerism in education, with parental rights to the fore, it could be expected that the default powers might assume greater importance as parents increasingly look to challenge LEA and governor decisions. The evidence so far, however, suggests that in this regard at least the Secretary of State will not bow to these consumer pressures. The Dewsbury dispute, referred to above, offers one illustration. Another occurred in Tower Hamlets when the LEA was unable to recruit sufficient teachers to its primary schools and children were denied an education (see above, page 20). The Secretary of State declined to declare the LEA to be in default of its duty under section 8 of the 1944 Act to provide 'sufficient schools', because it considered that the authority was doing all that it reasonably could to rectify the situation. (Community representatives later failed in a legal action to have the LEA declared to be in default of its duty, which suggests the Secretary of State acted lawfully in not interfering under section 99.[72]) The Secretary of State nevertheless announced later that he was 'exploring ways of tackling the situation' in Tower Hamlets.[73] But one can only assume that at no point did a solution which the LEA (the ILEA) might have agreed, or been directed (via section 99) to adopt present itself. Parents and others can, of course, challenge in court the Secretary of State's refusal to exercise his default powers. But they are likely to meet with little success. In the *Tameside* case (above) the House of Lords said that evaluation of an LEA's act or omission was for the Secretary of State alone; the court could not substitute its view for his. In cases concerned with the exercise of powers such as those in the 1944 Act, the courts generally seek to avoid a possible conflict between their view and that of the minister.[74] Whilst the court has an inherent discretion to review the Education Secretary's exercise of discretionary power, the House of Lords in *Tameside* said that the court could not intervene if the Secretary of State 'had directed himself properly in law and had in consequence taken into consideration the matters which on a true construction of the Act he ought to have considered and excluded from his consideration matters that were irrelevant to what he had to consider' (*per* Lord Diplock).

One successful legal challenge to a failure to use the power in section 99 has occurred, however. In *R v Secretary of State for Education and Science ex parte Chance* (1982), parents of a dyslexic boy had argued that the LEA had failed in its duty to make provision for his special educational needs. The Secretary of State's failure to intervene under section 99 was considered to be unlawful, because the minister had not properly addressed the facts of the case. However, in a remark that epitomises the court's perception of its role in these cases, Woolf J emphasised that if the Secretary of State exercises his functions properly under sections 68 and 99, 'that should have the beneficial effect of avoiding the courts getting involved in education matters, which they are much less equipped to deal with than the Secretary of State'. However, such lack of involvement seems, at the time of writing, a forlorn hope. The current question of whether white Christian parents should be allowed by LEAs to have their children transferred from schools where Asian religions and culture are to the fore, in which the Secretary of State has played an important role as arbiter,[75] is one of a number of contentious issues likely to presage further legal battles, in which the powers in section 68 and 99, as well as those in the ERA 1988, are likely to receive further judicial consideration.

Questions

1. What does the Education Act 1944 mean when it states that LEAs must provide 'sufficient' schools?
2. Ought there to be a greater willingness on the part of the Secretary of State to accord voluntary aided status to more schools catering specifically for ethnic minority groups?
3. What impact might a change to grant-maintained status have on a school?
4. What is the extent of the power of the Secretary of State to control the actions (or inaction) of LEAs?

Notes

1   Troyna B 1990 'Reform or deform? The 1988 Education Reform Act and racial equality in Britain'. *New Community* 16(3): 403–16.
2   See Audit Commission 1989 *Losing an Empire, Finding a Role – the LEA of the Future*, HMSO.
3   Dent H C (1969) *The Education Act 1944*, University of London Press, p. 13.
4   This issue is discussed in Harris N S 1990 'Education by right?: breach of the duty to provide "sufficient" schools'. *Modern Law Review* 53: 525–36.
5   See the remarks by Lord Goff in *Equal Opportunities Commission v Birmingham City Council* (1989) (HL), at 775.
6   Cane P 1981 'Ultra vires breach of statutory duty'. *Public Law* 11–18.
7   See, for example, *R v Hereford and Worcester LEA ex parte William Jones* (1981) (DC) – music tuition cut by LEA which was faced with severe financial constraints – not unlawful (although was unlawful to charge for music tuition).
8   See Meredith P 1982 'Individual challenge to expenditure cuts in the provision of schools'. *Journal of Social Welfare Law* 344–51. Meredith refers to an 'absence of a clear-cut definition of any essential minimum standard and content of the education which must be provided in schools', although his comments pre-date the ERA 1988 which provides for a National Curriculum.
9   Dent, *op.cit.*, pp. 13,14.
10 See *Watt v Kesteven County Council* (1955) and *Bradbury v London Borough of Enfield* (1967).
11 *Secretary of State for Education and Science v Tameside Metropolitan Borough Council (1976) (HL); Associated Provincial Picture Houses Ltd v Wednesbury Corporation* (1948) (CA).
12 Wringe C 1981 *Children's Rights: A Philosophical Study*, Routledge & Kegan Paul, p. 139.
13 EA 1944, section 8(2)(c).
14 EA 1944, s9(5); EA 1981, s.12; the Education (Approval of Special Schools) Regulations 1983 SI 1983 No. 1499 as amended by the Education (Approval of Special Schools) (Amendment) Regulations 1991 SI 1991 No. 450.
15 Education (Middle Schools) Regulations 1980 SI 1980 No. 918.
16 See, for example, Meredith P 1989 'Educational reform'. *Modern Law Review* 52: 215–31.
17 EA 1944, section 15(3).
18 H.L. Debs Vol 526, cols 1247–1308, 4 March 1991.
19 Poulter S 1986 *English Law and Ethnic Minority Customs*, Butterworths, pp. 203–4.
20 Cumper P 1990 'Muslim schools: the implications of the Education Reform Act 1988'. *New Community* 16(3): 379–89.
21 Anderson D 1990 *Sunday Times*, 29 Apr. 1990.
22 Maclure S 1988 *Education Re-formed*, Hodder & Stoughton.
23 Section 52(1) and (2).
24 DES 1987 *Grant-Maintained Schools*.
25 See, for example, Meredith P 1989 'Educational reform'. *Modern Law Review* 52: 215–31.
26 Maclure S 1988 *Education Re-formed*, Hodder & Stoughton.

27 *Times Educational Supplement*, 2 March 1990.
28 See ERA 1988, section 62.
29 *R v Secretary of State for Education and Science ex parte Avon County Council* (1990) and the same (No.2) (1990). For cogent analysis of these cases, see Meredith P (1991) 'Opting-Out Litigation: The City of Bath Litigation 3 (2) *Education and the Law* 65–70.
30 ERA 1988, section 60.
31 Education (Parental Ballots for Acquisition of Grant-maintained Status) (Prescribed Body) Regulations 1988, SI 1988, No. 1474.
32 ERA 1988, section 60.
33 *Ibid.*, section 74. For an attempt by an LEA to prevent the transfer of the site and buildings by lending money to a council-owned company which could then lease them to the LEA and subsequently the school when it opted out, see *R v Tameside Metropolitan Borough Council ex parte Governors of Audenshaw H.S.* (1990).
34 See, for example DES Circular 10/88, para. 53.
35 *Ibid.*
36 Education (Grant-maintained Schools) (Finance) Regulations 1991, SI 1991, No. 353, replacing SI 1990, No. 549 on 1st April 1991.
37 DES Circular 10/88, para. 60.
38 Meredith P 1989 'The Education Reform Act 1988: Grant-maintained schools'. *Education and the Law* 1(3):98.
39 Maclure S 1988 *Education Re-formed*, Hodder & Stoughton.
40 Education (Abolition of Corporal Punishment) (Independent Schools) Regulations 1987, SI 1987, No. 1183, as amended.
41 *The Times*, 25 April 1990.
42 EA 1944, section 114(1) as amended.
43 EA 1944, section 71(1).
44 *R v Secretary of State for Education and Science ex parte Talmud Torah Machzikei Hadass School Trust* (1985).
45 DES Circular 10/88, para. 33.
46 Education (Publication of School Proposals) (No. 2) Regulations 1980, SI 1980, No. 658. See *Coney v Choyce* (1975) for a challenge in respect of an LEA's failure to comply fully with the publication requirements. The court refused to uphold the challenge, holding that no one had been prejudiced by the failure. See also the Education (Grant-maintained Schools) (Publication of Proposals) Regulations 1989, SI 1989, No. 1469.
47 *Legg v ILEA* (1972).
48 Education Act 1980, section 12(2), as amended; ERA 1988, section 89(3) (significant changes to GM schools).
49 Education Act 1980, section 12(5).
50 *Ibid.*, sections 12(4) and 13(4).
51 *Ibid.*, section 12(9).
52 DES Circular 10/88, para.70. The procedure is contained in section 92 of ERA 1988.
53 See *Smith v ILEA* (1978), and generally Chapter 4.
54 See, for example, *Wood v London Borough of Ealing* (1967), *Bradbury v Enfield London Borough Council (1967) and Lee v DES* (1968). For a more recent consideration of the inter-relation of school closure and parental wishes provisions (in the Education (Scotland) Act 1980) see *Harvey v Strathclyde Regional Council* (1989).

55   *R v Secretary of State for Education and Science ex parte Avon County Council* (1990).

56   Meredith P 1984 'Falling rolls and the reorganisation of schools'. *Journal of Social Welfare Law* 208–21.

57   *R v Secretary of State for Wales ex parte Hawkins* (1982); *R v Secretary of State for Education and Science ex parte Collins* (1983); *R v Secretary of State for Wales ex parte Russell* (1983); *R v Brent London Borough Council ex parte Gunning* (1985); *R v London Borough of Sutton ex parte Hamlet* (1986); *R v Hertfordshire County Council ex parte George* (1988).

58   See *Council of Civil Service Unions v Minister for the Civil Service* (1985) on the concept of 'legitimate expectation'.

59   See *The Times*, 14 May 1988, on a challenge to Gateshead LEA's schools reorganisation plans.

60   *R v Secretary of State for Education and Science ex parte Birmingham City Council* (1985) and *R v Kirklees Metropolitan Borough Council ex parte Molloy (1988), cf Nichol v Gateshead MBC* (1989).

61   *Secretary of State for Education and Science v Tameside Metropolitan Borough Council* (1976).

62   ERA 1988, section 219.

63   Oral evidence to the House of Commons Education, Science and the Arts Committee, *Second Report* (1981–82), *The Secondary School Curriculum and Examinations*, HC 116–1, para. 9.16.

64   *Ibid.*

65   Bull D 1985 'Monitoring education appeals: local ombudsmen lead the way'. *Journal of Social Welfare Law* 1985: 189, 222.

66   *Ibid.*

67   *Initial Government Observations on the Second Report from the Education, Science and the Arts Committee, Session 1981–82* (1982), Cmnd 8551.

68   Salter B and Tapper T 1981 *Education, Politics and the State*, Grant McIntyre p. 106.

69   Lord Diplock, at p. 695b.

70   Viscount Dilhorne, at p. 687d.

71   E.g., *Meade v Haringey London Borough Council (1979)* (CA).

72   *R v ILEA ex parte Ali and Murshid* (1990).

73   *HC Hansard*, 20 June 1989, col 84w.

74   See, for example, *R v Secretary of State for the Environment ex parte Ward* (1984).

75   See, for example, *The Observer*, 22 and 29 April 1990.

CHAPTER 3

Governing bodies and their role

INTRODUCTION

School governing bodies have a long history. The Elementary Education Act 1870 provided for the election of school boards to provide public elementary schools; the Act empowered boards to delegate some of their functions to boards of managers. The Education Act 1902, which introduced local education authorities in place of school boards, required all elementary schools to have managers. The Education Act 1944 provided for managers of primary schools and governors of secondary schools (sections 17 and 18). Under the Education Act 1980, the term 'manager' was dropped, and all became 'governors'.

During the 1980s school government was affected significantly both by the reforms to the education system as a whole and by changes to the composition and role of governing bodies. The government set out to strengthen the involvement of parents and the local community in the running of schools, and to enlarge significantly the role played by governing bodies through an extension of their legal powers and responsibilities – most notably via financial delegation (LMS), although there are other important areas. These two major policy strands which run through the reforms of the 1980s are interrelated. For example, not only has parental representation on school governing bodies become a statutory requirement (it was not before the 1980 Act), but governing bodies themselves are on the face of it accountable to parents in a number of ways. Governors must publish information about the school and statements of policy on such matters as sex education, and must report annually to parents. Parents also have an opportunity to elect parent governors. A further element of 'accountability' to parents stems from the requirement to consult parents before instituting certain changes – for example, alteration of the starting and finishing times of school sessions (as stated in the Education (No.2) Act 1986, section 21(2)).

The reforms of recent years have not altered the basic requirement (contained in section 1 of the 1986 Act, or sections 53 and 58 of the ERA 1988 in the case of GM schools) that there is, for each school, an *instrument of government* which provides for the constitution of a governing body and *articles of government* which set out the way in which the school is to be conducted. The instrument of government basically reflects the requirements as to composition of governing bodies laid down in the Act (see below). The articles refer to the division of legal responsibilities of governors, the head teacher, the LEA and, in GM schools, the Secretary of State. Specific matters covered by the articles include admissions, discipline, reports and meetings. Model articles were specified in Annexes to DES Circular 7/87; they have recently been revised.

THE RE-SHAPING OF SCHOOL GOVERNING BODIES AND THE EXTENSION OF THEIR ROLE

The major impetus for reforming the composition of school governing bodies, which culminated in the conformations laid down by the 1986 Education (No.2) Act, came from the report of the Taylor Committee in 1977 – although its recommendations may be seen as a 'clarification, regularization and updating of the more defensible arrangements arrived at by many LEAs in the mid-seventies'.[1] The Committee recommended that on boards of governors there should be equal representation from four groups – parents, the LEA, staff and the local community – in addition to general consultation with parents.

Comprehensive reform of governing bodies necessitated changes in the law, for at this time the constitution of managing and governing bodies was in accordance with the requirements of the Education Act 1944. In authorities where there was no minor authority, the constitution of a county primary or secondary school's managing or governing body was to be determined by the LEA. In voluntary schools there were to be LEA and foundation managers or governors – in the ratio of 2:1 in controlled schools and 1:2 in aided and special agreement schools. Parents were not barred from managing/governing bodies, but parental representation was provided for in only a small minority of schools – usually in the form of parent-teacher association representation. The Plowden Report had recommended that parents of children attending a primary school should be represented on its managing body.[2] The demand for parental representation grew. In the 1970s, as a result partly of consumer pressure,[3] but also as a result of the intensifying debate about educational standards,[4] LEAs increasingly appointed parents to managing/governing bodies. In a 1975 survey, some 85 per cent of LEAs claimed to appoint parents to boards; four years later another survey showed that proportion had risen to 90 per cent.[5] The Taylor Committee's Report,[6] which backed the call for greater parental representation on governing bodies, added further impetus for reform.

Political interest in legitimising parent participation grew. Demands for increased involvement were coming mostly from middle-class parents; so the in-coming Conservative government in 1979 was thus able to reward many of its traditional supporters by guaranteeing parental representation on school governing bodies. The Education Act 1980 required all schools to have two parent governors, both (in the case of county schools) to be elected by secret ballot. But evidence emerged from a DES-commissioned study that parents elected as governors were frequently neither representative of, nor able effectively to represent the views of, parents with children at the school; however, this did not dissuade the Conservative government from proposing, in 1984, a parental majority on school governing bodies.[7] This proposal would clearly have been unworkable, and such was the opposition to it that the government abandoned the idea. But the government continued to advance the view that the involvement of parents, both generally and as school governors, would put pressure on schools and LEAs to improve standards. Fresh proposals were published in a White Paper in 1985.[8] The legislative changes needed to give effect to the White Paper proposals appeared the following year (in the Education (No.2) Act 1986). The opportunity was also taken to ensure that 'no single interest will predominate'.[9] The potential for a dominant political influence on governing bodies has been reduced, in that LEA representatives are clearly to be in the minority, and wider local representation comes from having representation from the local 'business community' (via co-option: section 6). As under the 1980 Act, teacher representation is limited to one or two teachers, depending on the size of the school (one if less than 300 pupils, otherwise two). The head teacher can elect not to be a governor; otherwise s/he serves as a governor in an ex officio capacity. The 1986 Act also makes provision for grouping schools so that two or more schools can be served by one governing body.[10] No provision is made for pupil governors – the minimum age for becoming a school governor is, in any event, 18. However, an 18-year-old pupil could, in theory, be co-opted as a governor. Both the White Paper and the Circular containing advice on governing bodies under the 1986 Act (7/87) are silent on this point. The Taylor Committee recommended that secondary school pupils be allowed to attend governors' meetings as observers, but felt there was also a case for changing the law so that they could acquire full membership.

So, under the Education (No.2) Act 1986 the basic composition of a governing body of a *county* or *maintained special school* is now as follows (the number of governors in each category is shown in parentheses):

A. *Schools with fewer than 100 pupils:* parents (2), LEA (2), head teacher (1), teachers (1), co-opted (3).
B. *Schools with between 100 and 299 pupils:* parents (3), LEA (3), head teacher (1), teachers (1) co-opted (4).
C. *Schools with between 300 and 599 pupils:* parents (4), LEA (4), head teacher (1), teachers (2), co-opted (5).

D. Schools with 600 or more pupils: parents (5), LEA (5), head teacher (1), teachers (2), co-opted (6).

In *controlled* schools there will be foundation governors in place of some of the co-opted governors: *A.* (2), *B.* (3), *C.* (4) and *D.* (4). In *aided* and *special agreement* schools, the number of teacher and head-teacher governors follows exactly the same pattern as for county schools. There will be more foundation governors than in controlled schools – the foundation governors must outnumber the combined total of the others (of whom the Act requires simply that there be at least one of each) by two, or three if there are 19 or more governors in all. The governing body of a *grant-maintained school* must be constituted thus: parents (5), teachers (1 or 2), head teacher (1) (note that s/he *must* be a member), and first or foundation governors[11] (eight or nine, or possibly more – there must be sufficient to outnumber the others by at least one). The total number of governors in a GM school will thus be either 15, 17 or any higher number – quite a large number given the fact that schools which opt out could be quite small.

In *Better Schools* the government argued that the changes in the required composition of governing bodies were necessary, *inter ali*a, to enable sufficient account to be taken of 'parents' natural and special interest in their children's education and progress'. The achievement of this via increased parental representation on governing bodies presupposed that most parents' interests would be represented by the tiny number (five for a school with 600 or more pupils) of elected parent governors. However, it is well known that parent governors are more likely to act as individuals, offering a parent's (subjective) perspective on an issue rather than as delegates for the parent community attached to any particular school.[12] The fact that parent governors generally have to be elected[13] gives an appearance of a democratic model of parental involvement in decision making. In reality, the real objective which has been achieved has been that of ending the potential for LEA domination of school government.[14] In any event, several aspects of the 1986 Act's school government regime are patently anti-democratic. For example, parent governors may hold office for up to four years. A parent could be elected near the end of his/her child's period at the school, and continue for some years after the child has left. A parent governor is not disqualified from membership simply because his/her child has left the school. This contrasts with the position relating to teacher governors (to be elected by the teaching staff from their own number) – they must relinquish their place on the governing body once they cease to be employed at the school. However, the democratic *process* is well served in the arrangements made for ensuring that election is by secret ballot and that all reasonable and practicable steps are taken to inform all persons who may be eligible to vote of their right to do so and of the voting arrangements.[15]

Apart from the need in some cases to belong to a particular social or occupational category – that is 'parent', 'teacher' or member of the 'local business community' – there are no specific qualifications which are a pre-requisite to governorship. Indeed, one of the criticisms of heaping so many additional functions upon governing bodies under the 1986 and 1988 Acts – in particular, control of the school's budget – is that governors are simply unqualified for the task now demanded of them. The government has sought to deflect this criticism by pointing out: (1) the power to co-opt experts to assist the governors in their task; and (2) the legal duty on LEAs to ensure that governors receive information and training,[16] for which the government has made significant sums available via education support grants (for example, nearly £5 million in 1989–90 simply for training on local financial management).

Nevertheless, certain major problems have beset the government's policy on parental involvement in the running of schools. First, there have been difficulties in finding enough persons willing to serve as parent governors since the 1986 Act arrangements came into operation in 1988 and 1989. There have also been complaints over the election of parent governors. Those responsible for the conduct of elections are given a great deal of discretion over the procedures to be followed and the method of deciding the issue.[17] In one case of alleged irregularity in the election of parent governors, redress was sought in the courts (although the court considered that the matter should have been pursued via complaint to the Secretary of State under section 99 of the 1944 Act).[18] Now there is now a real danger of large-scale resignation as the true burden of serving as a governor following the 1988 Act becomes evident. (A governor who simply stops attending meetings and who has not attended a meeting for twelve months would be disqualified from the governing body under the Education (School Government) Regulations 1989, which also prescribe disqualification for persons with certain criminal convictions, undischarged bankruptcy or more than four governorships at the same time.[19]) When the increased burdens placed on governors by LMS are taken into account it is clear that governors have a task of great magnitude. They are now responsible for decisions on: maintenance of buildings; appointment and dismissal of most teaching staff members; the school's policy on discipline; the effective discharge by the school of its responsibilities under the National Curriculum and in relation to religious education and collective worship; the provision of information to parents; whether sex education should be offered as part of the secular curriculum; the times of school sessions; admissions to school (aided schools only); and most important of all, (1) overall responsibility for the conduct of the school, and (2) control of expenditure of the school's budget share. This burden does not rest solely with parent governors; business community governors – local shopkeepers, solicitors, medical practitioners, water authority employees and others

– will find the task of school government both time-consuming and draining, and thus difficult to combine with career demands.

Of course, in many cases *de facto* control over those affairs of the school for which the governors have responsibility will rest with the head teacher, who will thus shoulder much of the day-to-day burden. In some cases, for example over exclusion of pupils, the law gives head teachers specific independent functions, in line with the government's wish to give the role of the head teacher 'a firm legal foundation, clarifying his responsibilities and preserving his authority'.[20] The nature of the relationship and division of responsibilities between head teachers and governing bodies will not be determined solely by the law; much will depend on the individuals themselves and how they perceive their own and one another's respective tasks. Moreover, although the 1986 Act aimed to establish a clear-cut division of responsibilities, the law has not fully achieved this and, in any event, it has not been so easy to put this policy into practice. The introduction of local financial management (LMS) has now begun to cloud the distinction in practice between the 'management' roles of governors and heads. For example, the government has explained that under LMS (which is discussed more fully below) 'the governing body and the head teacher will have freedom to deploy resources within the school's budget according to their own educational needs and priorities'.[21] The governors and the head will together produce a development plan, and the head will have a 'key role . . . in securing its implementation'. But in developing such a plan, governing bodies 'will need to take account of the full range of their responsibilities for the management of schools'.[22] It is inevitable that these power relationships will need to be worked out on a school-by-school basis as governors find that the new demands placed on them draw them more and more closely into the internal regime of the school. Establishing a good working relationship with heads will clearly be important. Some heads may find themselves seeking to thwart 'interventionist tendencies' by governors;[23] but the government hopes that governors will stand firm in demanding higher standards from schools. In order to play their new role effectively, governors will need to 'spend more time at the school . . . work hard and show great determination'.[24]

LOCAL MANAGEMENT OF SCHOOLS

Local management of schools (LMS) is presenting school governing bodies with their biggest challenge so far. In all schools covered by a delegation scheme control of the budget will rest with the governors. The ERA 1988 required all LEAs to submit delegation schemes in respect of such schools to the Secretary of State for approval.

The Secretary of State has a power to reject a scheme or ask for modifications – and in extreme cases to substitute a scheme of his own, although so far this has not happened. Not all LEA schools have to be covered by LMS. Delegation may not, as yet, be made to governors of special schools (although section 43 of the Act empowers the Secretary of State to extend LMS to these schools) or to nursery schools. Under the 1988 Act, primary schools with fewer than 200 pupils do not have to be included in a delegation scheme, although they may be. But at the end of 1990 it was announced that *all* primary schools would have to be given control of their own budgets in the near future.

Much of the discussion surrounding LMS has concentrated upon the role of governors under the new system, and clearly its success or otherwise hinges largely around the ability of governors to exercise financial management effectively and in a way that is responsive to the school's needs. A major justification for LMS according to the government is the fact that governors are more in touch with the needs of the school and are far more likely to have its interests at heart than the more distant LEA with its political interests to pursue. Staffing, maintenance of premises, catering, cleaning, teaching and learning resources and other equipment are among the matters with which governors will be directly concerned under LMS. Moreover, as a school's budget share will depend principally on pupil numbers (and ages), the provisions of the Act concerned with 'open enrolment' will also be an important area for governors. The implication is that governors will need to ensure that schools are able to attract the maximum number of pupils they can accommodate, and may have to employ marketing skills in order to do so. The spirit of competition which is being fostered will, the government hopes, pressurise schools into improving standards and thus secure their future by ensuring a continuing high level of demand for places. Critics point to the inability of some schools to 'compete' in this way, although provision is made for socio-economic and environmental factors which may affect a school's performance to be taken into account when determining its budget share.

If LMS is the key area of concern for school governors at present, what does it mean for the teacher? The fact that governors have control over most staff appointments, discipline and dismissals will clearly be relevant. This is discussed in Chapter 9, but it may be noted here that governors will have important decisions to make which will affect the teaching staff as a whole. For example, if funds are tight – and there is little doubt they will be, especially in schools with high salary costs as a result of having a large number of experienced staff but a budget share which reflects only the LEA's *average* teacher costs – decisions will have to be made about the grade at which an appointment should be made, whether part-time hours should be bought in, instead of replacing a full-timer, whether sorely needed administrative or technical support can be afforded, or even whether the photocopier can be repaired. But because the amount available for allocation to schools by LEAs in 1990 was severely limited by charge-capping in many local authorities, there has been talk of massive teacher redundancies. This effect of charge-capping is said to have compounded the problem of inadequacy of resources available to schools under the budget-share formulas in financial delegation schemes, and to have created the absurdity of threatened redundancies at a time of teacher shortages. It also gave rise to a curious legal problem. A number of charge-capped LEAs argued that because their schools' budget shares had already been determined the cuts on expenditure required by subsequent charge-capping could not be made. This argument was pursued in a June/July 1990 legal challenge, by way of an application for judicial review, to the charge-capping by Environment Secretary Chris Patten. The challenge, which was pursued all the way to the House of Lords, was unsuccessful.

The budget-share formula will determine the amount to which a particular school may be entitled under a delegation scheme in a particular year. But this amount will depend on the total sum that is available for distribution to schools. The starting point is the *general schools budget*, defined in section 33(4) of the ERA 1988 as the amount appropriated by the LEA for expenditure on schools in that financial year. From the general schools budget, certain items must be deducted – as *mandatory exceptions* – whilst others *may* be deducted as *discretionary exceptions*; once these deductions are made the residual amount will be the *aggregated schools budget*, from which each school's share will be allocated in accordance with the *budget-share formula.*

The mandatory exceptions, which must be deducted from the general schools budget, cover capital expenditure, repayments on loans to cover capital expenditure, expenditure falling to be taken into account in determining the amount of certain central government grants (such as education support grants and LEA training grants), and other prescribed items.[25] Schemes also make provision for exception of the cost of certain central administrative services (such as legal services) and advisory services. Advisory services can appear very expensive, and some head teachers have queried whether less should be withheld from delegation for LEA inspection and advisory services, which may be seen as something of a 'luxury' when, for example, schools do not have the resources to deliver the National Curriculum. Nevertheless, these services are clearly important if LEAs are to continue playing the residual monitoring role which the government has given them. Certainly, LEAs will resist any attempts to diminish any further their reduced opportunities to influence educational provision by schools.

In this initial phase of LMS, the discretionary exceptions are expected to amount in total to not more than 10 per cent of the general schools budget during the first three years of a delegation scheme, with a reduction thereafter to 7 per cent maximum.[26] Some items will not be subject to the initial 10 per cent limit, however, such as school meals and insurance for governors. The main item of expenditure to which the 10 per cent limit will apply is repairs and maintenance. In county schools LEAs will be expected to retain an amount to cover their responsibility for the structure and exterior of buildings, maintenance of playgrounds, and so on, whilst making sums available to governors in the delegation scheme for emergency repairs or routine maintenance such as replacement of broken windows or repairs to leaking roofs. The suggested division of responsibility between LEAs and governors for repairs and maintenance is set out in Annex A to DES Circular 7/88. (In aided and special agreement schools sums to meet all maintenance costs are expected to be delegated to governors.[27]) Various items which must or might most effectively be provided centrally, such as education welfare officers, educational psychologists, pupil support (uniform grants and educational maintenance grants and so forth), peripatetic and supply teachers and contingency moneys, are also expected to be included in the discretionary items covered by the initial 10 per cent limit. However, given the overriding principle of 'maximum delegation' which the government wishes to see applied, these items do not have to excepted. For example, many delegation schemes provide for schools to be allocated sums to cover the hiring of supply staff from the LEA's supply service. But such costs are difficult to predict, and often the scheme will have to provide for longer-term supply needs to be met by the LEA. This in turn requires the LEA to retain quite a large contingency fund, which ties up precious resources.[28]

The *budget-share formula* laid down in the delegation scheme determines an individual school's allocation for the financial year in question.[29] The formula is supposed to enable a school's 'objective needs' to be met.[30] The central determinant of these needs is the number of pupils at the school, weighted for differences in their ages – so that generally schemes will provide for more resources for a secondary school pupil than for a pupil attending a primary school. Thus, assumptions about teaching costs, of which teachers' salaries form the principal element, are reflected in the formula. But as shown above, it is *average* teaching costs across a LEA's schools which are taken into account, not *actual* costs. A survey of over 1,000 schools by the NAS/UWT in 1989 showed that over half would lose money as a result of actual teacher costs not being the basis of funding. Special account is, however, to be taken of the problems in small schools, whose low pupil numbers mean that the amount available to cover teaching costs could be insufficient to enable the school to meet its legal obligations under the National Curriculum, and in schools with large numbers of pupils with special educational needs where the pupil–teacher ratio may need to be lower. Allowance is also made for certain other factors – for example, the fact that a school may have higher heating costs because of the design of its buildings or higher repair bills because of the high incidence of vandalism in the area. Adjustment is also made to take account of the extent of social deprivation in the area which the school serves. In some cases a transitional period is allowed to operate, enabling adjustment to the new basis of funding to occur over a period of up to four years. This may be particularly useful for schools with highly experienced staff and thus higher than average teaching costs.

There are a number of control mechanisms. Schemes must make provision for monitoring and evaluation of their operation once actual delegation has taken place. LEAs can, in cases where the budget is not being managed satisfactorily or where the requirements of the scheme have not been met, suspend financial delegation on giving one month's notice (which is not required in the most serious cases). Reasons for the suspension must be given before it is to take effect. The suspension can be appealed against (to the Secretary of State) and must in any event be reviewed before the beginning of the financial year.[31] The 1988 Act and regulations made thereunder also provide for publication, before the start of each financial year, of a statement showing the various figures on which each school's allocation that year will be based – the general school's budget, aggregated budget, deductions, the allocation formula, planned expenditure per pupil and so on.[32] A further statement, showing the amount of actual expenditure per school and in aggregate, must be published at the end of the financial year to which it relates.[33]

It will be seen that the above requirements are intended to provide a basis for the allocation of resources to individual schools, whilst ensuring that a check is made on the way the governors exercise their powers of expenditure of the school's budget. Many of the fears which have been expressed about LMS have concerned the method of allocating resources, especially the pupil numbers basis, but there is also concern about whether governors will be able to perform their role effectively. It has been suggested that even though large sums have been made available for governor training, LMS has been introduced before proper training provision could realistically be established. So far as teachers are concerned, the most worrying aspects are the threat to jobs in schools for which the formula provides inadequate funding to meet actual teacher costs and the fact that LMS has put the school curriculum into the market-place, showing up inevitable disparities between staffing and equipment levels in different schools. Perhaps the major criticism overall, which can be heard from nearly all quarters, is that it is virtually impossible to produce 'a more effective and responsive school system' (which the Coopers and Lybrand report[34] which formed the basis for the government's thinking on LMS saw as the principal goal of financial delegation) at a time of major curriculum change, without additional resources.

Putting resources into the hands of governors has been presented as a way of enabling schools to become more responsive to their clients – parents, pupils, employers and the community in general.[35] But although meeting client needs might be the ultimate objective of any corporate enterprise, and one of which few might disapprove, allowing commercial factors to dictate the means to that end can have deleterious effects where many schools are concerned, as we saw above. On the other hand, the government might well argue that the benefits of LMS far outweigh the drawbacks. LMS has heightened financial/commercial awareness of teachers and governors, who, like business managers, will now appreciate the need to manage financial resources carefully and remain 'competitive'. Improved efficiency may well come about as a result of governors being able to spend money on meeting particular needs as they arise – for example, repairs which it may have taken the LEA weeks or months to have carried out, or the purchase of books which may have been subject to similar delay. But there are serious doubts about whether an overall improvement in the quality of provision, which is an aim LMS is intended to serve, will result from these reforms. One major obstacle is likely to be the difficulty of persuading head teachers and governors that all the extra work and time that is required, including numerous meetings and masses of paperwork, are really worth the effort – although several head teachers are reported to be seeing immediate benefits from the freedom to purchase much-needed items for their school.

SCHOOL GOVERNORS' MEETINGS

In view of the greatly increased functions of governing bodies under LMS and other provisions, it is important to consider the legal framework for decision making by governors, which is concerned primarily with governors' meetings and delegation of decision-making powers.

All teachers should take an interest in school governors' meetings, given the shift in power from LEAs to governing bodies. It is important for a teacher to be aware of the executive decision-making processes which operate in a school if s/he is to ensure that his/her view, or that of the department to which s/he belongs, is presented in the appropriate forum. Say, for example, the teacher considered that more money should be made available for the purchase of additional computers for use in teaching. This matter could be taken up with the head teacher, who may have been delegated a decision-making power over such matters, or could be put to a relevant sub-committee of the governors; but this might be part of a wider resource allocation issue which the governing body may have to address in a full governors' meeting. Governors may also have to consider staffing or pupil disciplinary matters in which the teacher concerned may have a particular interest. Personal interest in such matters may bar a teacher from attending all or part of a meeting at which they are being considered. But even so, the teacher may want to make representations to be considered at the appropriate time.

Neither notice of a governors' meeting nor an agenda need be given to all teachers at the school, however. Nor is there is a requirement to post an agenda on a school notice-board or similar place. Teacher governors would, of course, normally consult staff over any forthcoming agenda items in which they might have an interest, to ensure that their views on the subject in question are aired. Teachers might also be asked whether there are any matters they would wish to see raised as 'any other business' or included on the agenda for a future meeting. Reporting back to fellow teachers after a meeting would seem to be sensible, even though the governors must ensure that minutes of the meeting are kept and made available for inspection at the school premises.[36] Confidential matters in general, and the names of teachers or pupils about whom certain matters were discussed, would normally have to be excluded from the minutes on display.[37]

Normally the agenda and notice of the meeting must be provided to governors, the head teacher and the chief education officer at least seven days before the date of the meeting. The proceedings are not invalidated by a subsequent discovery that a member did not receive his/her notification. These requirements, and others referred to below, are contained in the Education (School Government) Regulations 1989.[38] Each governing body has a clerk who is to convene the meeting in accordance with a decision of the governors at their previous meeting or at the instruction of the chair of governors.[39] At least one meeting of the full governing body must be held each school term;[40] sub-committees, increasingly in use since LMS and covering separate functions such as curriculum or staffing, may meet as frequently as they wish. A full governors' meeting is to be chaired by the chair to the governors, or vice chair if the chair is not in attendance. Both must be elected from among the governing body, at the first meeting in each school year. The regulations bar teachers from election to either office.[41] The quorum for the meeting is stipulated as being the greater of (1) three governors or (2) one-third of membership (that is four, if there are 12 governors) or (3) the quorum specified in the instrument of government, provided that it is not more than two-fifths of the total membership.[42] For any decision to be binding it must have been approved by a majority of members participating in the vote.[43]

The 1989 regulations also make provision for attendance at meetings by non-governors, withdrawal from meetings and voting. In some cases the governors themselves have the final say on such matters. For example, the governors must decide whether they wish to permit teachers or parents to attend the proceedings.[44] It is a principle of natural justice that a person is given an opportunity to know the substance of any case being brought against him and to make representations to the 'judges'. The school government regulations partially reflect this by conferring a right on the governing body to allow any teacher or pupil who is the subject of a disciplinary hearing to attend and be heard. The governors may also request witnesses – for example, a teacher in a disciplinary hearing involving a pupil – to attend and answer questions or make representations.[45]

Governors themselves may only be required to withdraw from a meeting if one of the prescribed circumstances laid down in the Schedule to the regulations applies. Possibly the most important of these so far as a teacher governor is concerned relates to having a direct or indirect pecuniary interest in any proposed contract or other matter which is being considered. If a teacher governor with such an interest attended the meeting it might seem to those not on the governing body that his/her presence might have prevented the governors' decision from being wholly impartial, even if the governor concerned took no part in the discussions or vote. For example, if the governors were considering whether the school should be turned into a city technology college[46] (but not a grant-maintained school[47]) s/he would have a pecuniary interest in the outcome because his/her employment would change in a significant way (see chapter 2, p. 28). If a teacher governor's promotion, retirement, dismissal or similar matter is under consideration, s/he would be expected not to participate in the discussion and, unless the governors decide otherwise, to withdraw from the meeting. S/he could not vote on the matter. A teacher governor may also have an interest in the retirement and so on of another member of staff, in that it could create an opportunity for his/her promotion or the appointment of a spouse as replacement. The same rules on withdrawal, voting, and so forth, would apply.[48] The Schedule to the regulations also limits attendance by pupils whose admission or conduct are being considered, and their parents. If the governors are hearing an appeal in respect of a disciplinary matter, none of the governors who have previously dealt with the matter may participate or vote[49] – which usually rules out the head teacher (except in cases involving discipline of staff,[50] although even here withdrawal is considered desirable).

DELEGATION OF DECISION-MAKING AUTHORITY

The Education (School Government) Regulations 1989 legitimised what was probably an existing practice of delegating decision-making powers to head teachers, members (usually chairs) of governing bodies or committees of governors. As the extent of their responsibilities and functions had grown since the 1988 Act, it was felt that the 1987 regulations of the same name required amendment to enable the necessary delegation to take place within the law. The ability to divide their work among smaller sub-committees has relieved much of the pressure of time from school governors – indeed, in many cases it has most likely prevented the new system of school government from being unworkable in the context of LMS.

The government recognised that to enable decisions to be taken by individuals or small groups rather than the full governing body would appear to be incompatible with the policy of maximising community and parent participation in education decision making, and they offered the assurance that 'key policy decisions' would remain the responsibility of the whole governing body.[51] Accordingly, the regulations listed 17 broad and narrow areas where the function could not be delegated – for example, school admissions, curricular responsibilities and policy statements, times of school sessions and dates of terms, and initiation of procedure for grant-maintained status.[52] In most other cases delegation can be to the head teacher, a sole governor or a committee of governors constituted as the governors see fit. Persons other than governors can be co-opted on to these sub-committees; the intention is that where a particular form of expertise is needed it can be brought in. But such co-optees will have no voting rights.

In two specific cases delegation may only be to a committee and not to an individual. These are: (1) dismissal of a member of staff and appeals by him/her in connection therewith; and (2) reinstatement of a pupil and appeals relating thereto.[53] In these two cases the composition of the committee must be as prescribed for each respectively.[54]

Where a decision has been taken by a delegated body, it must be reported to the next meeting of the full governing body.[55]

CONCLUSION

Even with the not inconsiderable amount of governor training that is being undertaken at present, plus the welcome establishment by many LEAs of governor support units since 1988 and the recently acquired power to delegate functions, it is likely that far too much is being expected of governing bodies. It seems highly probable that governors will struggle to meet their new responsibilities and that effective school government and a more efficient model of local control may not be achieved despite government claims to the contrary.

It is said that despite their duty to provide various types of information to parents (see Chapter 5), and despite the election of parent governors, school governing bodies are not truly accountable to parents – and certainly not to teachers. There is an element of accountability, however. Governors do have to hold an annual meeting which all parents must be invited to attend;[56] and the governors' annual report to parents,[57] which is to contain an account of the governors' exercise of their functions over the previous year and the school calendar for the year ahead, must be laid for discussion at the meeting. The purpose of the annual meeting is to discuss the role of the governors during the previous year. The government has argued that the report and meeting should serve to secure the closer involvement of parents with the life of the school.[58] It is, therefore, rather surprising that there is no legal requirement for teachers to be present; nor do teachers have a legal right to attend – although there would be no reason to exclude a teacher from the meeting. In any event, these meetings have so far been very poorly attended in most schools, a reflection not so much of parental apathy but rather a perceived lack of clear purpose to the exercise.[59]

Questions

1. To what extent do you agree with the view that following the 1986 and 1988 Acts, too much is now expected of school governors?
2. What scope is there for the classroom teacher to play a role in the government of schools?
3. What impact is LMS (local management of schools) likely to have on the classroom teacher?

Notes

1 Beattie N 1985 *Professional Parents*, Falmer, p. 201.
2 Plowden (Lady) (Chair) 1967 *Children and their Primary Schools,* HMSO, vol. 1, para. 1150.
3 Richardson A 1983 *Participation,* Routledge & Kegan Paul, p. 38.
4 Beattie N *op. cit.* pp. 194–205.
5 *Ibid.*
6 Taylor Committee 1977 *A New Partnership for Our Schools*, HMSO.
7 DES 1984 *Parental Influence at School, Green Paper, Cmnd 9242, HMSO.*
8 DES 1985 *Better Schools*, Cmnd 9469, HMSO.
9 *Ibid,* para. 221.
10 See section 9 and Schedule 1.
11 If the school was formerly voluntary, it will have foundation governors. In other cases there will be 'first' governors.
12 Sutherland M 1988 *Theory of Education*, Longman, pp. 79–80.
13 In certain circumstances – for example, if too few parents present themselves as candidates – parent governors may have to be appointed (Education (No.2) Act 1986, section 5). Otherwise, elections must be arranged – by the LEA or, where voluntary aided or GM schools are concerned, by the governing body (section 15).
14 Possibly symptomatic of the frustration caused by their reduced influence on governing bodies has been the attempt by the ruling group on some councils not to appoint any political opponents as LEA representatives, which prompted a proposal by Jack Straw, MP, Labour's education spokesperson, for a bill which would ensure that all parties with

councillors would be represented: *The Times*, 8 Feb. 1990. Some LEAs have also abused or misused their power to remove governors they have appointed. In *R v Brent LBC ex parte Assegai* (1987) the LEA failed to adhere to natural justice when it dismissed a governor without giving a proper reason or an opportunity for a written explanation to be proffered by the governor concerned. Dismissal of two governors for failing to support LEA policy on the future of two voluntary controlled schools and of two others who objected to a trustee's scheme concerning a voluntary aided school resulted in the quashing of the decision by the courts in both cases: *R v Governors of Haberdashers' Aske's Schools ex parte ILEA sub nom; Brunyate v ILEA* (1989) (HL); and *R v Trustee of the Roman Catholic Diocese of Westminster ex parte Andrews* (1989). In *R v Warwickshire County Council v Dill-Russell and Anr* (1990) the LEA decided, following a council election, to dismiss all its governors and appoint new governors. The LEA argued that it had taken this step because, following the election, the numbers of LEA governors of each political affiliation were no longer in proportion with the representation of the political parties on the council. The Divisional Court and Court of Appeal held that the LEA had had a legitimate purpose for its action.

15 Education (No.2) Act 1986, section 15(6).
16 *Ibid.*, section 57(b).
17 See DES Circular 7/87, Annex 9.
18 *R v Northamptonshire County Council ex parte Gray* (1986), *The Times* 10 June 1986.
19 SI 1989, No.1503, regs 5–8.
20 Note 8, p. 227.
21 DES Circular 7/88 *Education Reform Act: Local Management of Schools*, para.21.
22 *Ibid.*, para.22.
23 Maclure S 1988 *Education Re-formed*, Hodder & Stoughton, p. 147.
24 *Ibid*, pp. 147–8.
25 See the Education (Financial Delegation to Schools) (Mandatory Exceptions) Regulations 1989, SI 1989, No. 1352.
26 DES Circular 7/88, paras 96 and 97.
27 *Ibid.*, para.71.
28 T. Blanchard *et al.*, *Managing Finance in Schools* (1989), London, Cassell, pp. 42–3.
29 Education Reform Act 1988, section 38.
30 DES Circular 7/88, para.99.
31 Education Reform Act 1988, section 37.
32 *Ibid.*, section 42(3)–(5).
33 *Ibid.*, section 42(6) and (7) and the Education (School Financial Statements) (Prescribed Particulars, etc) Regulations 1990, SI 1990, No. 353. A similar statement, for schools not covered by a delegation scheme, is also required: Education (Pre-Scheme Financial Statements) Regulations 1989, SI 1989, No. 370.
34 *Local Management of Schools* (1987).
35 DES Circular 7/88, para.9.
36 Education (School Government) Regulations 1989, SI 1989, No. 1503, regs 22 and 24(1).
37 Reg.24(2).
38 See note 36.

39 *Ibid.*, reg.19(1).
40 Reg. 12(1).
41 Reg. 9(5).
42 Reg.13. In a small number of prescribed cases a quorum amounting to three-quarters of governors entitled to vote on the matter in question is required (reg.13(3)).
43 Reg.14(1).
44 Reg.21.
45 Reg.14(4).
46 *Bostock v Kay* (1989).
47 Schedule, para.2(4), confirming the decision in *R v Governors of Small Heath School ex parte Birmingham City Council* (1989).
48 Education (School Government) Regulations 1989, Schedule, paras 3 and 4. See also *Noble v ILEA* (1984).
49 Para.5(1)(d).
50 Para.5(2).
51 DES 1989 *Amendments to the Education (School Government) Regulations 1987*. Consultation Document, May 1989.
52 Education (School Government) Regulations 1989, *op. cit.*, reg.25(2).
53 Reg 25(2) and (3).
54 Reg 26(5) and (6).
55 Reg 27.
56 Education (No.2) Act 1986, section 31(1).
57 Required by section 30 of the 1986 Act, and section 58(5)(j) of the 1988 Act in the case of grant-maintained schools.
58 DES Circular 8/86, para.13.
59 See Blanchard *et al.* 1989 *Managing Finance in Schools*, *op. cit.*, pp. 89–90.

CHAPTER 4

Parental rights and responsibilities

INTRODUCTION: PARENTS, CHILDREN AND THE STATE

The concept of parental rights in education could be said to be concerned with the ability of parents to extend the control they are able to exert within the family to their child's formal education, thus protecting their 'interest' in the child. But the concept of parental rights is not an unlimited one. The exercise of parental autonomy is constrained by various factors. One arises out of the need for state provision of education to be efficient and economical, which means that policy considerations might outweigh individual parental preference. This has been well illustrated by section 76 of the Education Act 1944, which provides that 'children are to be educated in accordance with the wishes of their parents', provided that this would be 'compatible with the provision of efficient instruction and training and the avoidance of unreasonable public expenditure'. The courts have made clear on several occasions that section 76 lays down a 'general principle' of parental choice which is only one of a *number* of factors to which an LEA could or should have regard when exercising their functions.[1] Nevertheless, despite a similar provision in section 6(3) of the Education Act 1980 (enabling, until the ERA 1988 restricted its effect to schools which are not yet subject to LMS, parental preference to be denied formally on economic efficiency grounds) considerable extensions of parental rights have occurred, as shown below. These have produced a conflict between state and parents' interests,[2] whilst failing to advance the independent rights of children.[3]

In another field, that of child care law, the relationship between parents', children's and state interests and rights has been affected by an increasing emphasis on the paramountcy of the child's welfare. It has been pointed out[4] that the legal protection of children's welfare is not the same as the conferment of rights on children, since it presupposes that welfare agencies, judges and even parents would have the right to take decisions on the child's behalf. The law might be seen to seek a balance between paternalism and liberation, accepting that whilst advancement of the autonomy interests of children to make their own decisions in respect of their own lives is an appropriate aim of the law, some restrictions are necessary to enable children to progress safely to maturity. There is, of course, room for disagreement about how much independence to grant children at different stages of their development. In any event, the real debate has focused on the question of how the 'paternalistic' or protective role should be shared between parents and state.

The law governing school attendance, which is discussed below, provides a good illustration of how the interests of state, parent and child interrelate. Put simply, LEAs have a duty to intervene when children are not being educated. Action is taken against parents, for it is they who carry the burden of ensuring that the child attends school. If the child is absent, parents will be in breach of the law unless they can, for example, demonstrate that an efficient education is being provided to their child outside the school system. Here it is assumed that the child's right to education is a correlative of the parent's duty to send the child to school. Despite the fact that the state system of education is over 100 years old, it is still regarded as a fundamental duty of parenthood to educate one's child. In his *Commentaries on the Laws of England* published over half a century before the 1870 Education Act, Blackstone wrote that 'it is not easy to imagine or allow that a parent has conferred any considerable benefit on his child by bringing him into the world, if he afterwards entirely neglects his culture and education, and suffers him to grow up like a mere beast, to lead a life useless to others and shameful to himself'.[5]

The distribution of legal responsibility for the education of children is such that parents have, in effect, a duty to send their children to school, and the state has a duty to educate them when they get there. The state is, in effect, assuming a *parental* responsibility, although the role of the state in the education of children goes much further than that, of course. In every society, the education system is fostering social reproduction through its inculcation of the values and ideas of the majority or dominant culture. It is not surprising then that areas such as sex education, religious education and the establishment of voluntary schools have proved contentious in view of the centrality of these matters to parents' own cultural values. Like the question of corporal punishment and school uniform, they lie at the heart of the parent–state conflict which flows from a disharmony between individual parental choice and the collectivist focus of the state.[6]

Among the manifestations of this conflict are cases where parents have challenged the content of their child's education by withdrawing him/her from school. The case of *Re S (A Minor)* was concerned essentially with the opposition of the parents of one child to comprehensive schools; they kept the boy, aged 11, away from school for 18 months before the Court of Appeal confirmed that the child should be taken into care so that he could be educated. It is a striking fact that although the court in this case clearly adopted its paternalistic role in deciding how the child's welfare would best be promoted, the chief emphasis was on the competing rights and responsibilities of parent and local authority rather than those of the child. This is emphasised by the fact that the parent claimed to be asserting a 'right not to be dictated to'[7] – at the expense of his/her child's right to education.[8]

But how far have the changes in child care law embodied in the Children Act 1989, with its focus on the paramountcy of the child's welfare (as a means to the child's better protection), and the increasing emphasis which has been placed on parental responsibility rather than rights by the courts in recent years,[9] been mirrored by changes in the balance of power between parent, child and state in education? The concept of parental rights may be in serious general decline – 'it has become increasingly difficult to reconcile its existence with the predominant emphasis which the law now places on the welfare of children'.[10] But in the sphere of education, the concept would appear still to be flourishing, even if in a somewhat limited form, as stated above. Even if the rights being asserted are in reality a reflection of parental responsibility to ensure that children receive a suitable education (although there is inevitably dispute between parent and state about the meaning of 'suitable' in this context), such responsibility gives rise to a considerable amount of power and authority.[11] So far as state education is concerned, increasingly free rein is being given to this power. As this happens, the level of conflict between parents and state rises. In the course of this conflict it is shown that whilst much of the relevant legislation – for example, on school admissions – may emphasise individual parents' rights, in practice it is not always easy to accommodate them. With the exception of the courts, those determining the issue will frequently take a policy-orientated approach in which individual claims are subjugated to the LEA's overall administrative goal.[12]

The dispute between parents and LEA in Dewsbury in 1987–88 exemplified this struggle between parent and state agencies over what is essentially the exercise of the paternalistic role concerning the formal education of a child. A group of white parents, each of whose children had been allocated places at a school (Headfield) where 83 per cent of the pupils were of Asian origin, challenged the LEA's decisions both individually, through separate appeals (some of which were successful), and subsequently through collective action. The parents of 26 children refused to send them to the designated school and instead made arrangements for tuition to be given to them by, *inter alios*, a volunteer retired teacher, in rooms above a public house. The parents argued that their action was not racially motivated, but rather reflected their concern that their children should be educated in a school with a prevailing Christian ethos, which they claimed would not be the case at the school designated by the LEA. But it seems that, regardless of the wider implications of the dispute (it has been bracketed with refusals of voluntary aided status in its impact on religious and cultural autonomy),[13] the issue was essentially one of parental choice rather than religion *per se*. The LEA refused to concede, even when the parents made application for judicial review; but when the application to the court was amended to focus on the legality of the LEA's admissions procedures and their operation, the authority finally backed down and found places for the children at two schools where non-white pupils were firmly in the minority (Overthorpe and Thornhill).

The outcome of the dispute was hailed by the parents and their supporters as a victory for the rights of parents. One parent is reported as saying: 'All we wanted was parental choice.' The parents' solicitor said that the Dewsbury parents' action had 'shown the tremendous value of parents fighting for their rights'.[14] Of course, it would be tempting to suggest that the independent rights of *children* are being forgotten in all of this. However, it has been suggested that often 'parents may legitimately be regarded as the child's representatives in what is a conflict between the family and the state'.[15] Thus, primarily whose interests or rights have been secured when parents such as those in Dewsbury succeed with their action is not at all clear. Despite the widespread feeling that there had been a victory for parental rights, many of the Dewsbury parents claimed to have been acting for the sake of their children.

The Dewsbury case also focused attention on the difficulties of accommodating the preferences of parents drawn from groups with diverse cultural and religious differences, especially where these interests conflict with the 'rights' of the state to promote a policy of multicultural education in the interests of racial harmony and integration.

In contrast to the increasing emphasis in child welfare on parental *responsibility* rather than rights, the Conservatives' policy since 1980 of making the education system far more responsive to parental demands has involved an extension of parental rights. In part, the new element of consumerism is reflective of a wider policy to bring market forces to bear in the field of state provision (for example, in the health service and public transport). In education, the best illustration of this policy, but also of the practical limitations to the concept of parental rights, is in the area of school admissions, and discussion of this occurs next. But a more complete understanding of the operation of and limits to parental rights in education requires a wider examination, of how the law deals with other areas where the interests of children, parents and the state are all in particularly sharp focus. Two further areas will, therefore, be considered: the legal enforcement of school attendance, and the law governing special education.

SCHOOL ADMISSIONS AND PARENTAL CHOICE

The 'parents' charter'

The Conservative governments of the 1980s saw school admissions as a key area in which to put into practice some of the New Right ideas about introducing free market principles into the education system, whilst at the same time deriving political capital from giving some legal recognition to parents' 'moral right' to choose how their children are educated.[16]

There can be little doubt about the lack of parental rights over choice of school prior to 1980. We have already seen how section 76 of the 1944 Act proved to be ineffective at forcing compliance by LEAs to parental wishes.[17] The Plowden Report on *Children and their Primary Schools* (1967) recommended no change to section 76, but said that parents should be given some choice whenever this was possible. Giving parents a measure of choice would, it was argued, be more likely to secure their involvement in the school and in their child's schooling: 'They are more likely to support a school they have freely chosen and to give it the loyalty which is so essential if their children are to do the same.'[18] The Report also noted, somewhat prophetically in the light of the present government's 'open enrolment' policy under the ERA 1988 – which is designed *inter alia* to identify bad schools by their lack of popularity with parents – that 'whenever a school is unpopular that should be an indication to the authority to find out why and make it better'.

By the 1970s the demand for an extension of parental choice was growing. The Labour Party supported the idea of greater parental involvement. The Conservatives' education spokesperson of the mid-1970s, Norman St John-Stevas, argued in favour of a 'parents' charter'; he called for clearer obligations on LEAs and the state to comply with parental wishes.[19] This 'charter' was put in place shortly after the Conservatives were returned to power.

An absolute guarantee of choice of school was always going to be impossible. For one thing, many LEAs had, during the late 1960s, turned their secondary schools into comprehensives. This policy, along with the policy of some LEAs to establish neighbourhood schools, had already reduced the element of choice available to parents.[20] Many parents wanted to send their children to grammar schools, but these were ceasing to be available. Several of the unsuccessful court actions brought during this decade arose out of opposition to LEA plans for the introduction of comprehensive schools. Although the Education Act 1979 removed the duty of LEAs to reorganise secondary schools along comprehensive lines (a duty imposed by Labour's Education Act 1976), the policy was not going to be easily reversible. Moreover, popular schools would seldom be able to accommodate as pupils the children of all parents who wanted to send them there. Parental choice was, therefore, always going to be 'a very limited concept'.[21]

The impossibility of guaranteeing adherence to parental wishes was acknowledged by the government in the provisions of the 1980 Education Act. Section 6 stated that although parents should be allowed to state a preference for a school, compliance with that preference was not required if it would 'prejudice the provision of efficient education or the efficient use of resources'. In the case of admission to voluntary aided or special agreement schools, or to selective schools, choice could also be denied on religious or ability grounds.[22] The courts have held that an LEA cannot, however, refuse to admit a child simply because s/he lives outside their district.[23]

Prior to the 1980 Act it had been observed that the law had been 'heavily weighed in favour of the local education authorities and schools with parents having few rights (although many duties) and little say in the decision-making process'.[24] On the face of it section 6 of the 1980 Act has added little in the way of parental rights to section 76 of the 1944 Act. However, the 1980 Act requires parental preference to be granted unless one of the exceptions applies. Moreover, at the heart of the 'parents' charter' is the appeals system, to which parents have a right (under section 7 of the Act) to refer their claim. Appeals are to be heard by an appeals committee, constituted in accordance with Schedule 2 of the Act. LEA-appointed members may outnumber by one the other members (persons with experience in education or knowledge of local educational conditions, or parents of pupils – but not of pupils at the school which is the subject of the appeal). Teachers are the only LEA employees entitled to serve as appeal committee members, but not in respect of appeals to their school.

The appeal committee's decision is binding on the LEA. Like the LEA, the committee must seek to grant parental preference, but subject to the exceptions contained in section 6 in so far as these have not been dis-applied by the 1988 Act (see below). The procedure for lodging an appeal, and various other procedural matters, are laid down in the Schedule, but the manner of conducting the appeal hearing is left to the committee itself. Nevertheless, there is a Code of Practice prepared by the Council on Tribunals for committees to follow. The Code reminds appeal committees of the apprehension and anxiety which many parents might feel when attending a hearing and of the need to adopt a welcoming and helpful approach, whilst remaining impartial. The legality of an appeal committee's decision would be open to legal challenge if there was a failure to comply with natural justice – for example, not giving an appellant an adequate opportunity to state his/her case. One recent case provides a good example of unlawful appeal procedure.[25] An LEA adopted the practice of hearing all secondary school admissions appeals before making any decisions on individual cases. This practice was held to be lawful in an earlier case,[26] in which Lord Justice Woolf referred to;

'the advantage of adopting this course if it is practical because children whose appeals are heard last could otherwise be prejudiced because of decisions which had been reached already by an appeal committee to send children to a particular school'.

In the later case a three-member panel had considered the applicants' appeal and had adjourned to hear the remaining appeals. One of the three members had been unable to attend the meeting at which these appeals were heard and a decision made on *all* the appeals. Nolan J said that the committee had to consist of the same people throughout. (Note that administrative errors could lead to an investigation by the Local Ombudsman.[27])

There have been complaints about the lack of independence of appeal committees (the majority of whose members are appointed by the LEA) and of legal deficiencies in the way that appeals are heard. There have also been suggestions that appeal committee hearings require closer monitoring. But, so far as two-thirds of appellants are concerned, the most dissatisfying aspect of the appeal process lies in a discovery that the appeal has been unsuccessful.[28] For them, parental choice may be somewhat illusory. As Buck states, 'there is, in reality, a lot of difference between the expression of a preference and a choice and it seems that some parents who have heard of the new rights sometimes confuse these two concepts.'[29] For LEAs, the appeals system has created administrative difficulties, such as delay in establishing school rolls (but see below). It was predicted that it might also 'destroy well conceived and equitable admission policies'.[30] On the plus side, the appeals system has undoubtedly caused many LEAs to tighten up their procedures.[31]

The appeals committees themselves have been faced with a difficult task. Like LEAs they have the problem of indivisibility in allocating school places. As there are too few places, comparison between competing claims is necessary. There will be the LEA's published admissions criteria to follow, of course. The DES has advised LEAs (or governors in the case of voluntary aided and special agreement schools) that they may apply 'any reasonable criteria'. Common practice is to consider: the presence of siblings at the school; distance of home from school; attendance at a 'feeder' school; medical or other domestic factors. Various orders of priority are given to these factors. But in the High Court, Parker LJ has stated that whilst the creation of an admissions policy is a matter of discretion for the LEA itself, that policy must enable consideration to be given to exceptional cases and therefore should not be too rigid.[32]

These admissions criteria will be part of the LEA's overall policy on admissions to its schools, which in the past may have reflected targets for enrolment. LEAs have tended to set targets which, when reached, cannot be exceeded in the year in question. The purpose of this practice is to ensure a more even distribution of pupils around the

LEA's schools. Schools would not, therefore, be allowed to become too small in terms of their pupil numbers: 'LEAs see it as necessary to balance allowance for parental choice against the consequences of choice for schools generally.'[33] This *general* policy could always be justified on the grounds of efficiency and cost-effectiveness, enabling parental choice to be denied under section 6(3)(a) (compliance would prejudice 'efficient education or . . . efficient use of resources'). However, the case of *R v South Glamorgan Appeals Committee ex parte Evans* (1984) showed that when looking at *individual* claims for a school place, it was necessary for an appeal committee to determine first whether the admission of one further child would prejudice efficient education at the school (with the onus on the LEA to show that it would): if they concluded that it would not, they would have to allow the appeal. If they decided the question in the affirmative, they then had to decide whether the prejudice was sufficient to outweigh the 'parental factors'. In *Evans* the school place had been denied because there were already 36 pupils in the class and the LEA's limit was 30. In the event it proved impossible for the appeal committee which re-heard the case after the court's ruling to find prejudice. Despite this, evidence shows that appeal committees have tended not to question LEA admission limits. Thus, whatever success individual parents may have achieved via the 1980 Act's appeal system, it seemed, by 1986, that 'rights of school choice do not appear to make much difference to the outcomes of school admissions or to the LEAs' management of school rolls'.[34]

'Open enrolment'

At various points in the early 1980s consideration was given by the Conservatives to the idea of introducing a 'voucher' system, designed to enable parents to exercise their choice by 'buying' a place at a particular school. Once doubts about the feasibility of such a system finally caused it to be shelved indefinitely, the government sought other ways of extending parental choice, once it had introduced reforms to school government to increase opportunities for parental *involvement* at school level (see Chapter 3).

The policy adopted was 'open enrolment' – described by the government as 'a significant enhancement of the ability of parents to secure the admission of their children to the school they prefer'.[35] LEAs would not be able to restrict admissions to schools by using artificial admissions limits. The government said that these limits had not only inhibited and delayed necessary rationalisation of schools provision but also had 'acted as a barrier to the exercise of effective parental choice'.[36] Under the new system (laid down in sections 26–32 of the ERA 1988) schools would be able to admit pupils until they were physically full – a stage reached when no additional pupils could be accommodated without the school being in breach of the law governing the use of school premises (see below). In this way popular schools could be allowed to 'expand' by increasing their pupil numbers, whilst unpopular schools would be allowed to contract – and in some cases would cease to be viable. With formula funding under LMS based on, amongst other things, pupil numbers at the school, it was clearly anticipated that there could be intense competition between schools to attract pupils. With allocation of places based ever more firmly around the notion of parental choice, it was expected that schools would be forced to raise their standards to meet the qualitative expectations of parents. In some cases the school's survival would depend on it, especially schools which were already threatened by falling rolls due to demographic factors. The requirements on schools to publish information about pupils' aggregated results of national curriculum testing (see Chapter 5), and the decision in 1983 to publish HMI reports on individual schools, are clearly intended to enable parents to evaluate schools' performance through a comparison of their academic achievements. Parents may also look at factors such as equipment levels, the state of decor and the perceived standard of discipline, and so on, as well as the attitude of staff, in forming such judgements.[37] Because of formula funding, the state of school premises and the amount and quality of equipment will tend to be dependent on pupil numbers. Thus schools which are having difficulty attracting pupils over a couple of years may find that they are powerless to avoid progressive deterioration in their position.

The law on open enrolment refers to a school's 'standard number'. This is an important concept, because the 1988 Act states that total admissions in any school year must not be restricted to a number below the school's standard number.[38] Admissions in excess of the standard number are, however, possible, provided the appropriate legal requirements have been met (see below). The existing standard number, determined under section 15 of the Education Act 1980 and generally set at the intake of pupils to the school in 1979–80 (a peak year), will be the new standard number – unless in 1989–90, the year before the law changed, admissions exceeded the 1980 Act standard number. If the 1989–90 actual intake is higher than the 1980 Act standard number, *it* will represent the standard number.[39] It is relatively easy for an admissions authority to admit in excess of the standard number, provided various conditions are met – of which the most important is that the school buildings are adequate to accommodate the new number. In some cases approval of the Secretary of State is required. Such approval is always required if the admissions authority seeks a *reduction* in the admissions limit, and thus a new standard number. Such reduction would have to be necessary because of a reduction in the school's capacity to accommodate pupils.[40] For example, it may be that admitting pupils up to the standard number would mean the school taking in more than it can accommodate by virtue of the Education (School Premises) Regulations 1981.[41] Schools will be able to calculate their physical capacity using a form set out in Annex A to DES Circular 11/88. There are various procedural requirements applicable to a reduction in the standard number, including a duty of the proposer to publish details of the proposals and to refer the proposals to the Secretary of State if objections to them are raised by 10 or more local government electors or by the LEA or governors (whichever of them is not the admissions authority).[42] The admissions authority is, in any event, required to keep the standard number under review.[43]

One important aspect of the new admissions regime concerns primary schools, to which open enrolment will not apply until the school year beginning in September 1992 (Education Reform Act 1988 (Commencement No. 9) Order 1991 SI 1991 No. 409). For the first time children aged under 5 years (other than those admitted for nursery education and those moving to a reception class from a nursery class in the same school) will be included in the standard number and parents of such children will have admission appeal rights above.[44]

The significance of these comparatively simple provisions on open enrolment should not be overlooked. On the face of it they may appear to do little more than give effect to the government's consistent promise to maximise the opportunities for parental choice in the education system. But they are clearly intended to form, in combination with formula funding under LMS, a system which will make schools subject to market forces in a direct and dramatic fashion. The message to schools is stark and simple: if you cannot persuade sufficient parents to exercise their freer choice by selecting your school, your allocation of resources will be less than your competitors'. As noted earlier, 'unsuccessful' schools could face terminal decline. Many head teachers are embarking on marketing courses, in the hope that they can learn the skills required to 'sell' their schools to parents, or are persuading governing bodies to co-opt persons with this area of expertise. Some schools may come to consider that the hard sell offers the only feasible way of gaining a firm position in the 'market-place', because it would be naïve to hold to the unrealistic idea that most schools can respond to the new spirit of competition by quickly raising standards to improve their school's popularity. Meanwhile, it is argued that LEAs' capacity for rational planning of educational provision is being replaced by 'the unpredictability of parental demand'.[45]

So far as new teachers are concerned, the implications of the new market ethos created by open enrolment and LMS are considerable. At a time of teacher shortages, the new spirit of competitiveness will almost certainly be reflected in the recruitment practices of schools and LEAs. Many teachers will have noticed the increasing efforts to sell an area or particular school to the potential recruit. New entrants to the profession and those seeking a new appointment will, though, have to be astute, in the same way that parents exercising parental preference are being encouraged to be. A bad choice could lead to an uncertain future.[46]

Sex and race discrimination

To conclude this section on parental choice of school we must consider the question of sex and race discrimination. To discriminate on the grounds of sex or race, either directly or indirectly, in relation to the admission of a pupil or group of pupils to a school is unlawful under the Sex Discrimination Act 1975 and Race Relations Act 1976. Both Acts contain provisions specifically concerned with education, of which those concerned with school admissions form part. (For provisions concerned with curricular provision, see Chapter 6.) *Direct* discrimination involves treating someone less favourably on the grounds of their sex or marital status (the 1975 Act) or colour, race, ethnic or national origins or nationality (the 1976 Act). Often discrimination in education is unintentional, although this is no excuse in law, and usually *indirect*. Indirect sex discrimination occurs when a person applies to a woman:

a requirement or condition which he applies or would apply equally to a man but –
(i) which is such that the proportion of women who can comply with it is considerably smaller than the proportion of men who can comply with it, and
(ii) which he cannot show to be justifiable irrespective of the sex of the person to whom it is applied, and
(iii) which is to her detriment because she cannot comply with it.[47]

An equivalent definition of indirect race discrimination occurs in the Race Relations Act 1976. So, for example, when the head teacher of a school refused to allow a Sikh boy to school because the boy wore a turban in contravention of the school rules on uniformity of dress, this was unjustifiable race discrimination. The court held that for the application of the rule to have been lawful it would have had to be justifiable irrespective of race or ethnic or national origins.[48] It would also be discrimination contrary to the Act if an LEA adopted an admissions policy of dispersing ethnic minority children.[49] In such a case the discrimination would be *direct*.

Discrimination and parental choice have come to be linked over a number of issues of current importance. One of these is the provision of single-sex schools. Many parents prefer to send their children to such schools if they are available. This is particularly true of certain ethnic and religious groups.[50] The provision of single-sex schools is not unlawful; nor is it unlawful to discriminate on the grounds of sex in relation to admission to a single-sex school.[51] Equally, parents have no right to insist on the provision of single-sex schooling, nor to payment by the local authority of fees for educating the child in a single-sex school in the private sector.[52] Nevertheless, there would be unlawful sex discrimination by an LEA if, *in toto*, there were more places available in its single-sex schools for boys than for girls and vice versa. In one case it was held that because such disparity would result from the closure by an LEA of the only two single-sex boys' schools in its area, whilst the authority permitted its two girls' schools to remain, there was unlawful sex discrimination.[53] Clearly there was not a deliberate act of discrimination here; nor was the LEA's decision taken without due regard for educational considerations. At a time of falling rolls and severe financial constraints as a result of central government policy of curbing spending by local authorities, LEAs are having to rationalise provision. But in doing so they must not restrict the opportunities for one gender or racial grounp.

One case of particular importance in this field was brought by the Equal Opportunities Commission which, in addition to its formal powers of investigation has legal authority to pursue cases in the courts. The case concerned the provision of single-sex voluntary aided grammar schools in Birmingham. There were 540 places for boys in such schools in the city, but only 360 for girls. This meant that on average a girl would have to obtain higher examination marks than a boy to secure a place at such a school. The LEA, which had an equal opportunities policy for its education service, was not the admissions authority. The schools' governors were responsible for admissions, and they favoured selection by ability. The House of Lords, to which the LEA appealed after defeat in both the High Court and Court of Appeal, held that the denial of selective single-sex education to a higher proportion of girls than boys was unlawful sex discrimination. Lord Goff said that it was the denial of *choice* that was the critical factor, rather than the denial of a form of education that may or may not be available in other of the authority's schools. In order to comply with the court ruling the authority was faced with a number of equally problematic options. The difficulty arose because for the most part the single-sex grammar schools did not want to become co-educational, in spite of the court's ruling. The authority has considered turning two of the boys' schools into co-educational schools. The governors of one school said they might invoke opting-out procedure to avoid the school's becoming co-educational.

After single-sex schools, the most contentious issue has been the admission of pupils to racially mixed schools. The best known dispute, in Dewsbury, was discussed earlier. As stated above, this is an issue over which parental feelings tend to run extremely high. Many of the parents who object to their child's attending a school at which a place has been allocated by the LEA claim to be opposed simply on religious or educational grounds. But there are clear racial overtones, which the press has been quick to highlight. The latest *cause célèbre* arose in Middlesbrough in early 1990. Mrs C asked her LEA if her daughter could change school, because at her school, where 40 per cent of the pupils were of Asian origin, the child was, in Mrs C's reported words, 'learning Pakistani'. Mrs C wanted the child admitted to a school where 98 per cent of the pupils were white. A place was available at the school in question, and the LEA had no ground under the 1980 Education Act for denying parental choice. The LEA's decision to allow the child's admission to the school was challenged by the Commission for Racial Equality, which asked the Secretary of State to use his default powers in the 1944 Act and quash the LEA's decision, on the ground that the decision was racist and would encourage other parents to pursue the same course as Mrs C and for the same reason. In reply, the Secretary of State said that parental wishes were paramount.[54] It is likely that a test case will be brought on this issue. According to the Commission for Racial Equality, one similar instance a week is being referred to them.

The case demonstrates the difficulties which the policy of parental choice in education is presenting for multicultural education in state schools. As multicultural education is cross-curricular in its scope, many parent groups regard the right of a parent to withdraw his/her child from religious education or collective worship[55] (but not sex education)[56] as offering insufficient choice where cultural or religious autonomy is at issue. This is especially so, given the emphasis on Christianity which the ERA 1988 seems to demand (see Chapter 6). Proponents of voluntary aided status for certain independent denominational schools could argue that the obstruction of their proposals is compounding the difficulties as well as denying them the choice which is available to other groups. It is clear that the racial/religious dimension to parental choice of school is likely to become one of the dominant issues in education in the 1990s, making the preference versus policy dichotomy all the more difficult to resolve.

PARENTAL RESPONSIBILITY AND SCHOOL ATTENDANCE

Compulsory education came to England and Wales in 1870, and was generally implemented by 1880 (by local by-laws). Responsibility for ensuring that children were educated was then, as now, placed on parents' shoulders. In the nineteenth century there was a need to protect children from exploitation by parents as juvenile labour. Nowadays, parental responsibility may be viewed in the same light for school attendance as for child care generally, namely: 'the duty to care for the child and to raise him to moral, physical and emotional health . . . the fundamental task of parenthood and the only justification for the authority it confers'.[57] Apart from the moral justification for such a legal responsibility, there are also the self-evident economic and social reasons why children should attend school. In simple terms, a well-educated work-force is necessary to meet the needs of an industrial age, and an education will equip a person to play his or her part in society.

As we shall see, these days the concept of parental responsibility seems to demand considerably more involvement in a child's education than simply packing him or her off to school every day.

How is this involvement to be achieved? The law on school attendance acts as a rather crude instrument in this regard, although the child-centred philosophy of the Children Act 1989 extends into the area of school attendance and perhaps offers a more appropriate method of enforcing parental responsibility.

As truancy is a major problem in many schools in England and Wales, it is important that all teachers are aware of the law governing enforcement of school attendance, and its limitations. There has been considerable discussion of the legal enforcement of school attendance in recent years, and wide disagreement about the effectiveness or otherwise of the law.

In the face of sustained high levels of non-excused absenteeism in Britain's schools, (up to one in ten pupils in some secondary schools), there have been increasing calls for more active legal intervention in truancy cases, from head teachers, school inspectors, the DES (Circular 2/86) and a number of MPs. Lining up in opposition are those who favour *less* use of the legal options in truancy cases, preferring policies which place greater emphasis on the causes of truancy. Many LEAs deliberately try to avoid invoking the formal legal procedures unless absolutely necessary and have developed procedures which enable individual truancy cases to be examined 'in the round', with diagnostic and remedial intervention which obviates the need to press for legal sanctions. Yet a number of head teachers believe that reluctance on the part of some LEAs at present to prosecute parents for the poor school attendance of their children is contributing significantly to high levels of truancy.[58] Nevertheless, some LEAs are adopting tough measures. In some areas, 'truancy patrols' have been set up, consisting of teams of usually two persons (an education welfare officer (EWO) and a police officer) who question youngsters who look as though they should be at school. Then, if the child's explanation is unconvincing, the team visits the parents.[59] The Elton Report advocated 'truancy sweeps' of this nature to maximise attendance and reduce juvenile crime.[60] In some cases LEAs operating such patrols are pressing magistrates to impose stiff penalties on parents of truants.[61] Meanwhile, the Children Act 1989 purports to offer LEAs a new legal solution to non-attendance at school – the Education Supervision Order.

Defining truancy

Before considering the legal enforcement of school attendance in depth it is necessary to understand what is meant by school absenteeism or 'truancy'. It has rightly been suggested that there is no legal definition of truancy.[62] But there are, of course, provisions governing compulsory education. In law, a parent is required by section 36 of the Education Act 1944 to ensure that his/her child of compulsory school age (5–16 years) receives 'efficient full-time education, suitable to his age, ability and aptitude, either by regular attendance at school or otherwise'. Leaving aside the possibility of the parental duty being satisfied by the child being efficiently (and so on) educated 'otherwise' than at school, in view of its relative practical insignificance,[63] parents are under a legal obligation to ensure both that the child receives a proper education and, if registered at school, that s/he attends regularly (Education Act 1944, section 39). Neither 'regular' attendance nor 'full-time education' are defined in the Education Act 1944. It could be argued that failure to attend for, for example, part of one school day during any particular week, would not be truancy under the law. This point is academic – first, because so much of this type of absenteeism goes unnoticed or unrecorded (it was described as 'hidden' truancy by the Pack Report),[64] and second, because, realistically, the use of legal procedures would probably not be contemplated by any LEA until the problem had worsened and discussion with parents had failed to resolve it. Much truancy in schools is of the 'hidden' variety (in one survey of fifth-formers, 52 per cent. admitted to playing truant for the odd lesson here or there);[65] as such it possibly lies beyond the scope of the law at present. In this respect, the law on compulsory school attendance clearly has its limitations. Cases of more persistent and 'regular' truancy fall squarely within the remit of the law (see below). It is in the context of such cases that discussion of the merits or otherwise of legal intervention is really centred.

Under the law, there is no truancy if a child has the school's permission to be absent or if his/her absence from school is occasioned by: sickness of the child (not of his/her parent);[66] or unavoidable cause affecting the child and generally involving an emergency;[67] or a day of religious observance; or 'the school . . . is not within walking distance . . . and no suitable arrangements have been made by the LEA for (the child's) transport . . . or for boarding accommodation'. This rather limited list of excuses, laid down in section 39(2) of the 1944 Act, must be regarded as exhaustive.[68] Note that the law relating to the last of these excuses, concerning distance to school from home and transport arrangements, has been amended following the decision of the House of Lords in *Rogers v Essex County Council* (1986). In this case a child's shortest distance to school along public thoroughfares was just less than 3 miles. Section 39(5) of the 1944 Act states that 'walking distance' is 2 miles, or 3 miles if the child is aged 8 or over, 'measured by the nearest available route'. It was argued by the LEA that it therefore had no obligation to provide transport. The parents contended that the shortest route in the case of their 12-year-old daughter was not truly 'available' because it was isolated and unlit and involved crossing difficult terrain. Lord Ackner felt that the route did not cease to be available simply because it was not possible for an unaccompanied child to walk it without danger. The test was whether a child 'accompanied as necessary' could use it with reasonable safety. More recently, the House of Lords held that in fulfilling his/her duty in relation to section 36 the parent had to do 'those things that are reasonably practicable to be done and which an ordinary prudent parent would do'. In the context of section 39(2) this might include 'accompanying the child in situations where it would be unsafe for the child to go to school unaccompanied', where the child did live (only just in this more recent case) within 'walking distance'.[69] It was felt that councils ought to consider the practicability of the child being accompanied in the particular circumstances.

Following the *Rogers* decision, an amendment was made to the law requiring LEAs to make such transport arrangements as they deem necessary for the purpose of facilitating the attendance of pupils at school.[70] LEAs must, when deciding whether to provide transport for a child, have regard (amongst other things) to 'the age of the pupil, and the nature of the route, or alternative routes, which he could reasonably be expected to take'.

The legal definition of truancy incorporates no distinction between its different forms. There are, perhaps, three categories of what a teacher might call 'truancy': simple non-attendance, parentally condoned absence, and school refusal/phobia. Parentally condoned absenteeism can, according to research studies over the past ten or so years, account for as much as 50–75 per cent of non-excused absenteeism.[71] Many recent government reports confirm its continuing presence.[72] But is parentally condoned absenteeism distinguishable from 'truancy'? There is a divergence of opinion on this question: Galloway, for example, argues that there is such a distinction,[73] whilst others (for example, the Pack Committee) have defined all cases of non-excused absence as truancy. In yet another classification, Reid distinguishes between truancy and less serious forms of poor attendance at school.[74] There clearly is much disagreement among academics and professionals about what is meant by 'truancy'. It is, therefore, perhaps understandable that the law continues to cover truancy in its broadest sense, using regular attendance as its yardstick.

The enforcement of attendance

So far as the enforcement of school attendance is concerned, increasing attempts are being made to control poor attendance from the fringe of the legal system and outside it.[75] Invocation of legal procedures, in particular court action, seems to have declined in recent years.[76] This has certainly been the case in Liverpool, where truancy prosecutions and care proceedings per annum fell by 40 per cent between 1981 and 1987 – although there has been a slight increase over the past couple of years. Meanwhile, the development of administrative networks has intensified and tactics from counselling to cajoling[77] have been employed, as the efficacy of the legal procedures and their sanctions in the fight against truancy increasingly comes to be doubted in some quarters. The pre-court 'tribunal' investigation employed in Sheffield[78] and the growing emphasis being placed on ways that schools can improve pupils' motivation to attend through curriculum development and new approaches to teaching,[79] serve as illustrations of the perceived inappropriateness of formal legal intervention other than in extreme cases.

There are several reasons for the dislike of the legal procedures. For one thing, they are perceived as essentially punitive since they ultimately involve criminal prosecution or the 'sanction' of a care order. If a child is not registered at school the LEA must issue a school attendance order (SAO) against the parents under section 37(1) of the Education Act 1944. Failure to comply with the SAO is a summary offence, as is failure to cause a pupil registered at a school to attend regularly (see section 39(1)). Before the changes contained in the Children Act 1989 came into effect the LEA, when contemplating prosecution, had to consider the appropriateness or otherwise of instituting care proceedings under section 1(2)(e) of the Children and Young Persons Act (CYPA) in the juvenile court (on the ground that a child was 'not receiving full-time education suitable to his age, ability and aptitude'), instead of or as well as prosecuting (see Education Act 1944 section 40(2)). Grenville pointed out that although no legal duty to attend school rests with the child, s/he might find her/himself the subject of 'welfare sanctions'.[80]

Prior to the Children Act 1989 there might be a care order (400 were made in 1987), transferring parental responsibilities to the local authority indefinitely, or a supervision order for a specified period (of up to three years), with a social worker attached to supervise the child's resumption of full-time schooling. Reid suggested that the CYPA had 'led to truancy being considered as a symptom of distress which is seen as being allied to the social and educational problems of the individual child'. Yet as he went on to say, the procedure, whatever its eventual remedial consequences, had 'punitive consequences'.[81] Moreover, care orders have been obtained on the education ground without much difficulty, the courts often taking the view that if the child was not receiving a suitable education it was likely that the separate care and control test would almost certainly have been satisfied. In one case, noted earlier, an order was made when a child from a good home was kept away from school because of the parents' opposition to comprehensive schools.[82] The Children Act 1989 will replace care orders in truancy cases with 'education supervision orders', likely to be seen as a more constructive and less punitive form of order (see below).

Although supervision was the most common form of disposal in truancy cases under section 1(2)(e) (and may become even more standard practice under the Children Act 1989), the practice adopted in

Leeds magistrates' court of adjourning such proceedings as a threat to the parents to improve the child's attendance or else the child might be made the subject of an order, was claimed to be more effective[83] as well as reducing overall levels of local juvenile delinquency.[84] Cases were sometimes adjourned repeatedly, with a review each time the child reappeared in court. Although the results achieved by the Leeds adjournment system appeared to favour its widespread adoption, this has not happened, although adjournment has been pressed for in some parts of the country – for example, in South Wales – and has been regarded as useful in certain cases by many authorities. However, the Leeds system has been criticised on various grounds, the major complaint being that repeated adjournment of individual cases, and randomised outcomes to test whether adjournment or supervision was the more effective, was illegal.[85] If cases were selected for a particular disposal at random, Galloway suggested,[86] how could proper consideration be being given to the welfare of the child in every case? Another criticism of the Leeds adjournment system was that it added further stress to socially disadvantaged people already living under stressful conditions. On the other hand, the Leeds researchers found that the effect of repeated court adjournments on the family, not least the inconvenience, was one reason for the system's success.

Under the pre-Children Act 1989 regime, between 10 and 25 per cent of care cases involving truants resulted in a residential care order. Not only does such an arrangement disrupt the child's schooling – although arguably it has already been badly disrupted by the child's absenteeism – but it can often also be a traumatic experience for the child, entrenching the resentment and disaffection which were among the major causes of the child's truancy in the first place.[87] Under the Children Act 1989 a child's lack of suitable education had ceased to be a specific ground for taking him/her into care. According to the minister, David Mellor, 'none of us wants . . . to continue with the care order on education grounds, even though its use is declining, because that would not meet the spirit of the times'.[88]

So far as prosecution is concerned, the most likely outcome, should a guilty decision be reached (most parents plead guilty), is a fine. (The Children Act 1989 has abolished a rarely used power in section 40(1) of the Education Act 1944 to imprison the parent for up to one month.)

Although prosecution followed by a fine can bring home to parents the reality of their child's non-attendance problem, a financial penalty is likely to be inappropriate when imposed on what is often a poor family whose financial problems are already one of the factors threatening family stability. For this reason, amongst others, Reid's recent suggestion that perhaps parents in Britain should, like those in France, lose some child benefit if it is proved that their children are truanting – 'Fines imposed on parents should be collected directly from child benefit' – deserves rejection.[89] (Note that the law seems to assume that it is the father who should be prosecuted unless the mother alone has custody.[90])

The Leeds researchers claim that the system developed there, the adjournment system, has resulted in lower truancy rates than elsewhere in the country.[91] But many other researchers have concluded that legal intervention is of extremely limited value in truancy cases. The findings of a major study in Sheffield between 1976 and 1978 lent 'no support to the view that formal action encourages parents to ensure that their children attend more regularly in the future'.[92] Although legal intervention is often seen as a means of last resort in cases of extremely persistent truancy, the problem may, by then, have become too firmly entrenched. Experience in Leeds suggests that intervention must take place at an early stage in order to be effective.[93] Truancy is most prevalent amongst young people approaching the end of their period of compulsory schooling when there is little point in taking legal action. It is increasingly being asked whether the solution to the problem of truancy beyond the age of 13 lies in changes at school to alleviate the boredom, and increase the motivation to participate, of less academic pupils. This point is considered further below.

Legal intervention in truancy cases has focused on the notion of parental responsibility. There is a tendency amongst teachers and EWOs to blame parents for most instances of truancy.[94] Such a viewpoint is mirrored in the legal procedures, which put an emphasis on a child's return to school via sanctions against parents as the solution to individual cases of truancy. But Galloway concluded from his study of procedures in Sheffield that prosecution will often be of little value, unless parents can be given a positive reason for insisting on their child's attendance at school. This would involve something more than the counselling which EWOs routinely provide in truancy cases. It requires changes in the way that parental involvement in their child's education is fostered by the school as well as changes in what the school has to offer the child. Meanwhile the procedure adopted in truancy cases should, rather than being geared towards punishment of parents, be a constructive process, involving parent and child.

Nevertheless, even the staunchest advocates of non-legal solutions to truancy seem to accept that legal procedures must continue to be available. Indeed there are some who will continue to argue that truancy rates would decline if tougher punitive measures against parents were taken, perhaps as a 'short, sharp shock' at an early stage of truancy, to 'forestall later persistent absence'.[95] But in the United States of America court sanctions are rarely used; there is an emphasis on personal and family *support*. A visit there convinced one EWO that there should be more emphasis on home–school liaison and an end to the practice of 'looking at school attendance as an enforcement issue'.[96] Many professionals feel that criminal proceedings are inappropriate and that care-type procedures, which place an emphasis on the welfare of the child, are to be preferred despite their limitations.

The DHSS Review of Child Care Law (1985) suggested that a new form of supervision order, the Education Supervision Order (ESO), should be introduced. Provision for this is now made in the Children Act 1989. Before instituting criminal proceedings for non-attendance, an LEA must consider whether it would be appropriate, instead of or as well as prosecuting, to apply for an ESO. Before applying for the order the LEA would normally have to consult the local authority social services committee.

An ESO may be made only if the court is satisfied that the child 'is of compulsory school age and is not being properly educated'. Under an ESO the supervisor will be under a duty to 'advise, assist and befriend, and give directions' to – (1) the supervised child; and (2) his parent(s); in such a way as will ensure that the child is 'properly educated'.[97] The supervisor will give directions to the parents (or persons exercising parental responsibility), but should take steps to ascertain and, so far as is reasonably practicable, take into account, the wishes and feelings of the child (as appropriate, having regard to the child's age and understanding) and parents. The element of parental responsibility is preserved by paragraph 18 of Schedule 3 under which a parent of a child who is the subject of an ESO commits an offence (maximum fine £400) for failing to comply with any directions given by the supervisor. However, there are various defences available – for example, that the parent took reasonable steps to comply with the direction or that the direction was 'unreasonable'. Moreover, it would appear that the supervisor would be expected to consider other possible remedies (such as making new directions) before referring the matter for prosecution. If there is a 'persistent failure' of a child to comply with directions the case must be referred to the local authority social services department for investigation of the circumstances. The purpose is clearly to determine whether any other forms of intervention would be in the child's best interests.

An ESO will remain in force for one year, but at any time within three months before its expiry date an application for its extension may be made to the court. The court could extend it for up to three years. Further extensions would be possible. The order will terminate when the child ceases to be of compulsory school age or if a care order is made.[98]

The ESO provisions above have certain of the characteristics of the CYPA supervision order. But the important difference is that truancy *per se* is more clearly separated from other child welfare issues, and this is confirmed by providing for LEA supervision in the Act. The ESO has the advantage of offering greater scope for really getting to the root of truancy problems by keeping the education welfare service in close contact with the families with which it has been working. Social workers, who have carried out routine supervision under CYPA, are said to concentrate too much on family dynamics whilst ignoring the child's educational difficulties.[99] On the other hand, research has shown that in their dealings with families, EWOs, many of whom are not qualified social workers, are not likely to focus on the surrounding causes of truancy.[100] In any event, the education welfare service is frequently too busy and inadequately staffed to exercise the kind of supervision which enables the causes of truancy to be explored fully (nor to work with schools in order to develop links with parents, as advocated by the *Better Schools* White Paper in 1985). The Elton Report called on LEAs to maintain adequate numbers of EWOs.[101] Unless extra resources and training are made available, the ESO procedure laid down in the Children Act 1989 may not herald a new emphasis on the causes of truancy. An encouraging sign was the availability in 1990–91 of education support grant (covering 60 per cent of the cost of specific projects) for initiatives to improve school attendance, including the improvement of home–school liaison via extending the role of EWOs.[102]

Schools and absenteeism

Given the emphasis currently being placed on the role that schools should be playing, by providing a more socially relevant curriculum, more student-centred learning and a less alienating environment so as to prevent truancy,[103] it is clearly important that education becomes the focus of any intervention. It may be observed that the object of EWO intervention under the ESO is to ensure, in the words of the Act, that the child is 'properly educated'. The 'education' focus offered by the law should extend into closer monitoring and intervention by teachers. Indeed, another type of initiative which was eligible for three-year education support grant from 1990–91 was projects enabling teachers to play a more active role in relation to non-attendance. Some researchers have observed that teachers are prone to ignore truancy, being less than sympathetic to those whom they regard as 'non-conformers' and whose absence means a smaller and easier class to manage. The Elton Report advocates senior school staff carrying out random attendance checks on individual lessons.[104] School-based initiatives are far more likely to prevent either casual truancy or its exacerbation into persistent truancy.

Truancy and the law: some conclusions

Truancy is a matter of grave social concern; but is a solution possible? Galloway has commented that 'teachers and magistrates who see legal sanctions as the solution to the problem of poor attendance might be more happily occupied in search of the Holy Grail'.[105] (It remains to be seen whether the ESO is seen as a 'sanction'). Suggestions about school-based strategies, including changes in schooling, emanating from researchers and Her Majesty's Inspectorate will appeal to some teachers;[106] others will regard the law as rightly emphasising parental responsibility and in need of tougher enforcement. A similar schism has emerged in the education welfare service between those who favour sanctions and those who prefer a more supportive role by EWOs. Going to law in truancy cases is undoubtedly the 'easier' option, and accords with the prevalent notion in child law of parental responsibility. For this reason, amongst others, it may be anticipated that many parents of children who truant will, at the end of the day, continue to be dealt with in punitive fashion. This is unfortunate, for there is evidence that much more effective methods of tackling the problem can be adopted, without necessarily undermining in any way the principle of parental responsibility.

RIGHTS AND RESPONSIBILITIES IN RESPECT OF CHILDREN WITH SPECIAL EDUCATIONAL NEEDS

Since April 1983, when the Education Act 1981 was introduced, LEAs have had important responsibilities regarding the identification and assessment of children with special educational needs and the provision of suitable education for such children.[107] But in addition to imposing duties on LEAs, a major feature of the Act, the regulations made under it, and the Circulars issued in respect of it, is an emphasis on securing parental involvement. As we shall see, some argue that while the law, modelled on the recommendations of the Warnock Committee, establishes a range of parental rights and duties, parental involvement in practice is hindered by a number of factors. Singled out in particular has been the poor record of LEAs in involving parents effectively in the assessment process[108] – something which the latest government circular on special educational needs seeks to redress.[109]

The rights of parents under the Act concern consultation, information and appeal (in each case within limits). In a number of cases there has been recourse to the courts by parents anxious to secure appropriate provision for their child in the face of local authority opposition.[110]

There is not the space here for a detailed examination of the regime laid down in the 1981 Act and the Education (Special Educational Needs) Regulations 1983, as amended. However, an outline is offered because it is important for all teachers to be aware of the legal framework of special education, and not just those working with the disabled in special schools. Approximately one-fifth of all school children are believed to have special educational needs of one sort or another. Moreover, an important principle in the 1981 Act is that of 'integration' – the education of many of the children with special needs must, so far as practicable, take place in ordinary schools.[111] Because parental involvement is such a key feature, teachers also need to know about parents' rights and responsibilities under the legislation, in addition to those of the school and LEA.

Special educational needs defined

Under the Act, a child has special educational needs if s/he has 'a learning difficulty which calls for special educational provision to be made for him'.[112] 'Learning difficulty' is thus a key concept. It is consonant with the Warnock Report's recommendation of a broader definition of special educational needs than one based simply on disability or deficiency. One of the problems to have emerged is, however, the relativity of the concept of special educational need, which is said to be causing 'uncertainty and confusion' amongst LEAs, and consequently 'variations in the extent of and provision for special educational needs from LEA to LEA'.[113] 'Learning difficulty' is defined in the Act[114] in a less than precise manner. The House of Commons Select Committee which examined the operation of the legislation concluded that on balance the definitions should remain as they are, although better guidance for LEAs would be desirable.

The first type of learning difficulty is where a child 'has a significantly greater difficulty in learning than the majority of children of his/her age'. The second type is where the child has a disability which prevents or makes it difficult for him or her to make use of educational facilities of a kind generally provided in schools – within the LEA's area – for children of his/her age. A child who is under the age of 5 and who is likely to have a learning difficulty when s/he reaches that age also has a learning difficulty.

If a child is aged under 2 then any provision which is made for him/her by the LEA is stated to be special educational provision; in the case of a child aged 2 or over it is 'educational provision which is additional to, or otherwise different from, the educational provision made generally for children of that age in schools maintained by the LEA'.[115] The combined effect of these provisions is that the question of whether or not a child has special educational needs depends not so much on the child's specific needs considered in isolation, but rather on the appropriateness or otherwise of existing provision.[116]

As stated above, if a child has a learning difficulty which calls for special educational provision to be made for him/her, the child has special educational needs under the Act. The emphasis on 'learning difficulty' has given rise to several problems, identified by the House of Commons Select Committee on Education in 1987. They found that 'learning difficulty' was being interpreted as poor achievement in traditional academic subjects and was not regarded as an appropriate description of emotional and behavioural difficulties. They also found that some combined health and education needs were not considered to be adequately covered by the definition, citing speech therapy as a prime example.[117] In fact, the courts have now ruled (in the case of *R v Lancashire County Council ex parte CM*) that speech therapy could be special educational provision. Provided that a need for speech therapy is, on the facts of any particular case, an educational need, then an LEA will have to ensure its provision.[118]

Ex parte CM was one of several important cases in this field, and demonstrates the determination of some parents to secure appropriate provision for their child. Another important case, which reveals a good deal about the workings of the legislation, is *R v Hampshire County Council ex parte J*.[119] Here the LEA had argued that a child (J) with dyslexia did not have special educational needs requiring special educational provision for the purposes of the 1981 Act, because he was an intelligent child whose needs could be provided for in an ordinary school. J was aged 13½, was of small stature and was asthmatic. His dyslexia caused a significant weakness in his capacity for continuous reading, spelling and essay writing. His high intelligence resulted in his being depressed and frustrated by his inabilities. The LEA proposed to place the boy at a comprehensive school. His mother, who was opposed to this, sought medical opinion. According to a doctor with considerable experience of cases of dyslexia, the boy was 'moderately dyslexic, but the effects . . . are offset by his exceptionally high IQ which means that those effects are modified but not eliminated . . . . He is immensely creative'. In the doctor's opinion the boy clearly had special educational needs for the purposes of the 1981 Act. The doctor recommended a place at a named independent special school. But the LEA refused to offer the applicant's mother a grant for the child to be educated at that school. She then initiated the statutory procedure under section 9 of the Act to have an assessment made of J's educational needs. The authority made an assessment, but did not consider that the boy's needs were such that it should determine in a statement the special educational provision that should be made for him. (This aspect of 'statementing', which falls under section 7 of the Act, is considered below.) The authority took the view that J's difficulties did not preclude him from following 'a normal mainstream curriculum suited to pupils of his age'. It did not accept that J had a learning difficulty.

In the High Court, Taylor J found it 'very difficult to see how one could come to any other conclusion than that J had a learning difficulty'. His Honour said that J's dyslexia 'would appear to give him significantly greater difficulty in learning than the majority of children of his age', and that J's high intelligence was 'neither here nor there' in relation to the specific cause of the learning difficulty. Moreover, Taylor J felt that J's dyslexia was a 'disability' and thus was covered by the second definition of learning difficulty (above).

There was also a fair amount of discussion in this case about the meaning of the phrase 'special educational provision'. This, as mentioned above, is defined as 'educational provision which is additional to, or otherwise different from, the educational provision made for children of [the child's] age in schools maintained by the LEA'. The LEA had argued that if a particular type of educational provision was generally available to children of the applicant's age in their schools, then it was not a *special* educational provision. Thus, logically, any generally available additional provision for deaf or partially blind or disturbed children, and others such as dyslexic children, was not special educational provision. Taylor J rejected this contention, holding that special educational provision was different from provision made to 'the general run of normal children, to the normal majority'. Thus provision intended to help dyslexic children with their special difficulty is special educational provision.

Identification and assessment of special educational needs

Parental rights and responsibilities are built into the arrangements for the identification and assessment of special educational needs. Formal assessment of a child believed to have special needs which require special educational provision must be conducted, once the child has been identified either by the school, via its non-statutory assessment monitoring of pupils and assessment under the National Curriculum regime, or by the parents. The school has a duty (which rests with the governors) to identify pupils with special educational needs and to ensure that appropriate provision is made.[120] Whilst the manner of non-statutory assessment is a matter for the school or LEA the Act prescribes a *formal assessment procedure*. The relevant DES guidance has been revised to improve the advice to LEAs about how to secure effective parental involvement in the assessment process (see DES Circular 22/89).

Parents, who have no right to prevent an assessment, must be informed of the LEA's proposal to assess the child, given the name of an officer of the LEA from whom further advice may be obtained, and notified of the right to make representations (orally or in writing) within a minimum period of 29 days from service of notice by the LEA.

Once the period of notice has expired the LEA must proceed with the assessment, provided it considers it appropriate having regard to the representations which have been made.[121] Advice from a variety of professional sources (teachers, educational psychologists, doctors and others) must be sought by the LEA when carrying out the assessment.[122] This advice should relate to the child's home background and medical history, and to his/her difficulties and the provision required in respect of them.[123] The child will be examined as part of the assessment process. Parental responsibility appears here in the form of a duty to ensure that the child is examined; there is an offence on failing without reasonable cause to comply with requirements of a notice requiring the child to be examined at a stipulated place and time.[124] Parents do have some important rights, however. They may attend the examination (but not any case conference, although the Circular advocates their presence whenever possible) and may submit information. The House of Commons Select Committee found that insufficient weight was being given to parents' views in the assessment process.[125] The Circular emphasises that parents must be seen as 'partners' in the assessment process, although the evidence is that parents are by no means equal partners here. The language used and the complexity of the procedures – both of which cause parents some difficulty[126] – reinforce the seemingly inevitable 'distancing' of parents from the professionals. The same may also be said of the existence of a right of appeal. Parents have a right to appeal to the Secretary of State when the LEA has decided, following the assessment, that it is not required to determine the special educational provision that should be made.[127] The Secretary of State can only direct the LEA to *reconsider* its decision.[128]

The fact that there is a right of appeal here demonstrates the importance of the LEA's decision on this matter. If the LEA's decision is that it should determine the provision that should be made, it must make a statement of the child's special educational needs, in a form prescribed by regulation.[129] The existence of such a statement confirms that the child has greater special educational needs than most other children with such needs.[130] About 2 per cent of the school population has statements,[131] but across LEAs the proportion varies from 4.2 per cent to 0.04 per cent.[132] This compares with an estimated proportion of the school population with special educational needs of 20 per cent.

In the case of *R v Hereford and Worcester County Council ex parte Lashford*,[133] the Court of Appeal confirmed that there is no duty on LEAs to maintain a statement in respect of every child with special educational needs. The case concerned a 13-year-old girl whom the LEA accepted was a slow learner with special educational needs. The LEA considered that the child's needs could be met in an ordinary school and that no statement was necessary. The parents had come to the conclusion, after soliciting expert opinion, that her needs could best be met in a special (and, as it happened, private) school.[134] The parents had appealed to the Secretary of State, but had been unsuccessful. The Court, in upholding the LEA's right not to determine the special educational provision that should be made for the child, drew an important distinction. They distinguished between a child who has special educational needs, and a child who has special educational needs which are such that the LEA may be of the opinion that they should determine the special educational provision that should be made for him – in the words of Nicholls LJ, 'not special needs *simpliciter*, but special needs that satisfy a further condition'.

Part of the parents' case had rested on the following argument: within the school which the child attended a decision had been taken to include her in a remedial class; thus, the special educational provision that should be made for her had already been determined; so a statement (under section 7(1) of the Act) should follow. But Dillon LJ said:

if the [LEA] does not itself decide the special educational provision that should be made for the child, but leaves that to be decided by the school, with remedial classes and other facilities as may be available in the school, the [LEA] is not itself determining the special educational provision for the child within the meaning in section 7(1); consequently, the [LEA] is not obliged to make and maintain a statement . . . . A decision to leave what is to be done for a particular child . . . to the school is not itself, in my judgment, a determination of the special educational provision for the child . . . which would necessitate the making of a statement.

The *Lashford* case thus demonstrates the extent of LEA discretion under the 1981 Act.[135] Hannon's prognosis of the Act, that 'LEAs will be able to draw the line between the "statemented" and the "unstatemented" where they please',[136] would appear to have been accurate.

The case also confirms the limitations to the patchwork of parental rights provided by the 1981 Act. Parents have various opportunities to question aspects of any statement which the LEA is proposing to make. They are entitled to receive a copy of the proposed statement and to make representations, or arrange a meeting with an officer for discussion of the statement, within 15 days.[137] They must be notified of the LEA's subsequent decision concerning the statement (the LEA can modify the statement, leave it as it is, or determine not to make it).[138] If and when the statement is actually made, parents are entitled to a copy of it. They must also be informed of their right of appeal to an appeal committee under section 8 of the Act and the name of a person from whom advice and information concerning their child's special educational needs may be obtained.[139] The appeal committee's decision is not binding on the LEA,[140] but there is a further right of appeal to the Secretary of State who can confirm, amend or revoke the statement.[141] If the LEA *declines* to make a statement, the value of an appeal is somewhat limited in that the Secretary of State may direct the LEA to reconsider its decision, but cannot impose a decision on the authority. Parents of children have a right to request a reassessment of their children; the LEA must comply unless to do so would be 'unreasonable' (in the case of children who are not statemented) or 'inappropriate' and there has been no assessment in the previous six months (in the case of statemented children).[142] A reassessment of statemented children must, in any event, take place within six months either side of a child's fourteenth birthday.[143] But it has been held that although all statements must be reviewed at least once a year,[144] a LEA is not obliged to re-assess a statemented child's special educational needs before s/he is that age unless the parents so request.. [145]

Some conclusions

The House of Commons Select Committee on Education found that although the Act had enhanced the position of parents in many respects, there were 'still situations in which parents feel their contribution . . . to be insufficient or ineffective'.[146] Thus perhaps the fact that a number of legal cases have been brought is indicative of some parents' resistance to the subservient, rather than partnership, role which some say they are forced to assume by the Act (regardless of exhortations to LEAs to extend parental involvement). Wolfendale argues that the involvement of parents has been fostered by professional and parental convictions rather than the law.[147] Edis and Brabazon have suggested that parental involvement would be improved if parents were given more extensive rights.[148] They argue that in some cases parents' contribution depends on their 'tenacity, willingness to fight for their rights and a belief in their children's educational capacity'. One suspects, however, that the lack of appropriate provision stems most often from the inadequacy of resources, about which parents can do little. Although supporting the Act at the time of its enactment, the Labour Party's education spokesman, Neil Kinnock, highlighted lack of resources as likely to be the major impediment to the legislation's success. The Select Committee on Education has found that the lack of specific resources has restricted the 1981 Act's implementation. The Committee concluded that a commitment of extra resources was needed if significant further progress was to be made.[149] Evidence suggests that some LEAs have been redistributing resources to meet their obligations under the 1981 Act. But given the fixed level of those overall resources, the inevitable result has been a reduction in resources for the remainder of the school population.[150] In any event, Her Majesty's Inspectorate have concluded that special education in England and Wales is 'not well prepared' for the challenges of the ERA 1988 reforms.[151]

(Note: discussion of special educational needs and the National Curriculum appears in Chapter 7.)

Questions

1. Consider, in the context of education, the legal relationship between parent and state.
2. To what extent is it erroneous to talk of 'parental choice of school'?
3. How can the exercise of parental choice sometimes be racially divisive? How can this problem be resolved?
4. What role should the legal system play in securing the attendance of children at school?
5. Is there a case for extending parental rights in relation to children with special educational needs? What changes might be required?

Notes

1   *Watt v Kesteven County Council* (1955); *Cumings v Birkenhead Corporation* (1972); *Smith v ILEA* (1978).
2   On which, see Milman D 1986 *Education Conflict and the Law*, Routledge & Kegan Paul; and Adler M *et al.* 1989 *Parental Choice and Educational Policy*, Edinburgh University Press.
3   See Bainham A 1988 *Children, Parents and the State,*. Sweet & Maxwell.
4   *Ibid.*, p. 5.
5   Vol. 1, p. 446.
6   On the subject of parental choice and voluntary aided status for Muslim schools, see Cumper P 1989 'Muslims knocking at the classroom door'. *New Law Journal* 139: 1067–71.
7   *The Times*, 29 Sept. 1977.
8   Marson, P (1980) Parental choice in State education, *Journal of Social Welfare Law*, 193–208.
9   Most notably by the House of Lords in *Gillick v West Norfolk and Wisbech Area Health Authority* (1985).
10 Bainham, *op. cit.*, p. 5.
11 Hoggett B 1987 *Parents and Children: The Law of Parental Responsibility*, 3rd edn, Sweet & Maxwell, p. 17.
12 Tweedie J 1986 'Rights in Social Programmes: The Case of Parental Choice of School'. *Public Law* 407–36.
13 See Bradney A 1989 'The Dewsbury Affair and the Education Reform Act 1988'. *Education & the Law* 1(2): 51–7.
14 *The Times,* 14 July 1988.
15 Bainham, *op. cit.*, p. 187.
16 Taylor W 1981 'Contraction in context', in Simon B and Taylor W (eds) . *Education in the Eighties*, Batsford, p. 29.
17 Above, p. 60. For a recent case confirming the limitations of the equivalent of section 76 in Scottish Law (s.28(1) Education (Scotland) Act 1981), see *Harvey v Strathclyde Regional Council* (1989).
18 Para.120.
19 See Bull D 1980 'School admissions: a new appeals procedure'. *Journal of Social Welfare Law* 209–33, at p. 212.
20 Taylor and Saunders 1976 *The Law of Education*, 8th edn, Butterworth, p. 34.
21 Marson, *op. cit.*, p. 193.
22 For comparison of these grounds of exception and those contained in the Education (Scotland) Act 1981, see Tweedie, *op. cit.*, p. 411.
23 *R v Greenwich London Borough Council ex parte the Governors of John Ball Primary School* (1989); *R v Bromley London Borough Council ex parte C* (1991); *R v Royal Borough of Kingston upon Thames ex parte Kingwell* (1991); Education Act 1980, s.6(5).
24 Freeman MDA 1980 'Children's education and the law'. *Legal Action Group Bulletin* 62.
25 *R v Camden London Borough Council ex parte S*. 1990.
26 *R v Commissioner for Local Administration ex parte Croydon London Borough Council* (1989).
27 For an assessment of the role of the Ombudsman in this context, and a critique of the appeals system itself, see Bull D 1985 'Monitoring

education appeals: local ombudsmen lead the way'. *Journal of Social Welfare Law* 189–226.

28 Caroline St John Brooks observed that 'parents who lose their cases tend to feel very bitter': 1982 'Parental choice: con or compromise?' *New Society*, 26 Aug. 1982.

29 Buck T 1985 'School admission appeals'. *Journal of Social Welfare Law* 227–51.

30 Report in *The Times* (31 Oct. 1982), citing the view of the Association of Metropolitan LEAs.

31 Buck, *op. cit.*, p. 247.

32 *R v Greenwich London Borough Council ex parte Governors of John Ball Primary School* (1989).

33 Tweedie, *op. cit.*, p. 425.

34 *Ibid.*, p. 426.

35 DES Circular 11/88 *Admission of Pupils to County and Voluntary Schools*, para.1.

36 DES/Secretary of State for Education & Science 1987 *Admission of Pupils to Maintained Schools*, Consultation Paper DES, para.3.

37 On the range of factors which influence parents exercising choice of school, see Elliott J 1982 'How do parents choose and judge secondary schools?' in R. McCormick (ed.) *Calling Education into Account*, Heinemann, pp. 41–2; West A and Varlaam A 1991 'Choosing a secondary school'; Hunter J 1991 'Which school? A study of parental choice of secondary school', both in *Educational Research* 33(1): pp. 22–30, 31–41.

38 ERA 1988, section 26(1).

39 *Ibid.*, section 27.

40 *Ibid.*, section 28(7).

41 See further DES Circular 11/88, para.14.

42 ERA 1988, section 28(3) and (5); Education (Publication of Proposals for Reduction in Standard Number Regulations) Order SI 1991 No. 411, see also SI 1988 No. 1515 and SI 1991 No. 411.

43 *Ibid.*, section 27(8).

44 *Ibid.*, section 29.

45 Meredith P 1989 'Educational reform' *Modern Law Review* 52: 221–2.

46 See, for example, 'Drastic LMS job cuts', *Times Educational Supplement*, 1 June 1990.

47 Sex Discrimination Act 1975, section 1(1)(b).

48 *Mandla v Dowell Lee* (1983).

49 See Commission for Racial Equality 1983 *Secondary School Allocations in Reading. Report of a Formal Investigation*. A Welsh comprehensive school sent home a boy wearing an ear stud when girls were not disciplined in such circumstances. This was unlawful. See *The Observer* 28 April 1991.

50 See Poulter S 1986 *English Law and Ethnic Minority Customs*, Butterworths, p. 191.

51 Sex Discrimination Act 1975, section 26(1).

52 Poulter, *op. cit.*, p. 193.

53 *R v Secretary of State for Education and Science and Anr ex parte Keating* (1986).

54 See *The Times*, 23 April 1990, p. 4.

55 ERA 1988, section 9(3).

56   Schools have a discretion to permit the withdrawal of a child from sex education lessons. DES Circular 11/87 advises schools to pay regard, when exercising this discretion, to the strong religious objections felt by some parents towards the imparting of sex education by schools. The Education (No.2) Act 1986 requires sex education to be given in such a way as to emphasise morality and the value of family life (section 46). The Circular (at para 15) says that due consideration should also be given to religious or cultural factors bearing on the discussion of sexual issues. In the case of *Kejedlsen, Busk Masden and Pedersen* (1976) the Eurpean Court of Human Rights said that compulsory sex education in Danish Schools did not contravene Article 2 protocol 1 of the European Convention on Human Rights (respect for parents' religious and philosophical convictions).

57   Department of Health 1989 *An Introduction to the Children Act 1989.* HMSO, para. 1.4.

58   HMI 1988 *Secondary Schools: An Appraisal by HMI,* HMSO, p. 74.

59   For a discussion of these patrols, see Grenville M P 1989 'Police truancy patrols', *Education and the Law* 1(2): 65–7.

60   Lord Elton (Chair) 1989 *Discipline in Schools: Report of the Committee of Enquiry Chaired by Lord Elton,* HMSO, R 105. On the link between juvenile crime and truancy, see Brown I 1990 'Truancy, delinquency and the Leeds adjournment system'. *Education and the Law* 2(2): 47–53.

61   See *The Times Educational Supplement,* 28 Oct. 1988.

62   Galloway D 1985 *Schools and Persistent Absentees,* Pergamon, p. 21.

63   See Sutherland M 1988 *Theory of Education,* Longman, pp. 66–7, for a discussion of home schooling by parents (or 'education otherwise').

64   Pack D C 1977 *Truancy and Indiscipline in Schools in Scotland: Report of the Committee Chaired by DC Pack,* HMSO.

65   Gray J and Clough E 1984 *Choices at 16, a Survey: Summary of Results,* University of Sheffield.

66   See Grenville M P 1989 'Sickness and compulsory school attendance'. *Education and the Law* 1(3): 113–17.

67   *Jenkins v Howells* (1949) – girl staying away from school to perform domestic duties for mother. Held: Not an unavoidable cause affecting the child. See also *Jarman v Mid-Glamorgan Education Authority* (1985) *The Times,* 11 Feb.

68   See *Spiers v Warrington Corporation* (1954).

69   *George v Devon County Council* (1988).

70   By section 53 of the Education (No. 2) Act 1986.

71   Reid K 1986 *Dissaffection from School,* Methuen, p. 23.

72   DES 1985 *Better Schools,* HMSO, Cmnd 9469, para 191; HMI (Wales) 1985 *Attendance and Achievement in Secondary Schools,* Welsh Office, p. 13; HMI 1988 *Secondary Schools. An Appraisal by HMI,* p. 74.

73   Galloway, *op. cit.,* p. 21.

74   Reid K 1985 *Truancy and School Absenteeism,* Hodder & Stoughton, p. 23.

75   *Op. cit.,* p. 95.

76   Pratt J and Grimshaw R 1985 'An aspect of welfare justice: truancy and the juvenile court'. *Journal of Social Welfare Law* 257–73.

77   Grenville M 1988 'Compulsory school attendance and the child's wishes'. *Journal of Social Welfare Law* 4–20.

78   See Pratt J and Grimshaw R 1985 'Restructuring a juvenile justice pre-court tribunal'. *Journal of Social Welfare Law* 4–15.

79   E.g., Gray J, McPherson AF and Raffe D 1983 *Reconstructions of Secondary Education*, Falmer; HMI (Wales), *op. cit.*

80   Grenville 1988, *op. cit.*, p. 5.

81   Reid K 1985 *op. cit.*, p. 31.

82   *Re S (A Minor)* (1977).

83   Berg I 1980 'Absence from school and the law', in Hersov L and Berg I (eds) *Out of School*, Hodder & Stoughton; Berg I *et al.* 1987 'School attendance, visits by EWOs and appearances in juvenile court'. *Educational Research* 29: 19.

84   Brown I 1990 'Truancy, delinquency and the Leeds adjournment system'. *Education and the Law* 2(2): 47–51.

85   Most recently by Grenville M P 1988 'School attendance: supervision by the courts'. *Family Law* 18:488–492.

86   *Op. cit.*, p. 117.

87   Reid 1985, *op. cit.*, pp. 32–3.

88   Official report (House of Commons) *Standing Committee B*, col. 248, 23 May 1989.

89   Reid K 1988 'The Education Welfare Service – some issues and suggestions', and 'Combating school absenteeism: main conclusions' – both in Reid K (ed.) *Combating School Absenteeism*, Hodder & Stoughton.

90   Poole K 1987 *Education Law*. Sweet & Maxwell, p. 151.

91   E.g. Brown I *op. cit.*

92   Galloway 1985, *op. cit.*, p. 113.

93   Hullin R P *et al.* 1987 'Truancy: legal solutions', *Family Law* **17**: 324–6.

94   Brown D 1988 'The attitudes of parents to education and the school attendance of their children'. in Reid K (ed.) *Combating School Absenteeism*. Hodder & Stoughton.

95   Reid 1985, *op. cit.*, p. 38. See also Ruddick J and Wood T 1990 'In search of the Holy Grail – an alternative view'. *Education and the Law* 2(1): 13–16.

96   Wingham G 1989 'Tackling school dropouts in the Big Apple'. *Social Work Today*, 7 Dec. 1989, pp. 20–1.

97   Children Act 1989, Schedule 3, para.12(1).

98   *Ibid.*, para. 15.

99   Blyth and Milner 1988, writing in K. Reid (ed.) *op. cit.*, chap. 14.

100   Pratt J and Grimshaw R 1988 'Truancy: a case to answer?' in Reid K (ed.) *op. cit.*, p. 149.

101   Lord Elton (Chair) 1989 *Discipline in Schools Report of the Committee of Enquiry Chaired by Lord Elton*, HMSO, R 104.

102   Draft circular (DES), July 1989.

103   HMI (Wales) 1985 *Attendance and Achievement in Secondary Schools*. Welsh Office; Felstenstein 1988 'Strategies for improving school attendance', in Reid K (ed.), *op. cit.*

104   Lord Elton (Chair), *op. cit.*, R 100.

105   Galloway 1985, *op. cit.*, p. 121.

106   See HMI 1989 *Education Observed 13*, DES.

107   For a discussion of the historical development of the law on special educational needs, see Hannon V 1982 'The Education Act 1981: New rights and duties in special education'. *Journal of Social Welfare Law* 275–84. For a more conceptual analysis of the development of law and

policy on special educational needs, see Welton J and Evans J 1986 'The development and implementation of special education policy: where did the 1981 Act fit in?' *Public Administration* **64**:209–27.

108   House of Commons Education, Science and the Arts Committee 1987 *Session 1986–87, Third Report Special Educational Needs: Implementation of the Education Act 1981*, vol.1. HC 201–1, HMSO, para. 16.

109   DES 1989 Circular 22/89 *Assessments and Statements of Special Educational Needs: Procedures within the Education, Health and Social Services*, para. 21.

110   For a review of the cases, see Milman D 1987 'The Education Act 1981 in the courts'. *Journal of Social Welfare Law* 208–15. In a more recent case, *R v Mid Glamorgan County Council ex parte Grieg* (1988), parents unsuccessfully sought compensation for school fees paid and for their child's lost potential opportunities resulting from 'allegedly reduced academic and social attainments'.

111   Education Act 1981, section 2. Integration, which includes a child with special educational needs engaging in activities at the school with children who do not have such needs (section 2(7)), is hedged about with various conditions: for example, integration of the child must be compatible with both the provision of efficient education for the children with whom the child will be educated and with the efficient use of resources (section 2(3)). The LEA can determine that the child be educated wholly or partly away from school (section 3); a new provision (section 3A) enables LEAs to arrange for some children to be educated outside England and Wales, for example at the Petó Institute in Hungary which offers conductive education for pupils with cerebral palsy. There are now 20,000 fewer children in special schools than in 1981.

112   Education Act 1981, section 1(1).

113   Note 106, para. 24.

114   Section 1(2).

115   Section 1(3).

116   See Solity J and Raybould E 1988 *A Teacher's Guide to Special Educational Needs; A Positive Response to the 1981 Education Act*, Open University Press, p. 23.

117   Note 108, para. 25.

118   *R v Lancashire County Council* ex parte CM (1989) (CA); cf. *R v Oxfordshire Education Authority ex parte W* (1986). There is still the problem of an acute shortage of speech therapists. As as 30 Sept. 1986 there were just 2,510 whole-time equivalent speech therapists employed in England: HC Official Report, vol 121, col. 417w, 29 Oct. 1987.

119   (1985).

120   Section 2(5). Once the needs have been identified, they must be made known to all who are likely to teach the child (section 2(5)(b)).

121   Education Act 1981, section 5(4).

122   *Ibid.*, Schedule 1; The Education (Special Educational Needs) Regulations 1983, SI 1983, No. 29, regs 4–7.

123   DES Circular 22/89 para.18 and Annex 1.

124   Education Act 1981, Schedule 1, para. 2(4).

125   Note 108, para.16.

126   *Ibid.*, paras 16 and 32.

127   Education Act 1981, section 5(7).

128   *Ibid.*, section 5(8).

129   *Ibid.*, section 7(1); Education (Special Educational Needs) Regulations 1983, *op. cit.,* reg.10. The statement must also now refer to any non-educational provision which is to be made, either by the LEA or another body: reg. 10(1)(c), substituted by the Education (Special Educational Needs) (Amendment) Regulations 1990, SI No. 1524 (reg. 2(9)). It must also specify the provision to be made in respect of *all* the special educational needs referred to in it: *R v Secretary of State for Education & Science ex parte E* (a minor) 1991.

130   For a discussion of the 'statemented'–'non-statemented' divide, see Whalley G E 1989 'A critical view of the Education Act 1981'. *Education and the Law* 1(2): 47–9.

131   DES Circular 22/89, para.14.

132   Note 108, para.33.

133   (1988) (CA).

134   The Education (Special Educational Needs) (Approval of Independent Schools) Regulations 1991 SI 1991 No. 449 prescribe the requirements which an independent school must satisfy before it can be approved to admit statemented children.

135   A fact also demonstrated by the case of *Re D* (1988), in which parents failed to have a child with special educational needs made a ward of court in order to inhibit the LEA's plans for the child's education.

136   Hannon Note 107, *op. cit.* p. 284.

137   Education Act 1981, section 7(4) and (7).

138   *Ibid.*, section 7(8).

139   *Ibid.*, section 7(9).

140   Milman argues that appeal committees should have the right to overturn the provision suggested by the LEA: Milman D 1987, *op. cit.* at 215.

141   *Ibid.*, section 8(7).

142   *Ibid.,* section 9(1) and (2).

143   Education (Special Educational Needs) Regulations 1983, *op. cit.*, reg.9.

144   *R v Newham London Borough Council ex parte D* (1991).

145   Education Act 1981, Schedule 1, para. 5.

146   Note 108, para. 16.

147   Wolfendale S 1983 *Parents' Participation in Children's Development and Education.* Gordon & Breach, p. 112.

148   Edis F and Brabazon E 1982 'Inequality before the law'. *New Statesman,* 10 Dec. 1982.

149   Note 108, para. 23.

150   Goacher B *et al.* 1986 *Policy and Provision for Special Educational Needs,* Cassell, p. 165.

151   Her Majesty's Inspectorate of Schools 1990 *Special Needs Issues,* HMSO.

CHAPTER 5

Access to information

INTRODUCTION: THE POWER OF INFORMATION

Education provides two major areas for arguments over access to information. The first concerns the individual pupil's curricular record, what is in it and who may see it. It is a fairly quiet fight, involving privacy and confidentiality, professionalism and relationships and the respective roles of parents and their children. The second is the broader area of information about the education authority's policies and arrangements and about the individual school itself. The clash of government policy may be heard here and there is some confusion between consumer and democrat. Here the battles over sex education and opting out will take place, but there will be further battles over the ability to govern and effective use of resources. Consumers do not always win, and free lunches are in decline.

Information and power have a very close relationship. If it is true that 'Political power and the effective control of communication go together'[1] and political power at a local level may concern formation of council or school policy; equally, consumer power depends on knowledge for choice and accountability while producer power needs control of the base materials, including know-how. Power over individuals or autonomy rely on the control of personal information. Power of professionalism involves both submission of the client to the professional's better judgement and a network of professional and inter- professional relationships, and probably rivalries, buttressed by exclusive sharing of information. It is well to recognise that decisions about information-holding or access are, to an extent, always decisions about power. We can then properly assess the value and consequence of an acquisition or transfer of power.

It is also well to recognise the confusions that arise in this area from the use of words or phrases with ill-defined but sometimes emotive meanings or with very different meanings. 'Confidentiality' may mean my right (or wish) that you do not pass on what I have told you (or don't identify me as the informant), or it may mean my wish (or right) that you do not pass on information about me, or, with 'professional' prefixed, it may mean that our group will support each other by saying nothing about each other's judgements, competencies or foibles. In one statute 'confidential information' means information disclosure of which is forbidden by statute or by the civil servant who gave it to the local authority. It should be said at the outset that this is not the usual legal meaning of the word. 'Privacy' is a word even less susceptible of exact meaning, though probably everyone could define something they considered to be private. In the present context the nearest to a definition might be the right to control who knows information about me. Someone has pointed out that this would require an ability to control the Royal Mail to ensure that letters did not get lost! 'Right to know' is an emotive phrase used in campaigns to widen access to information. But paradoxically the public right-to-know argument, which may be a pure power argument for involvement in decision making or an argument just to know what has been decided (and why), may conflict fundamentally with the individual right to know argument which may say, 'I have a right to know information and decisions about me and to prevent anyone else from knowing' – the confidentiality argument (or one of them).

'Professionalism' and 'relationships' (or 'confidential relationships') are also relevant words in this discussion which may be used in a way that is highly supportive of, or very antagonistic to, access to information by the person to whom it relates. Thus professionalism may be seen as expertise applied to and building up the relationship with the individual pupil, where a trusting relationship which can share information and build autonomy is seen as a goal. The professional takes power to give to the client self-determination. Or professionalism and relationships may be seen mainly within the professional group. Information may be shared within the group but its cohesion depends on limiting the sharing of information outside the group. The strength, and even survival, of individuals depends on the cohesion of the group. The loyalty of confidentiality is seen to be owed to members of the group and those relationships are the crucial ones which must be protected.

For many years the arguments for access to information have emphasised on the one hand the private values of privacy and autonomy and on the other hand the public values of democratic involvement in decision making. In the last decade a new basis for argument has been that of consumerism and accountability. As a general argument it straddles the two others, being more limited than either but broader than each. A consumer is not the only person to whom information relates, but the consumer seeks more than personal information. Accountability or value for money is not the only reason for knowing what government is doing and having a say in it, but the consumer may have a more direct effect on policy and the producer than any number of democratic arguers.

THE PUPIL'S RECORD

The development of a right of parents and pupils to see the pupil's personal school record has not been a specifically education issue but has arisen as part of the wider campaign for access to personal records. Until recently what was on the child's school record and whether parent or child could see it was a vexed question. There was little consistency on record-keeping, some authorities having extensive personal files while others kept only the minimum information. Some of the tragic child-abuse cases publicly investigated in the 1970s and 1980s highlighted the need for schools both to record information about possible child abuse and to share it with other agencies. In less extreme circumstances others were expressing concern that the holding of information and its transmission from teacher to teacher and from school to school might unfairly label and prejudice a child. The NUT, reporting to the Younger Committee on Privacy in 1972, proposed that reports about a child's misbehaviour should be kept from parents and that information on the pupil or his home background 'which might be gleaned from hearsay or possibly based on malicious gossip' should not be kept on a permanent record. Any information on parents should not be passed from one school to another.[2]

For information which was on the file, there were very different approaches to letting parents or children have a look. Most authorities kept files well away from parents and children. Arguments against allowing access included that people would not write frankly if they knew their comments would be seen, it could be important to record facts which could not be proved and suspicions or impressions, the child or parent might be made unhappy by a teacher's judgement and it might impair the relationship or discourage the child, and access would lead to constant arguments about fairness or relevance of information.

A few authorities, however, have long had a formal policy of allowing parents to see their children's school records, and individual schools have sometimes had an open files policy and reported beneficial results to the motivation of pupils and relations with parents.[3] A general shift of attitude by teachers towards openness arose, at least in part, from their arguments in support of a right to see reports and references on the teachers themselves. In 1984 the NUT reported 'considerations of natural justice which led the union to adopt a policy opposed to confidential reports and references on teachers apply equally to the current demand from many parents for a right of access to files kept on their children'. The union proposed that in principle parents should have access to their children's files.

The Assistant Masters and Mistresses Association (AMMA) in 1985 studied the arguments for and against access and concluded, 'the opening up of school records to parents and older students would greatly reduce understandable, if unfounded, fears of needless secrecy, . . . serve to strengthen the relationship between educational establishments, parents and pupils . . . [and] improve the quality and value of the records.'[4]

OPENING THE RECORD

The law now reflects this basic right of access. The Data Protection Act 1984, whose only specific reference to education concerns examination results, gives a general right of subject access (with few exceptions) to all computerised personal information.

The Act requires data users to register, declaring the sources of data, uses and people to whom it may be disclosed. It also provides a general right for the data subject to see and have copies of the data relating to him. Information relating to another or which would identify another as its source may not be shown unless that person consents. Names may have to be blanked out. Health information is also subject to the doctor's right to refuse disclosure on the ground that it would be likely to cause serious injury to the health of the subject or another. Apart from these exceptions the subject can see the whole computerised record. If he disagrees with any part he can have it rectified or removed by agreement or have his dissent recorded and his own version put alongside.

For manual files (which includes the majority of school files) the relevant law is the Education (School Records) Regulations 1989.[5] The Regulations require from September 1989 that each maintained school, special school and grant-maintained school must keep a curricular record annually updated for each registered pupil at the school. 'Curricular record' is defined as a formal record of a pupil's academic achievements, his other skills and abilities and his progress in school (Regulation 4). The authority and the school have wide discretion as to how the records should be compiled, given the two major purposes of providing basic data on a pupil's progress for other teachers and the parents and providing evidence to support the teacher's assessment of the pupil's level of attainment. Other information such as behaviour and home circumstances may be included in the record but, if not entirely factual, it should be sufficiently well founded to bear scrutiny by the parents.[6] The Regulations recognise that a teacher may keep notes on a pupil simply for his or her own use. These are not part of the formal record (Regulation 7 (2)).

One year's notice was given to enable schools to get the records into order. From September 1990 parents, and in some cases the pupils themselves, have a right to see the record in so far as it is made after 31 August 1989. Earlier material may be shown but at the discretion of the school. Thus all material to be shown will have been compiled in the knowledge that it would be made available.

There are exceptions to access. There is no duty to disclose information provided by or on behalf of another person other than an employee of the local education authority, an education welfare officer or the person seeking disclosure. Thus reports from social services and the medical service and probation service reports are not bound to be disclosed. On analogy with subject access in social services and housing one might expect the governors to seek the consent of the person compiling the report and for such consent normally to be forthcoming since otherwise the record may clearly be incomplete. However, it is not even clear in the Regulations that the governors have any such discretion. It is suggested that an active policy to gain consent and then disclose would be supported by the law. There is no liability for breach of confidence if consent is obtained. In an extreme case the European Court of Human Rights decision in *Gaskin*[7] could be invoked. Mr Gaskin had been a child in care of the local authority. He asked to see his social services file and eventually the local authority agreed, provided the donors of information consented. Most did not. The European Court held the refusal was a breach of his right to a private and family life, since the file was the major record of his childhood, and there should have been an independent body which could override an improper refusal of consent. Such a body is now being provided in relation to social services but has not yet been provided for education. Another perhaps rather negative exception concerns references to a prospective employer or higher education or other training body, though here there is a discretion. Other exceptions are understandable. Information concerning or identifying another pupil should not be disclosed, and information, the disclosure of which might cause serious harm to the mental or physical health or emotional condition of the pupil or anyone else, or which indicates that the pupil has or may be likely to suffer child abuse, should not be disclosed. The law does make provision for a person on a child-abuse register to know and to challenge that decision but the information does not have to come through the school record.

Some other sensitive information has limited disclosure. Thus only a parent may see information on the record concerning the pupil's racial group, language or religion, and only a parent may see a statement of special educational needs (under the Education Act 1981–see Chapter 4) or results of the pupil's assessment. (On the duty on schools to provide information to parents on the pupil's National Curriculum assessment, see the Education (Individual Pupils' Achievements) (Information) Regulations 1990, SI No. 1381 and circular No. 8/90.)

Part of the value of parents having access is to enable inaccuracies to be challenged and corrected. The Regulations require the governors to arrange procedures for complying with requests for access within 15 school days and for correcting or removing any parts agreed to be inaccurate and to hear appeals. If the record holder does not agree that an item is inaccurate, the parent is entitled to have a note of his disagreement added to the record.

ACCESS FOR PARENT OR PUPIL?

In much of the discussion it has been assumed that it is a parent who seeks the information. If access is seen as part of the right of autonomy of the individual, one might ask why parents, rather than the children themselves, should have access. If it is seen as part of control over quality of education, the parent might ask why the child should be given access at all. In most cases the issue raises no problems, but estranged parents using the child to fight their battles or rebellious teenagers seeking recognition of their maturity and autonomy against over-protective or interventionist parents may see it as an important issue of principle. The teacher may thus stand in the cross-fire between them. It is as well to know the legal position. The general law is somewhat ambivalent on parents and children, and indeed the rights of children have only recently begun to be recognised. The House of Lords case of *Gillick v West Norfolk and Wisbech AHA* (1985) is important in setting out the basic principle. A mother sought a declaration that the doctors, health authority and Department of Health had no right to provide contraceptive advice and treatment for her children under 16 without parental[8] knowledge and consent. The rights of parents in relation to their children were thus an issue. The House of Lords held that parental rights are recognised in law only for so long as they are needed for the protection of the child. Lord Scarman said: 'The principle is that parental right or power of control of the person and property of his child exists primarily to enable the parent to discharge his duty of maintenance, protection and education until he [that is, the child] reaches such an age as to be able to look after himself and make his own decisions.'

The principle is thus clear, though difficult to apply in the many practical situations which arise.

In the present context, however, there are further provisions. The Data Protection Act 1984 makes no distinction between adults and children. The data subject is entitled to access personally or to authorise another. The Registrar advises that if the data user is satisfied that the child understands what he is asking and is acting on his own volition his request must be obeyed. For a child too young to make an informed request the information may be disclosed to a parent on his behalf. In *Gillick* terms, the ability to make an informed request assumes the child to be old enough to make at least that decision for himself. The Regulations for manual records make the position much easier to administer for the school though they may perhaps cause more family friction. For a pupil under 16, the parent alone is entitled to access, for a pupil aged 18 or over he alone is entitled and when he is 16 and 17 they both have the right. The exception to this is that only a parent may receive the results of the pupil's assessment. Other particular provisions allow parents to be given special information relating to their child. Thus if the school head decides to disapply or modify the National Curriculum in respect of a particular child, or to revoke such a direction, a copy of the notice must be sent within three days to at least one parent of the pupil at the registered address. If necessary the head must take steps to enable the parent to understand the Regulation.[9]

DISCLOSURE AND TRANSFER OF THE CURRICULAR RECORD

Another aspect of the rights of the pupil in relation to his record is his right to have the record disclosed where it will be to his benefit and to prevent disclosure elsewhere. It may also be very important to him that the record is transferred to his next school. If the record is computerised, the Data Protection Act 1984 does not give any right to the subject to ensure disclosure. Rather, the data user, the school or educational authority, has a right to disclose to any registered disclosee though not to anyone else. The Act makes no provision about transfer of the record. The position with manual records is again more clear. The governors are under a duty to ensure that, on receipt of a written request, they transfer the curricular record to the head of a new school or place of education or training to which the pupil has transferred or, from September 1990, disclose the record to one which is considering the pupil for admission. The institutions in question may not insist on receiving results of assessments ascertaining the pupil's educational achievements though there is nothing to stop the parent passing it on. The institutions are also not entitled to receive information about the pupil's racial group, religion, home language or court reports.

Thus the Regulations aim to ensure that useful information will be passed on but possibly prejudicial information will not. It cannot exactly be described as a right of the pupil, however, since he cannot ensure that the other schools and so on ask for the record. Neither do the Regulations say anything about limits to any other disclosures of the record (apart from the exempt parts). The general law of confidential information would impose a duty to the donors of information not to use or disclose it beyond the purposes for which it is given without consent of the donors. Schools entering into an entrepreneurial spirit should not, for example, sell school records to promoters of consumer goods or allow journalists or public relations consultants to leaf through them for good stories. All staff must be aware that they are confidential and so must not be the topic of gossip. Relations with the press may cause difficulties and advice should be taken before talking about a pupil.

THE EFFECT OF ACCESS ON RECORD-KEEPING

It is inevitable, and probably salutary, that an open records regime affects the way in which records are kept. Items stated as fact should be accurate, and often the benefit of access is that their accuracy can be checked. Care must be taken not to read more than is said into reports from others, particularly since the Regulations exclude access to the original report but a teacher's use of it may be on the record. For example, a small boy was seen once by an educational psychologist at his parents' request on a problem of which hand he should write with. The specialist's report to his school mentioned also some transitory emotional difficulties the child was having (while a loved schoolteacher was ill). Two schools later (his parents having moved house) the boy was ill, and his then head wrote to the consultant treating him that he 'had previously attended two schools, having transferred from the first because of "transitory emotional difficulties" (Ed. Psych.)'. The result was that his serious physical illness was assumed to be a form of 'school phobia' and his parents were threatened with a court order if he did not return to school.[10] Access to the file, including the head's letter, would have enabled correction of the factual errors at least and perhaps an accurate diagnosis of his illness to be made. Accuracy of recorded facts is in everyone's interests.

More difficulty arises over recording a suspicion or allegation, whether about the pupil or his family. 'A bit concerned over X's honesty, though as yet no evidence' and 'Mother professes an interest in his welfare but we hear stories of drinking and late night parties' – both come from school records[11] but could not stand parental scrutiny. Is it necessary to record the item? If so, is there supportive evidence?

It may be helpful for the record to include a brief pen-picture of the pupil, to assist the next teacher or school in getting to know the pupil and helping his development. There is a danger that by remaining on the file the picture acquires a spurious aura of eternal truth. 'Very much inclined to sulk. Wants to be liked and likes to hang around and curry favour with teacher. Very much inclined to cheat. Rather lovable in spite of all' – was recorded at age 7 and still remained on the secondary school record at age 14. Schools should have a policy of removing obsolete material.

Some recorded comments would be merely offensive if they were not so potentially damaging. Another example found in school records, 'this boy is big, black and smelly'[12] indicates a use of the school record for quite unjustifiable venting of a personal spleen. Anyone recording or passing on such a comment is in danger now that records are open. May critical or unflattering things no longer be written about pupils? It is possible for teachers to keep a personal notebook which does not form part of the record and is not open to subject access, but if information is intended to be used officially and passed on to the next teacher it should be treated in the same way as the formal record. The law of libel reflects this difference.

Access to files sometimes leads people to worry that they will be sued if the record contains unprovable statements. By the law of defamation the publisher of an untrue statement which brings the subject into 'hatred, ridicule or contempt' may have to pay damages. But qualified privilege exempts the person who made or published the statement without malice in the course of their work to a person with a duty or interest to receive it. This should be sufficient to protect the teacher preparing or passing on the records in any reasonable circumstances where what is written has a valid purpose. Comments like 'big, black and smelly' can only be malicious and would not be protected. Liability could follow simply from passing on the statement. How the law would view the personal notebook is uncertain. It is quite likely that qualified privilege would not apply here as there is no duty, as part of the teacher's work, to compile an informal, unofficial record. The teacher who uses this aid will have to be particularly careful to keep it secret and so not publish any libel to anyone at all.

CONFIDENTIALITY OF THE PUPIL'S RECORD

Although the pupil or parent may now see what is in the file, it should otherwise be held in confidence. In this context, this means used and disclosed only for the purposes for which it is compiled, or for which authority is given, or with the donor's consent or for certain other limited purposes. There is a general rule that the holder may disclose information held in confidence if necessary to protect his own interests, and it may be that disclosure is justified if needed to protect someone from harm.

These grounds reflect some of the reasons some of the time for compiling records. It may be necessary to chart events and actions to be able to show later that teachers acted promptly and appropriately; in child abuse particularly, but also in other cases, careful records may be helpful in protecting the child or someone else from harm. The following sections describe some exceptions to the general rule of confidentiality. Some of them have been used as an indirect way of seeing the file by parents denied access for themselves. Now that access by parents and pupils is the normal rule, these indirect routes will become less important. However, they may still be needed for information which for one reason or another is not made available by subject access.

DISCLOSURE OF INFORMATION FOR LITIGATION

Any information which is relevant may have to be disclosed to the parties in respect of any court case. There are exceptions, but the fact that information is held in confidence is not as such a sufficient reason for exemption. A school record on a child may have to be disclosed as may any other record held by the school or authority. The court has a discretion, and a record holder who would prefer not to hand over the file is entitled to refuse unless the party gets a court order to disclose.

Mrs Campbell was a schoolteacher in her fifties who suffered what many teachers fear. She was violently attacked in the classroom by an 11-year-old pupil and suffered injuries so severe that she had to take early retirement. She wished to bring an action against her employers alleging that they had been negligent in failing adequately to protect her against the known risk of injury from this pupil. She knew that a record had been kept on the child, including an educational psychologist's report, and that the school logbook would record other incidents, so she sought disclosure of these documents to help her in her case against the authority. The Court of Appeal allowed her to see them, deciding that although the reports might contain information given in confidence, yet the public interest in parties to litigation being able fully to prove their case and so not be denied justice outweighed the public interest in maintaining the confidentiality of pupil files. [13]

By contrast, in *D v NSPCC* (1976) parents wished to see a report which alleged that they had injured their child. The House of Lords accepted evidence that the NSPCC relied on anonymous informants for much of its work in child protection and held that the public interest in informants coming forward with information outweighed the parents' interest in being able to sue a malicious busybody. The name of the informant must not be disclosed.

GETTING THE COUNCILLOR TO SEE THE FILE

Councillors vary tremendously in the extent to which they expect to be involved in day-to-day matters of administration in the authority. Some leave it all to officers and concentrate on policy issues in council and committee meetings, whereas others wish to know details of particular cases and administrative decisions. Most councillors expect to be lobbied by constituents and asked to intervene on their behalf. It has always been clear that a councillor must be allowed to see any information he needs to carry out his duties, but it has been unclear how far that goes. A councillor member of a housing committee wanted to see information in a social services file on prospective adopting parents as she doubted their suitability as adopters. The House of Lords eventually upheld her right, recognising that she had a genuine interest, [14] but providers of information (particularly the BMA) and social services staff were extremely uneasy about the apparent danger to confidentiality of client files. Eventually the local authority associations agreed a self-denying ordinance and in many authorities councillors do not seek access to records on individuals.

The general right to information was confirmed, and perhaps extended, in the Local Government (Access to Information) Act 1985. Any council member has a right to inspect any document held by or under control of the authority and relevant to any business to be transacted in council, committee or sub-committee. Controversy about need to be a member of the committee is thus removed. But the Act exempts some information from all its provisions, and exempt information includes information about a particular pupil or about the education of a particular person. The Act does not override the common law rights decided in the *Birmingham* case, and under that decision a councillor could claim to see the individual file if he could show a need to know. Since rights of subject access have been given, this is obviously less important than it was, but getting the councillor to see the file could still be important for pre-1989 information and reports from third parties which the parents and pupil still have no right to see.

Whether the councillor will press his claim to disclosure will depend on political factors (for example, in councils which regularly change political complexion it is much easier for an opposition party councillor to get information than in one which is solidly of one political complexion). The parents have no right to insist that the councillor should get involved.

ACCESS BY THE OMBUDSMAN

If an individual claims to have suffered injustice because of maladministration by a local authority, the Commissioner for Local Administration may investigate the complaint on his behalf. The investigation is held in private but the authority and individuals concerned may comment on the allegations. The Commissioner has wide powers to receive information and look at documents.[15]

The Commissioner's report is made public, and the authority must consider it if an adverse finding is made. The authority has no duty to implement any proposals for redress but clearly refusal to do so may lead to unwelcome publicity.

Maladministration is particularly concerned with procedural matters (as well as such obvious things as malice and discrimination) so the maintenance of accurate records is particularly important in countering any such allegation.

PUBLIC ACCESS TO SCHOOL INFORMATION

As part of the policy of accountability and choice, local education authorities and school governors have a duty to provide information not only for parents but also for prospective parents and the public generally. This information is broadly of two kinds – that relating to the education authority's policy and arrangements, and that relating to the individual school.

Information about local authority policy and arrangements is clearly intended to provoke public awareness and discussion of local education policy generally. Given the substantial resource committed to education and the consistent government policy of the last 10 years of shifting the balance of power from local authorities to individuals, this is not in any way surprising. Authorities and teachers should welcome the policy of openness since informed debate is vastly more constructive than ignorant criticism and the determinedly ignorant can be reminded to do their homework! That the policy is not restricted to increasing the knowledge of parents of pupils is seen by the access provisions under the various Regulations. No special interest need be shown by a person seeking to see particular items, and availability must usually be given in local public places as well as in relevant schools. Thus the main regulations[16] of 1981 (as amended) provide that the authority must make available information on all its schools and the authority's policies on such matters as examination entries, special educational needs and charging and remission on charges. This must be sent to parents of prospective pupils but also be made available in schools, public libraries and education offices. Similar provision is made, for example, by the Education (Publication of Schemes for Financing Schools) Regulations 1989, whereby a copy of any such scheme must be available for reference 'by parents and other persons at all reasonable times and without charge' at the school, public libraries and education offices. Not only future proposals but also information about the present financial position of schools must be made available for reference both to parents and to others, in education offices and public libraries.[17] A more extreme example of very local publicity relates to the publication of proposals in relation to grant-maintained schools under sections 89(1) or 92(2) of the ERA. As well as being published in a local newspaper, the proposal must be posted at or near the main gate of the school and in 'a conspicuous place' in the area and made available for inspection at the school 'or at any other place within that area to which members of the public may conveniently have access' (SI 1989, No. 1469). It is to be hoped that this is not early warning of the demise of public libraries!

Access to the policy making of the LEA is already provided by law. The Local Government (Access to Information) Act 1985 requires each local authority to make available to the public before the meeting agendas, agenda papers and minutes of council and committees; and there is a statutory right to attend council, committee and sub-committee meetings. Information exempt from disclosure is defined and includes information relating to an individual's education. Meetings may only exclude the public if exempt information is likely to be considered or if 'confidential information' would be disclosed. The particular definition of confidential information in this Act is information given by a central government department on terms forbidding disclosure to the public, or information, the disclosure of which, is forbidden by statute or court order. On this basis education committee business and that of its sub-committees should be open to the public except when dealing with individual pupils.

INFORMATION ABOUT THE SCHOOL

Since the Education Act 1980 began the emphasis on parental choice of schools, it became obvious that comparable information must be available about the various schools. The 1981 Regulations have been much amended and extended so that now each school must provide a School Prospectus containing a long list of prescribed information, including information about the curriculum, qualifications obtainable and careers education, and an Annual Report, including updates to the prospectus and dates and times of the school term. Both documents must be given freely to parents of pupils on request and must be made available at the school for reference by parents and others. The head must also make available for inspection at the school information on syllabuses, schemes of work and school hours as well as details of the arrangements for dealing with complaints and providing access to pupils' records and documents, such as any HMI Report on the school.[18] It might be thought that those seeking detailed information about a particular school should show a special reason for wanting it, but there is no suggestion in any of the Regulations that availability of the information should be limited. In the past the courts have construed statutory and common law rights to information restrictively and have either required an applicant to show a special reason for wanting the information[19] or have denied access to a person with an 'indirect motive' such as a councillor helping a constituent in a complaint against the authority.[20]

In another case the court upheld an elector's right to see council documents (a statutory right without qualification, as here) unless his request 'was so oppressive as to amount to an abuse of the right'.[21] It remains to be seen whether similar restrictions or limits will be placed on these public rights to information.

GOVERNORS' MEETINGS

If complete public openness is the policy, it might have been expected that the public would have free access to governors' meetings so that they could hear the arguments for policy and resource allocations within the school. This could have been provided under the Public Bodies (Admission to Meetings) Act 1960 (as amended) under which local authority meetings are open to the public with limited exceptions. Instead, the matter of attendance is left to the discretion of the governors with no restriction on their discretion. Agendas, minutes and related papers are available for inspection at the school,[22] but this is no substitute for attendance at meetings if public information and debate is fully intended. The School Government Regulations even allow the governors to decide that any matter 'by reason of its nature' should be treated as confidential and so exclude papers and minutes about it from public scrutiny. Thus the general scheme of the Regulations is to give public information about the authority and the school but to leave the governors free to make controversial decisions behind closed doors and without public knowledge.

ACCESSIBILITY OF ACCESS

All the relevant Regulations make provision for the translation of information, where appropriate, into languages other than English. Ethnic minority groups for whom English is not their first language may find this very useful. None of the Regulations refers to the possibility of translations into Braille or on to cassette to facilitate access to information by the many people who have a sight impairment. For them, access to information, whether about themselves or their children, will remain an illusory right. Perhaps that is the next campaign.

Questions

1. Your education authority is considering transferring all pupil records in all local schools on to a common computer system.
   Consider the implications of this proposal for access by parents and pupils and disclosure to others.
2. Susan transfers into your class from another school. You receive a hand-written note from her previous teacher saying that Susan was thought to have bullied some younger children though no proof was found.
   What should you do with this information?
3. Mr Brown comes to your classroom and demands to see his son David's file. You know the file contains, amongst other things, (a) a letter from a youth club leader telling of a fight between white and Asian boys and naming David and another boy as ringleaders;

(b) a report from a neighbour that David had been seen with some known drug users and suggesting that he is involved in a drug ring at school; and (c) a psychiatrist's report suggesting that family problems are a cause of David's anti-social behaviour. What steps should be taken before Mr Brown sees the file?

4.   You are asked to write a reference for Michael, aged 16, who is applying for a job. On his file is a note from his junior school teacher saying that he was thought to have stolen some money and a report from a class teacher that Michael, then aged 13, had told her when tackled about unexplained absence that he had been visiting his father in prison. The prospective employer specifically asks you to report on Michael's trustworthiness, attendance record and any relevant family details. Michael's attendance and behaviour in your class have been excellent. Will you use any of this information?

Notes

1   Hill D 1974 *Democratic Theory and Local Government*, Allen & Unwin, p. 62.
2   Report of the Committee of Privacy 1972, Cmnd 5012, paras 348, 350.
3   Frankel M and Wilson D 1985 'I want to know what's in my file'. Campaign for Freedom of Information, p. 18.
4   'Confidence and confidentiality'. AMMA, 1985.
5   SI 1989, No. 1261, made under Education Reform Act 1988, s.218.
6   DES Circular 17/89, para 18.
7   Gaskin v United Kingdom (1990).
8   The Family Law Reform Act made clear that over 16 the child could consent.
9   Education (National Curriculum) Temporary Exceptions for Individual Pupils, Regulations SI 1989, No. 1181.
10   Reported in 'I want to know what's in my file'. Campaign for Freedom of Information.
11   *Ibid.*, p. 9.
12   See Note 10.
13   *Campbell v Tameside Metropolitan Borough Council* (1982).
14   *R v City of Birmingham DC ex parte O(1983).*
15   Local Government Act 1974, s.32(3) Amended by Local Government Planning and Land Act 1980, s.184 *Re a complaint against Liverpool City Council 1977.*
16   Education (School Information) Regulations, SI 1981, No.630.
17   Education (School Financial Statements) (Prescribed Particulars, etc.) Regulations 1990, SI 1990, No.353 – budget statements and outturn statements in prescribed form.
18   Education (School Curriculum and Related Information) Regulations, SI 1989, No.954; Education (School Hours and Policies) (Information) Regulations, SI 1989, No.398.
19   *R v Bradford on Avon Rural District Council ex parte Thornton* (1908).
20   *R v Hampstead Borough Council ex parte Woodward* (1917).
21   *Evans v Lloyd* (1962).
22   Education (School Government) Regulations 1989.

CHAPTER 6

The school curriculum and the law

INTRODUCTION

Following the Education Act 1944, the school curriculum in England and Wales was (with the exception of religious instruction) unregulated, and the teachers who taught were not subject to legal constraint over curriculum content. Little changed until the mid-1980s. The equal opportunities legislation of the 1970s was and is important, but was regarded by most members of the teaching profession as a positive rather than constraining factor and had no influence over the locus of power or control over the curriculum.

The 1944 Education Act had heralded a 'Golden Age' of teacher freedom, according to commentators. But in the late 1960s the relative autonomy of the teaching profession over the curriculum came increasingly under attack. By the late 1970s the impetus towards central control was well established. The situation today is quite different from that which prevailed following the 1944 Act. Dent's comment at the time when that Act was still before Parliament as a bill has a curious irony to it, which will become all the more apparent from the discussion which ensues later:

I was asked . . . the other day whether the Bill would lay down the curricula for schools. My reply was 'God forbid!' Stereotyped curricula would mean the end of democratic education. We want infinite variety of curricula, to develop the infinitely various capacities of children . . . ; we want teachers to experiment freely, research workers to carry out investigations, and the general public to make suggestions. What we do *not* want is lessons laid down by law.[1]

The Education Reform Act 1988 has produced a degree of prescription and central control to which the government was apparently resistant only a couple of years before its enactment.[2] This is, of course, symptomatic of the rapid move over the past few years away from a consensus-based approach to education policy making towards one based on central autonomy. Its implications for teachers are profound.

This change in the law and in the locus of power will not end the debate, which has prevailed for a number of years,[3] about control of the curriculum of schools; such a debate emerged once the content of the curriculum become a controversial subject in the 1960s[4] and has continued since. A central concern must now be exactly that which was identified by Dent nearly 50 years ago – the 'threat to democracy', which it has been argued is also present, although manifested in a different form, in the changes in the legal framework to the university sector.[5] The threat in schools is posed by the degree of control which the executive is able to exert over the education of children, or rather by the possibility that the power to dictate (by inclusion or exclusion) the content of education could be abused by a government with extreme views. The other alleged threat to democracy has been a threat to *local* democracy, as LEAs have lost their power to control the secular curriculum in their schools. The government defended this charge by arguing that some LEAs manipulated the curriculum for ideological purposes rather than solely seeking to accommodate electors' wishes and meet children's needs. It claimed to have wide support from parents for its provisions concerning homosexuality, the coverage of political issues in the classroom, and the 'moral' dimension to sex education. Claiming a widespread dissatisfaction with the quality of education being provided by LEA schools, and promising greater opportunities for parent power to preserve local accountability, it was able to seize control over the curriculum with considerable public support.

A consequence of these changes to the control of the curriculum has been a considerable increase in the number of legal provisions. The first 25 sections of the 1988 Act, and many other parts of that legislation and of the Education (No.2) Act 1986, concern the school curriculum. These provisions are discussed in this chapter under two main headings. The first is concerned with the legal regulation of the curriculum, and in particular with the requirements of the Education Reform Act 1988 concerning the National Curriculum – the most important educational reform since the 1944 Act. The second section looks at the various legal provisions which can be said to be concerned with certain specific social and moral educational objectives: the law on sex and race discrimination, religious education and collective worship, sex education and the coverage of political issues in the classroom.

REGULATION AND CONTROL OF THE CURRICULUM

Writing about the future development of education following abolition of the Schools Council, which had had curriculum development and examination monitoring functions and which had managed to stem temporarily the growth of DES curricular involvement,[6] Plaskow commented that without the achievement of consensus within a workable framework, there would be central direction, with 'prescription through authority'.[7] A few years later there were proposals for a National Curriculum in England and Wales under the law – a law which would provide, according to the government, 'a framework not a straitjacket'.[8] Now that the National Curriculum is enshrined in law and is being phased in, how closely does the new system conform either to Plaskow's 'prescription through authority' or the government's consensus-backed 'framework'?

Traditionally, architects of educational reform in England and Wales have held the view that, as the 1943 White Paper *Educational Reconstruction* put it, 'Legislation can do little more than prepare the way for reform'. True to this tradition, the DES/Welsh Office National Curriculum consultation document of July 1987 stated that while, to be effective, a national framework for the secular curriculum required the backing of the law, 'legislation alone will not raise standards'.

Nevertheless, over the years the curriculum has become increasingly regulated, in the face of concern about the need for reform – expressed with increasing regularity once James Callaghan's Ruskin College ('Great Debate') speech in 1976 had acted as a catalyst for debate. Part of this new regulation has involved a shift towards central rather than local control. The Education Act 1944, after stipulating that LEAs should 'contribute towards the physical, moral, mental and spiritual development of the community' through educational provision (section 7), basically placed control of the secular curriculum in their hands (section 23). Central government's role was to promote, plan and guide the system (section 1). In extreme cases of default, powers (under sections 68 and 99) were, and still are, available to the Secretary of State, although they have rarely been used. These powers have traditionally been regarded by the DES as 'dangerously punitive measures, difficult to enforce in the courts, and . . . measures of absolute last resort'.[9] A House of Commons Select Committee found that local authorities had a considerable amount of discretion over what to include in or exclude from the secular curriculum. The Secretary of State would, at that time (1981/82), not have considered using his default powers if, for example, a school failed to offer a modern language (other than English). A High Court judge held that there was no basic statutory provision of education, so that if an LEA had (instead of, as in this case, charging for it) decided to cut music tuition altogether (because of financial constraints) it would not have been acting illegally.[10]

Whilst not advocating the imposition of a national curriculum, the Select Committee called for greater powers for the Secretary of State to intervene in circumstances where 'a nationally agreed guaranteed provision appears to be at risk'.[11] The government rejected this, claiming it to be contrary to the notion of partnership between central and local government which the 1944 Act had established. Instead they would continue to work towards what they had earlier described as 'a national consensus on a desirable frame-work for the curriculum' in the quest for 'improvement in the consistency and quality of school education across the country'.[12] Rather than prescription, there would be guidance for LEAs and schools, which would be reviewed periodically.

Lord Joseph's reign as Secretary of State for Education saw an even greater emphasis on the improvement of quality in education, a theme pursued in his *Better Schools* White Paper in 1985. So far as the curriculum was concerned, the policies and practices of many LEAs were seen as detrimental to quality. Following on from *Better Schools*, the Education (No.2) Act 1986 removed control of the secular curriculum from LEAs (section 23 of the 1944 Act, above, being revoked). Under section 18 of the Act, control of the curriculum in county schools has shifted to head teachers, although they must ensure that the curriculum is compatible with their LEA's statement on curricular *policy* – as modified by the governors in their own such statement.

,The 1986 Act also regulated certain specific curricular areas – notably sex education (section 46) and political education and activities (sections 44 and 45) (see below). But aside from this, and not forgetting the important duties laid on LEAs by the Education Act 1981 in relation to children with special educational needs (discussed in Chapter 4), there was little prescription. Control had shifted away from LEAs, but central government claimed to lack the power to secure the improvement to education that it sought and which the Conservatives promised the electorate in 1987. It was granted this power by Parliament in July 1988, when the Education Reform Act was enacted.

The Education Reform Act

The government regarded a solid legal framework as fundamental to the achievement of the main objectives of the proposed National Curriculum. These were stated in the 1987 consultation document to be:

1   *Raising standards*: by guaranteeing that all pupils get a balanced curriculum which prepares them for adult life; and by setting objectives over the full range of abilities – via 'attainment targets' backed up with appropriate assessment arrangements.

2   *Raising levels of accountability*: by measuring schools against each other locally and nationally (whilst 'taking account of [a school's] particular circumstances'), enabling LEAs and others to assess schools' strengths and weaknesses, through publication of National Curriculum assessments.

It was said that, as noted above, the law would provide not a straitjacket but, rather, scope for the 'imaginative application of professional skills at all levels of the education service, within a statutory framework which sets clear objectives'.[13] But when the list of prescribed core and other foundation subjects was scrutinised, along with the suggested allocations of curricular time spelled out in the consultation document, many teachers wondered whether what they would be getting would not be a 'straitjacket' after all.

Although the Education Reform Bill, published in the autumn of 1987, failed to dispel these fears, there were some modifications. The provisions, discussed more fully below, allowing a departure from all or part of the National Curriculum in certain cases or where certain individuals are concerned, were introduced when the bill was before the Commons in early 1988. Allocations of time for individual subjects were omitted from the bill. (Later the bill was amended to provide that the Secretary of State would be prohibited from prescribing periods of time or proportions of school timetables to be allocated to programmes of study: see now ERA 1988, section 4(3).) But going into the House of Lords, the clauses concerning the National Curriculum in the Bill were still 'frighteningly prescriptive and inflexible'.[14] In the Lords, Lord Joseph proposed an amendment to remove compulsion from the National Curriculum provisions – arguing that a mandatory National Curriculum was not working satisfactorily in France. But the amendment was defeated.

Before examining the legal structure of the National Curriculum, it is important to identify the other areas of curricular regulation in the Education Reform Act. These centre on what has been described in DES guidance as 'the whole curriculum'.[15] Under section 1 of the Act, a duty rests with the Secretary of State, LEAs, governing bodies and head teachers (of maintained schools)[16] to ensure provision of 'a balanced and broadly based curriculum which – (a) promotes the spiritual, moral, cultural, mental and physical development of pupils at the school and of society; and (b) prepares such pupils for the opportunities, responsibilities and experiences of adult life'.

Religious education and collective worship (provision of which is compulsory under sections 2 and 6) do not form part of the National Curriculum. The government diffused pressure to include RE in the National Curriculum by arguing that it would form part of the statutory 'basic curriculum' provided for by section 2(1) of the Act. (The National Curriculum forms the rest.)

So far as the National Curriculum is concerned, the Act (in section 3(1)) provides for foundation subjects, in two categories:

A. *Core subjects*: mathematics, English and science (and, in Welsh-speaking schools, Welsh).
B. *Other foundation subjects*: history, geography, technology, music, art, PE, and (in secondary schools only) a modern language.

Welsh is a also a foundation subject, in non-Welsh speaking schools in Wales. A list of prescribed modern languages is laid down in an Order:[17] Danish, Dutch, French, German, Greek (Modern), Italian, Portuguese and Spanish. Other languages which may be offered by a school as a foundation subject, provided one of the above languages is available to a pupil as an alternative, are also prescribed by the Order: Arabic, Bengali, Chinese (Cantonese or Mandarin), Gujerati, Hebrew (Modern), Hindi, Japanese, Punjabi, Russian, Turkish and Urdu.

For each of the foundation subjects there are to be 'attainment targets', 'programmes of study' and 'assessment arrangements'. These terms are defined in section 2(2):

A. *Attainment targets* (ATs): the knowledge and understanding expected of pupils of various ages and levels of maturity at different stages;
B. *Programmes of study* (PS): 'the matters, skills and processes' to be taught to pupils;
C. *Assessment arrangements*: the arrangements for assessing pupils' achievement of the attainment targets 'at or near the end of each key stage' (that is basically at ages 7, 11, 14 and 16).

The 'key stages' referred to above are defined in section 3(3). There are four such stages:

Key stage 1 (ages 5–7) (years 1 and 2): begins on attainment of compulsory school age and ends at the end of the school year in which the majority of pupils reach the age of 7.
Key stage 2 (ages 8–11) (years 3–6): begins with the school year in which the majority reach the age of 8 and ends at the end of the school year in which the majority are 11.
Key stage 3 (ages 12–14) (years 7–9): as in 2, with ages 12 and 14.
Key stage 4 (ages 15–16) (years 10 and 11): as in 2, but with ages 15 and 16.

ATs and PS for mathematics, science, English, technology, Welsh, history and geography have now been prescribed.[18] The Orders refer to the ATs and PS numerically and in relation to key stages, and stipulate commencement dates. The actual ATs and PS are set out in separate documents (for example *Science in the National Curriculum*) which have recently been issued to schools (and are also available for purchase through HMSO). The Act permits the ATs and PS to be prescribed via such documents.[19]

Introduction of the National Curriculum began in September 1989. Only key stages 1–3 were affected during this first year. Prescribed

ATs and PS for maths, science and English applied to those in the first year of key stage 1, and (with the exception of English) in the first year of key stage 3.

Also in September 1989 pupils in key stages 1–3 were brought within the scope of section 10(3) of the Act – which provides that prior to the introduction of the prescribed ATs and PS the subjects should be covered for a 'reasonable time', taken to mean sufficient for 'worthwhile study' in each subject. This applied in relation to all the foundation subjects in England, but only the core subjects in Wales. It was extended to the remaining foundation subjects in Wales, and the core subjects in first year of key stage 4, from September 1990.

September 1990 also saw the prescribed ATs and PS for the core subjects in the first year of key stage 2 and for English in the first year of key stage 3 brought into effect. ATs and PS for maths and science were introduced in the second year of key stage 3, and those for design and technology in the first year of key stages 1–3.

The first non-core subjects to have prescribed ATs and PS brought into effect will be geography and history – in key stages 1–3 from September 1991.

The full implementation timetable is set out in *National Curriculum: From Policy to Practice*, published by the DES.[20] Further Orders will be required to give the timetable legal effect. Implementation will not be complete until 1997.

As the National Curriculum is implemented, it will be possible to carry out a check of the curriculum of each school. Governors will be responsible for the submission to their LEA of a detailed 'Annual Curriculum Return' on a standard form. Either copies of the forms, or appropriate information drawn from them, will have to be submitted to the Secretary of State.[21] (In grant-maintained schools – that is, those which have been allowed to opt out of LEA control – the information will be sent by the governors direct to the Secretary of State.)

'Assessment arrangements' may be (and some have already been) prescribed by the Secretary of State.[22] There will, for the first time, be a national standard against which a pupil's performance may be measured. Assessment will be by a combination of national external tests and assessment by teachers. Teachers will be able to identify pupils' weaknesses, which they will then be expected, so far as is possible, to correct. Parents will be informed of the results of their child's assessment. Aggregated results for key stages will be published so that comparisons between schools will be possible – enabling governors, LEAs and parents to judge the performance of a school. Work on the development of the tests ('Standard Assessment Tasks') is being carried out under the direction of the School Examinations and Assessment Council (SEAC) (see below).

It is probably true to say that the likely arrangements for assessment and recording of pupils' achievement have provoked more concern among the teaching profession than almost any other area of the National Curriculum. The SEAC has identified the key areas of concern: 'How do I assess so many attainment targets? How can I observe one pupil and supervise the whole class? Is it not all going to take more time?'[23] Moreover, in January 1991 it was announced that the tests for 7 year olds had been modified and would take up half of teaching time for three weeks. Despite the fact that attainment targets may be grouped into 'profile components' for the purposes of reporting achievements, teachers are expected to 'keep a record of pupils' progress in relation to each attainment target',[24] a particularly onerous requirement. Teachers are relieved that the Secretary of State (albeit belatedly) decided to restrict compulsory testing at age 10–11 to the three core subjects. But many feel that they are being forced to spend large amounts of time unnecessarily testing pupils and recording achievement. One primary school head teacher in whose school pilot testing of pupils was carried out has expressed a willingness to 'break the law unless the tests are drastically changed' and another school's head (probably illegally) later suspended the tests in the face of parents' objections.[25]

If the above constitutes only a 'framework', it is undoubtedly an elaborate one. The degree of prescription is reinforced by section 10(2) of the Act, which lays a duty on LEAs, governors and head teachers to secure that the National Curriculum is implemented in their school(s).

Other legal requirements

The impact of other legal requirements relating to the curriculum also warrants mention here.

The confusing rules prohibiting charging for educational provision (including anything provided as part of the National Curriculum) and examination entry (see Appendix to this chapter), and the requirement that a course of study leading to a qualification authenticated by an outside body be approved by the Secretary of State or a designated body,[26] have imposed further constraints on what may be offered. Meanwhile the new regulations on provision of and access to information (discussed in Chapter 5) will, in addition to raising levels of public accountability, increase the already substantial administrative burden resulting from the Act. Public accountability is further emphasised by the existence of arrangements for the consideration of complaints by parents about educational provision and the achievements of individual pupils. LEAs are obliged, by section 23, to establish such arrangements.[27] The complaints procedure applies also to RE and collective worship. The Secretary of State cannot interfere on a parent's behalf over a curricular matter until the complaint has been pursued via the local complaints machinery.

Flexibility?

The freedom of the Secretary of State to depart from the recommendations of the National Curriculum Council (to which proposals on attainment targets and programmes of study must be referred),[28] as in effect happened in the case of the history curriculum, stands in marked contrast to the restrictions binding teachers under the National Curriculum. The tone of the guidance issued in 1989 suggests little flexibility:

Head teachers are responsible for ensuring that teachers do teach and carry out assessments as required . . . . Teachers and schools will not be free to pick and chose . . . . They can always do *more* than is required, and how they do it is left open; but they may not do less. The starting point will be that teachers should know what will be expected of them.[29]

What freedom teachers may have in this area centres principally on their delivery of the National Curriculum. In this regard reference may be made to the original consultation document,[30] which explained that 'within the programmes of study teachers will be free to determine the detail of what should be taught', although it urged teachers to prepare schemes of work to ensure consistency within a school. There will be 'full scope for professional judgment', both in relation to teaching and organisation of the curriculum; and there will be 'sufficient flexibility in the choice of content to adapt what they teach to the needs of the individual pupil'.

It would appear that all teachers will be placed in a similar position to that of teachers preparing pupils for external examinations, in that they will have set objectives, or learning outcomes, to be achieved, but will be free to plan their lessons as they think fit – especially where the core subjects are concerned. Some of the other foundation subjects, such as art or PE, will have far less detailed ATs and PS.

A key concession towards greater flexibility was made in January 1990, when the Secretary of State, in a speech to the Society of Education Officers, stressed the need for a more flexible framework for the curriculum at key stage 4. Mr MacGregor suggested that schools should be free, amongst other things, to offer vocational courses which might include material outside the National Curriculum and, exceptionally, enable the ablest pupils to drop a non-core foundation subject in order to take a non-statutory option.

To some extent the charge of inflexibility can also be countered by reference to the provisions sanctioning *exception from the National Curriculum*. First, the Secretary of State has a power, in section 17, to provide, by regulation, that the National Curriculum shall not apply, or shall apply in a modified form, in cases or circumstances which may be specified. This power, which can be used in respect of an entire category of pupils, has so far been exercised only in respect of English and Welsh teaching in Wales (SIs 1989 No. 1308 and 1990 No. 2187). Second, where a child with special educational needs is 'statemented' under section 7(1) Education Act 1981 (see Chapter 5), the statement may exclude the application of the National Curriculum or specify its provision in a modified form (section 18). Third, under section 19 temporary exception or modification can be directed by a head teacher in respect of an *individual pupil* – for a period of six months initially, with the possibility of two further three-month periods of exception. Regulations,[31] which came into force on 1 August 1989, prescribe the circumstances in which a direction by the head teacher under section 19 may be given. Basically, the head teacher must consider it inappropriate for the time being for the pupil to follow the National Curriculum *and* that *either* (1) circumstances giving rise to that opinion are likely to change within six months *or* (2) that the pupil may have special educational needs requiring modification of the National Curriculum and temporary exception is necessary while those needs are assessed. A direction in relation to (1) is a 'general direction' and in relation to (2) a 'special direction'. A general direction could, for example, be necessary in respect of a recently immigrated child who speaks little English and who needs intensive language support.[32]

Adjusting to regulation

As the legal regime for the National Curriculum comes into effect, it becomes increasingly apparent that it represents not so much a 'straitjacket' but a 'corset' – holding things in place, while restricting, but not totally, freedom of movement! Teachers will become ever more conscious not only of their increased administrative responsibilities but also of the fact that conformity to the prescribed ATs and PS is expected, under the law. Opportunities to depart from the National Curriculum are severely limited, except where children with particular learning difficulties are concerned, although teachers will have freedom over how they teach the National Curriculum.

Teachers in this country are unaccustomed to operating in such a regulatory environment where the curriculum is concerned; and local authorities have for the most part exerted little control over what is taught. Despite the fact that many western European countries have had a core curriculum for some years, prescription through central authority is associated, at least in the public mind, with authoritarianism.

In many Latin American countries teachers lack the freedom to devise and organise their own teaching plans, Peru being one of the few exceptions (and even here there is a general curriculum laid down by the ministry).[33] In the Soviet Union, central state control of the curriculum and syllabuses is said to be 'virtually total'.[34] Curricula are devised by the USSR ministry or a body responsible to it. Contrasting the Soviet and English systems, Muckle points out that traditionally in England the task of working out what subjects should be taught was 'replicated in every school'.[35] Now, following the enactment of the ERA, it may be observed that the contrast is less marked. Nevertheless, one ought not to underplay significantly the degree of consensus aimed for in England and Wales through consultation and extensive teacher participation in National Curriculum syllabus working groups, even if this system was rather undermined by the government's rejection of several of the history working party's recommendations. Nevertheless, the ERA has given the Secretary of State considerable powers. He can, after appropriate consultation, change the content of the National Curriculum as he thinks fit. This is an unprecedented and far-reaching power, with constitutional implications.

In any event, it may be asked whether all this regulation is necessary or desirable? In the United States, academics have for some years been engaging in what has been termed the 'deregulation critique' of the federal role in education. The 'deregulation' thesis has been described by Clune thus:

. . . it is possible to reduce the number and intensity of legal obligations on educational organizations without decreasing the quantity or quality of education in any respect. Legal intervention, with its categorical rules and sanctions, is said to be incompatible with the adaptive, flexible, social interaction of teaching and learning.[36]

There are arguments in both directions where regulation is concerned. Legal regulation tends to create administrative burdens, resentment and loss of self-esteem through the undermining of professional autonomy. On the other hand, it can create a system through which goals may be achieved, having taken them out of the realm of pure ideology.

The National Curriculum represents a middle course – the present government believing that law by itself cannot raise standards. Experience has shown that social goals, such as equal opportunities in education, above all require personal and professional commitment. As Clune puts it: 'Being required to do *anything* and especially being required to do something *specific* cannot match the effectiveness of internally motivated, adaptive behaviour directed at the same underlying end.'[37] The Secretary of State urges teachers in England and Wales to work with commitment towards the improvement of standards in education, within a legal framework. But proponents of the 'deregulation critique' might well question the degree of regulation which has been imposed.

Whatever the arguments, teachers face a challenging period of adjustment – not just to the procedural formalities of the National Curriculum and its prescriptive content, but also to the psychology of regulation.

RELIGION, SEX, RACE AND POLITICS: THE ENFORCEMENT OF MORAL, CULTURAL AND SOCIAL VALUES

It is a general feature of the education system that both through its programmed and 'hidden' curricula it plays its part in the socialisation of the individual and in social reproduction. Whilst *any* legal provisions concerned with the curriculum may be said to add further legitimacy to the instillation of moral, cultural and social values by the education system (via the so-called 'affective curriculum'), there are provisions associated in a particularly identifiable way with certain values – for example, those concerned with sex and race equality, which may be said to have almost universal support amongst policy-makers and practitioners.

Anti-discrimination measures are, of course, reflective of liberal values, many of which are in fact currently under attack. The New-Right Conservatives have challenged the educational establishment's alleged over-liberalism which they claim has resulted in abandonment of the inculcation of traditional values by schools. The law has been used to impose a structure in which traditional values are reasserted – for example via a provision which says that sex education should emphasise 'the value of family life' – and in which the dominant religious tradition, Christianity, is emphasised – via the provisions concerning RE and collective worship contained in the Education Reform Act 1988. Even before the National Curriculum swallowed up most teaching time, 'Peace studies', regarded as ideologically unsound by the government, was effectively killed off (by the Education (No. 2) Act 1986 – see below).

Religion

Religious education is part of the 'basic curriculum' to be provided in all maintained schools. It is not part of the National Curriculum, for which, as we have seen, there are prescribed attainment targets and programmes of study. Instead, religious education in county schools must be provided in accordance with a locally agreed syllabus. (Voluntary controlled schools may be expected to follow the locally agreed syllabus. In voluntary aided and special agreement schools the syllabus is to be determined by the governors and will be based on the requirements of the trust deed or the arrangements which prevailed before the school acquired voluntary status.) A conference, in which the Church of England, representatives of principal religious traditions in the area, teachers' associations and the LEA may be represented, is to be drawn up by the LEA for the purpose of agreeing the syllabus.

The part of the 1988 Act which has upset certain religious minorities has been section 8(3), which states that all religious syllabuses adopted on or after 29 September 1988 must 'reflect the fact that the religious traditions in Great Britain are in the main Christian whilst taking account of the teaching and practices of the other principal religions represented in Great Britain'. The pre-eminence apparently accorded to Christianity here may reflect the position in the country as a whole; but it is easy to see how some religious groups would identify an implicit suggestion by the section that the other religious traditions in Great Britain are less important. The fact that the section seeks to justify its own requirements by stating a fact – 'the religious traditions in Great Britain are in the main Christian' – implies anticipation of this criticism. Poulter argues that it would have been inappropriate to have given all the principal religious traditions represented in Great Britain equal weight in the RE syllabus, since it would leave Christianity being reflected in just one-sixth of the course. He suggests that section 8(3) will probably be 'sensibly construed as an attempt to strike a realistic balance' and points out that there will be 'room for legitimate differences of emphasis among the various agreed syllabuses, as at present'.[38]

Ealing LEA's syllabus, which has been challenged by one parent for failing to give sufficient attention to Christianity, apparently states that, 'whilst our children need to understand that Christianity is a living faith which has shaped the history, institutions, art and culture of Britain, they also need to explore the other living faiths in our borough so that the richness of our religious experience can be shared and appreciated'. On the face of it, this approach is consonant with the requirements of the Act. Moreover, the law continues to require that RE syllabuses should be non-denominational; RE must not be given 'by means of any catechism or formulary which is distinctive of any religious denomination'.[39] The law now explicitly states that the study of any such catechism or formulary is not prohibited.[40] Thus detailed comparative analysis of different religions is possible. As Poulter points out, this is in line with the modern ethos of concentrating on the broadly educational role of RE, which is underlined by the reference to RE instead of 'religious instruction' to which the 1944 Act referred previously.[41]

Given the emphasis on Christianity in the ERA 1988, parents from religious minority groups may now feel more inclined to exercise the right to withdraw their children from religious education at school, and perhaps also the right to have their children receive a particular form of RE away from school premises during school hours if appropriate arrangements can be made.[42] If, in the case of a child attending a county school, convenient arrangements for the RE to take place elsewhere cannot be made, the LEA is to allow it to be given on school premises provided that it does not consider that it would be unreasonable in the circumstances to do so and provided the authority does not have to meet the cost.[43] In either case, it is clear that a parent who wants his/her child to receive denominational RE at school may have to pay for it. Although there is a general principle that education in the state sector must be provided free of charge, there are exceptions to this in the case of, for example, 'optional extras' (see Appendix to this chapter). According to the government, this form of RE would, in the above circumstances, be considered an 'optional extra' for which a charge could be made.

Collective worship is also compulsory in the maintained sector. The Education Act 1944 provided for the school day in every county and voluntary school to 'begin with collective worship on the part of all pupils in attendance at the school'.[44] The Act required the whole school to meet for the daily act of collective worship unless the school premises made this impracticable.[45] It had become clear over the ensuing years that the requirements concerning collective worship had increasingly been disregarded by schools, and there were calls for the introduction of a more flexible system as well as suggestions that as a concept collective worship in school was outmoded and out of line with the more secular society in Britain, and should, therefore, be abandoned altogether.[46]

The government chose to retain collective worship in schools, but to change the law to reflect 'present practice' in schools.[47] The law, now in section 6 of the ERA 1988, still requires all pupils to take part in an act of collective worship; however, there may be a single act for all pupils or separate acts for different groups of pupils. Furthermore, whilst the act of worship must normally take place on school premises, it may take place elsewhere on a special occasion.

Given the ecumenical spirit which has prevailed in many school religious assemblies for a number of years, it was hardly surprising that serious objection would be taken to the emphasis on Christian traditions that was incorporated into the law on collective worship. Like section 25(1) of the 1944 Act, which has now been repealed, the ERA provides that the act of collective worship should be non-denominational. However, in county schools it must now be 'wholly or mainly of a broadly Christian character', reflecting 'the broad traditions of Christian belief without being distinctive of any particular Christian denomination'.[48] (In voluntary schools the governing body may determine the character and content of collective worship.) The emphasis on Christianity in this part of the Act came about as a result of a House of Lords amendment to the Education Reform Bill originally tabled by Baroness Cox and finally presented in a more pragmatic form by the Bishop of London after extensive consultation with interested parties.[49]

Opposition to the emphasis on Christianity in the provisions on collective worship from non-Christian religious minority groups has continued. One the other side of the coin, there are some parents who believe that their LEAs are ignoring the new law. A white parent of a child attending a Wakefield school where one-third of the pupils come from Asian families has asked the Secretary of State to declare the school to be in default of its duty by continuing to offer a multi-faith assembly, in the face of claims by the LEA that the arrangements for collective worship had been carefully designed to comply with the law.[50]

But in fact there are several provisions which, as Poulter puts it, offer 'plenty of scope for maintaining the pattern of multi-faith assemblies which schools have followed in recent years'.[51] For one thing, the 1988 Act specifically states that it is not necessary for every act of collective worship to be of a broadly Christian character providing that most of such acts are.[52] Furthermore, the Act allows pupils' family backgrounds, ages and aptitudes to be taken into account by the school in determining whether an act of collective worship which is not of a broadly Christian character takes place in the school.[53] These factors must also be taken into account when deciding whether the act of collective worship reflects Christian traditions and the ways in which such traditions are to be reflected in the act of worship.[54] The family background of pupils must also be taken into account by the local statutory advisory council on religious education (SACRE)[55] when it is considering an application by the head teacher of the school under section 12(1) of the 1988 Act for lifting or modifying the requirement for Christian collective worship at the school.[56]

Race

The Report of the Swann Committee in 1985[57] added weight to the widely held view that in Britain's culturally and racially pluralistic society the education system has a crucial role to play in promoting racial harmony. The Secretary of State for Education and Science has referred to LEAs' and schools' 'important responsibility to work towards the promotion of equality of opportunity for the different ethnic groups who are part of our national life'.[58] One of the principal means of fulfilling this responsibility has been the development of the concept and practice of 'multicultural' education, which the Swann Report endorsed.

Multicultural education does not specifically form part of the National Curriculum. However, the 1988 Act does make provision for the 'whole curriculum' (in section 1). As discussed earlier, this requires schools to prepare pupils for the 'experiences and opportunities of adult life' and to promote their spiritual, moral, cultural, mental and physical development. The DES has explained that a range of cross-curricular issues is intended to be included within this concept of the whole curriculum – including 'coverage across the curriculum of gender and multicultural issues'.[59] In fact, it would appear that other aspects of the new curriculum, and in particular the National Curriculum, have been given more immediate priority, although the National Curriculum Council has issued some guidance on multicultural education and linguistic diversity. It has been suggested that there is a danger that because the 1988 Act is silent on the subject of multicultural and anti-racist education these areas will be largely overlooked, to the detriment of race relations in this country.[60]

The Race Relations Act 1976 deals only in a very indirect way with the causes of racism and is more concerned with its effects. In particular, the law focuses on less favourable treatment of a person on the grounds of his or her 'colour, race, nationality or ethnic or national origins'.[61] The courts and tribunals have had to determine the meaning of racial/ethnic group for the purposes of the Act where doubts have existed. They have looked at a clear historical development, distinct traditions and geographical origins in determining this question, and so far have confirmed that Sikhs, Jews, and Gypsies, but not Rastafarians, are ethnic groups.[62] This means that only groups identifiable by their religion but not race, or national origins etc., are not protected by the Act.

In the sphere of education, the Act applies to direct and indirect discrimination (defined at page 70) or victimisation (treating someone less favourably because they are asserting their right not to be discriminated against) by schools and LEAs in a variety of contexts. There could be unlawful discrimination in the admission of pupils (as discussed in Chapter 4), in a pupil's access to benefits, facilities and services provided by the school, or by the LEA in the way it fulfils its broad duties under the Education Acts.[63] Local authorities also have a specific duty to carry out their functions in such a way as will promote racial harmony.[64] Many LEAs pursue anti-racist policies vigorously. Nevertheless, such policies must not be applied in a heavy-handed manner, as the MacDonald Report concluded, otherwise they could have the opposite effect to that which was intended.[65]

In practice the Act requires teachers to avoid racial bias in the performance of their teaching and pastoral duties. This requires a conscious effort, because it is clear that discrimination is more often unintentional than intentional. The fact that discrimination is unintentional has no bearing on its legality or otherwise. The Commission for Racial Equality's Code of Practice advises teachers that the form that discrimination takes could 'vary from crude racist remarks to subtle differences in assessment, expectation, provision and treatment'.[66] It could occur in the disciplining of pupils, careers advice or work experience.

It should be noted that positive discrimination would also be unlawful under the Act, since it inevitably results in one racial or ethnic group being treated less favourably than another on the grounds of their race, and so on. In some circumstances it may, however, be desirable to afford an ethnic minority group greater access to specialist facilities such as language support, because of the group's special needs. This would not be unlawful under the 1976 Act.[67] However, if such pupils were removed from the mainstream for this purpose, this would be a form of segregation and would be unlawful indirect discrimination.[68]

Discrimination in education, as in other spheres covered by the Act such as employment (see Chapter 9) is also permissible if it can be shown to be 'justifiable'.[69] The school or LEA would have to show that, for example, a requirement which affected one group more than another and which therefore resulted in indirect discrimination, was justifiable irrespective of a person's race.[70] The question of justifiability has been considered by the courts in a number of employment cases, where it has been construed most recently as meaning that the discriminatory effect of the requirement or condition must be weighed against its 'reasonable necessity' for the purposes of the business enterprise in question.[71] The justifiability rule has yet to receive widespread judicial consideration in the context of education, but it might be expected to be applied more strictly. Take, for example, the question of dress. There have been several examples of ethnic customs with regard to dress conflicting with school rules on uniform. In *Mandla v Dowell Lee*, (1983), a school was unable to convince the court that its policy of playing down cultural diversity to create a harmonious, racially integrated environment justified the decision to refuse to allow a Sikh boy to attend the school wearing a turban. It is highly likely that the decision of the governors of Altrincham Grammar School for Girls to suspend two Muslim girls who wished to wear head scarves to school for being in breach of school uniform rules would also have been unlawful.

So when would a rule or practice which had a discriminatory effect be 'justifiable'? The answer is probably that it would rarely be so. If the rule is justifiable on safety grounds, however, it would be. For example, the Altrincham governors could have argued that there was a safety risk in the girls wearing scarves in the laboratory or workshop – although it is by no means clear that they would have succeeded on this basis. It may be that the wearing of jewellery (such as ear studs, as favoured by some groups) could also pose a risk to safety in certain situations. But what if a school wished to ban Sikh girls from wearing trousers, and sought to justify its action with the argument that to create an exception from school rules for Sikhs would cause resentment from whites and thus work to the detriment of racial harmony? The answer, in the light of the *Mandla* case, would appear to be that the school would be acting unlawfully.

To take a further example, suppose that a school had arranged a school trip abroad during a week which coincided with a Jewish religious festival. A Jewish pupil was unable to attend the trip as a result. If the school refused to reschedule the trip, would this amount to unlawful indirect discrimination, or would the school's decision have been 'justifiable'? Obviously, it all depends on the circumstances.

Assuming that the school had not confirmed its booking, so that rescheduling was still a possibility, it might depend on, for example, whether there was any other suitable time during the year for the trip to take place. If the timing of the trip was important in terms of the curriculum of the school group in question in that year, the decision would clearly be justifiable.

The above example also prompts discussion of the extent to which a school might be required to go towards accommodating the diverse needs of various ethnic minority groups represented amongst the pupil body. The obvious response to this question would be to say that the school should do all that it reasonably can. But even if a school fulfils its legal obligations there will be some parents who will remain dissatisfied. Some, for example, would argue that if the well -established indigenous white population are taught in their mother tongue, English, those originating from the New Commonwealth deserve a similar right to be taught in their mother tongue – Urdu, Punjabi, Bengali and so on. But whilst these languages can be offered as subjects under the National Curriculum, it seems that the denial of an opportunity to be taught in one of these subjects across the curriculum would not *per se* be unlawful under the Act.[72]

The framework for the enforcement of the Act may briefly be mentioned. If the complaint centres on anything other than the broad duty resting with LEAs to provide their services without discrimination,[73] a complainant can institute proceedings in a designated county court.[74] Provided the discrimination was not indirect *and* unintentional, damages can be awarded to take account of injury to feelings. The Commission for Racial Equality can carry out a formal investigation and issue a non-discrimination notice. A complaint of breach of the LEA's broader duty must be made to the Secretary of State under sections 68 and 99 of the Education Act 1944 (see Chapter 2).

Gender

The law on sex discrimination has provoked very little litigation in the educational context until the past few years, in contrast to the wealth of judicial consideration of the provisions concerned with sex equality in employment (see Chapter 9). This is perhaps symptomatic of the fact that the principle of equal opportunities between the sexes has been so heavily promoted by educationists, in addition to being supported by the DES and politicians, that the law has been viewed as having a very much secondary purpose in this area.[75]

On the few occasions when parents have taken their grievances over sex discrimination to the courts, the question has concerned school admissions and single-sex schooling, which was discussed in Chapter 4 in the context of parental choice. But the Sex

Discrimination Act 1975, which outlaws direct or indirect discrimination and victimisation against men or women on the grounds of sex or marital status, has a much broader scope. Like the Race Relations Act 1976 it applies not only to discrimination in relation to admissions, but also to the benefits, facilities and services offered by the school and the arrangements for discipline, including exclusion from school. The duty not to discriminate rests with the 'responsible body' – the governors or LEA or proprietor of an independent school.[76] LEAs are under a duty not to discriminate in the carrying out of any other of their functions. LEAs and responsible bodies are also under a separate duty in section 25 of the 1975 Act to 'secure that [their] facilities for education . . . and any ancillary benefits or services are provided without sex discrimination'. This duty appears to overlap with the other duties *vis-à-vis* education which are imposed by the Act. But it seems that the principal focus of the section 25 duty is not on correcting cases of illegality but rather on ensuring that LEAs and responsible bodies play 'a positive role in relation to the elimination of sex discrimination'.[77]

So far as the curriculum is concerned, equality of access to 'benefits, facilities and services' means that in relation to subject choices and the way they are taught, stereotypical assumptions about the respective roles of men and women in society should be avoided. A formal investigation by the Equal Opportunities Commission on West Glamorgan schools showed that there was separate curricular provision for boys and girls in the areas of craft, design and technology (boys) and home economics (girls). Although there was not a deliberate effort to discriminate on the grounds of sex, it was clear that the opportunities for girls to take CDT or for boys to take home economics were severely limited by the way the curriculum was organised. The provision of separate facilities for boys and girls is not unlawful under the Act provided the facilities can be regarded as equal.[78] The crucial factor is that boys and girls must be given equal choice. This does not necessarily mean that girls will necessarily choose subjects traditionally associated with boys and vice versa. Nationally, girls still outnumber boys as candidates in biological and health sciences and boys still easily outnumber girls in physics and mathematics.[79] The National Curriculum will, however, give a greater number of girls exposure to the physical sciences, in which as pupils and employees in industry they are still under-represented. At the same time, progress towards greater equality could be hampered by schools necessarily giving higher priority towards the development of the curriculum in the light of the National Curriculum changes in general.[80]

Damages may be awarded to a complainant on complaint to the county court.[81] As with race discrimination, damages cannot be awarded if the discrimination is found to have been unintentional. The court has no jurisdiction if the complaint concerns breach of the broad duty in section 25; the complaint must be made to the Secretary of State under sections 68 and 99 of the Education Act 1944.[82]

The Equal Opportunities Commission was established under the 1975 Act to monitor its implementation, give advice and play a part in its enforcement. Not only can the Commission assist complainants by bringing proceedings on their behalf, but it can also conduct a formal investigation, as it did in West Glamorgan. The Commission likes to play a positive, enabling role, working with schools and LEAs to ensure that best practice is adopted and that, once it has been identified, illegal practice is replaced in line with the Commission's recommendations. The Commission has, for example, been monitoring closely the various measures attempted by Birmingham City Council to bring its admissions policy into line with the House of Lords judgment in respect of its school admissions arrangements (see Chapter 4).

Sex education

If a school is going to prepare a pupil for the 'opportunities and experiences of adult life' as it is required to do by section 1 of the Education Reform Act 1988, it surely cannot ignore his/her sex education. Thus the guidance given to governors by DES Circular 11/87 that, although it is expected that at least some sex education would be provided by the school, they have freedom to decide whether or not sex education should be offered[83] should now be revised. It is clear that knowledge of how human sexual reproduction takes place is required by the attainment targets for science.[84] But DES Circular 11/87 exhorts schools to acknowledge that some parents have strong religious or cultural objections to the imparting of sex education by schools and to comply with a request to withdraw a child in such circumstances. This could not be handled via temporary exception from part of the National Curriculum, referred to earlier (see p. 118), because a 'general direction' can only be issued if the head teacher considers that it is inappropriate for the child to follow the National Curriculum and in his opinion that situation is *likely to change* within six months.[85]

Withdrawal of a pupil from sex education in fact presents schools with something of a dilemma – whether to accede to parental wishes, which may reflect the parent's philosophical or religious convictions, or whether to make the welfare of the child the paramount consideration. In fact, to refuse a parent's request would not be a breach of the European Convention on Human Rights, even though it requires such convictions to be upheld. In one case, Christian parents argued that compulsory sex education (in Denmark) was contrary to their religious convictions. But the Court held that while those beliefs should be respected, the overriding requirement was for schools to present information and knowledge with an objective, critical and pluralistic approach.[86] Moreover, to comply with the request may be a breach of the school's duty under the curriculum requirements of Chapter I of the ERA 1988 as well as detrimental to the child's welfare. If the request were denied, the parent would have to pursue the matter via the local curriculum complaints procedure established under section 23 of the ERA 1988, then via the Secretary of State under sections 68 or 99 of the Education Act 1944, before the matter could then be referred to the European Commission on Human Rights.

Assuming sex education is given to the child by a school, the question of what form it should take must be considered. The governors' policy will be relevant: the 1986 Act requires the head teacher to ensure that there is compliance with the governors' policy statement on sex education at the school. But that policy statement must surely be consistent with the other legal requirements as to the content of sex education.

The 1986 Act states (in section 46) that sex education should be given in such a way as to encourage pupils to 'have due regard to moral considerations and the value of family life'. The government was predisposed to see a 'moral framework' established for the conduct of sex education, emphasising the responsibilities attached to sexual activity and awareness of its possible consequences, and especially of 'casual and promiscuous sexual behaviour'. There was the suggestion that if pupils were 'helped to appreciate the benefits of stable, married and family life and the responsibilities of parenthood'[87] such behaviour might be discouraged. However, this assumption seems flawed. For one thing, it ignores the social reality that teenage sexual experience is extremely common amongst young people; pupils may well appreciate the benefits of stable family life and so on without perceiving any need to desist from their sexual activity. Second, it ignores the other social reality, that many pupils come from homes in which there is no stable and married family life and so will not be able to relate easily to this concept. In any event, it may be noted that the science attainment targets seek to put the scientific aspects of human reproduction into a social and emotional context, in a way that is consistent with the requirements of the Education (No. 2) Act 1986.

Leaving aside the moral issue, it is obviously desirable that schools should foster awareness of the physical risks of sexual activity, and especially of the danger of contracting a sexually transmitted disease. The government's advice to those engaging in casual sexual relations to use a condom to reduce the risk of contracting AIDS has rendered the suggestion in the Circular that contraception is a 'controversial' subject only to be discussed when pupils ask questions about it somewhat inappropriate, as well as inconsistent with the later advice in the Circular that in sex education 'particular attention should be given to . . . ways in which risks [of infection with AIDS] may be avoided or lessened'.[88]

So far as individual counselling on sexual matters is concerned, schools are advised that whilst pastoral care of pupils is an important aspect of the teacher's role, parents are expected to play their part, so that if a pupil were to approach a teacher for advice the teacher should, wherever possible, encourage the pupil to seek it from his/her parent whilst at the same time warning the pupil of the risks attached to the pupil's behaviour. The case of *Gillick v West Norfolk and Wisbech AHA* (1985) established that doctors may, in certain circumstances, give advice about contraception to under 16-year-old girls without parental consent. The Circular points out that the decision should not be taken as sanctioning such advice given to such girls by teachers.

Sexual orientation

Considerable controversy was provoked by the government's measure, still known by the name of its previous incarnation as 'Clause 28', in which it sought to ban the promotion of homosexuality by local authorities. So far as education is concerned, it is known that the government has been concerned for some time about an alleged willingness on the part of some teachers to bring the question of homosexuality out into the open in a way that seeks to normalise it as a form of human relationship. DES Circular 11/87, referred to above, said that there would never be a case for a teacher advocating homosexual behaviour to pupils.

It is doubtful, however, whether section 46 of the Education (No. 2) Act, which as shown above requires sex education to be given in a way that encourages pupils to have regard for 'moral considerations and the value of family life', prohibits discussion of homosexuality. For one thing, 'moral considerations' will inevitably be viewed subjectively. For example, would not fidelity be a 'moral consid eration'? Moreover, is the concept of 'family life' restricted to heterosexual relationships? There is a similar doubt about 'Clause 28' (actually section 2A of the Local Government Act 1986, inserted by section 28 of the Local Government Act 1988). This prohibits *local authorities* from intentionally promoting homosexuality or publishing material 'with the intention of promoting homosexuality', or promoting 'the teaching in any maintained school of the acceptability of homosexuality as a pretended family relationship'. It has been suggested the phrase 'pretended family relationship' is directed at the book *Jenny Lives with Eric and Martin*, which shows a girl living with her father and a male partner who have a homosexual relationship;[89] the presence of this book in an ILEA school was seized upon by the tabloid press.

Doubt about whether section 28 bars the promotion of homosexuality in the course of teaching stems from the wording of the section. It is actually outlaws the promotion by *local authorities* of teaching of the acceptability of homosexuality, and so on, or their intentional promotion of homosexuality. It is not at all clear whether the failure of a Local Authority to prevent one of its teachers from teaching the acceptability of homosexuality would be construed as promotion by the Local Authority itself. There is the added complication here that, following financial delegation, the governors of the school have many of the rights of an employer previously resting with the Local Authority.

Political issues and activities

The Conservatives have been concerned about what they have regarded as bias, especially left-wing bias, in the way issues have been presented to pupils by some teachers. In *Better Schools* (1985) the government singled out 'peace studies' for criticism, saying that it had no place on the school curriculum because it failed to deal with certain issues in a balanced and objective manner. Under provisions contained in the Education (No. 2) Act 1986 Parliament has sought to remove all scope for political bias in teaching and in extracurricular activities. Section 44 states that LEAs, head teachers and governing bodies are required to forbid the pursuit, at a junior school, of 'partisan political activities' by pupils, and, at any school, 'the promotion of partisan political views in the teaching of any subject'. These bodies are also required to ensure that pupils at primary and secondary schools are offered a 'balanced presentation of opposing views' when political issues are brought to their attention at school or during extracurricular activities organised by or on behalf of the school (section 45).

These measures could quite justifiably be regarded as something of a sledgehammer to crack a very small nut, since they are intended to deal with a problem the existence of which is almost totally unproven. DES Circular 8/86 referred to the 'important safeguards' offered by these sections against what the side note to section 44 refers to as 'political indoctrination' – indicating a somewhat alarmist approach overall.

'Political issue' may extend beyond the merely party political – to environmental issues or the prison system, for example. So far as balance is concerned, would a teacher in a school with Afro-Caribbean children on the register have to present a case for as well as against apartheid when covering South Africa? Clearly, many teachers would have great difficulty with strict compliance because of their own convictions.

APPENDIX TO CHAPTER 6

Charges for school activities

(in maintained schools, including grant-maintained schools)
Note: References are to sections of the Education Reform Act 1988

Nature of provision	Is a charge possible? Yes/No (If Yes, parent to pay, unless stated otherwise.)
A. Admission to a school	NO (s.106(1))
B. Provision of the National Curriculum to pupils	NO (s.106(2))
C. Religious education	NO (s.106(2))
D. Education required as part of a syllabus for a prescribed public examination for which the pupil is being (wholly or in part) prepared by the school; and entry for the examination	NO . . . (s.106(4)(a), (5) and (11)) . . . but exam fee may be recovered from parent if pupil fails 'without good reason' to meet any exam requirement (s.108(1) & (2)) (would not apply to simple failure on ability grounds).
E. Individual music tuition	YES (s.106(3)(a)) – the charge to include the teaching cost of providing tuition (s.109(8))
F. Education provided by a grant-maintained school for the LEA, which is neither primary nor secondary education.	YES (s.106(3)(a)) – the LEA to pay.
G. The supply of any 'materials, books, instruments or other equipment' for use for the purposes of or in connection with B–D (above)	NO . . . (s.106(6)). unless the pupil has used the materials to produce in the course of

	education provided to him/her an 'article incorporating those materials' and the parent has indicated beforehand that 'he wishes the article to be owned by him or the pupil' (section 118(3)).	
H.	Transport incidental to educational provision for the purposes of B–D above	NO (s.106(7) & (8))
I.	Education provided partly during and partly outside school hours (non-residential trip)	NO – unless less than 50 per cent of the time (inc. travel) spent on the activity is spent during school hours, in which case *the whole activity* is treated as falling outside school hours and is thus chargeable (s.107(1) & (2))
J.	Board and lodging on a residential trip (i.e. involving at least one night away from home)	YES (s.106(9) & (10))
K.	Education provided on a residential trip (i.e. at least one day spent away)	YES – provided that of the time spent away from school (inc. travel) more than half occurs outside school hours (s.107(3)).[*]
L.	'Optional extras' (ie education provided in school other than that falling within categories B–D (above))	YES – provided the parent has agreed to the education or exam entry in question (s.109(2)). The charge is known as a 'regulated charge' (s.109(3)) and must not exceed the cost of provision (s.109 (5)–(7)).

* There is a special way of calculating time for this purpose. School time is divided into AM and PM sessions. Time spent away is divided into half-days (12 hours, ending at noon or midnight (section 109(4)), although if at least six of those 12 hours are spent on the trip the whole half-day is treated as part of the trip (DES Circular 2/89, para 31). If, during the period covered by the trip, the number of half-days outside school hours exceeds the number of school sessions occurring during this period, a charge may be made in respect of the entire period of the trip.

Voluntary contributions: In cases where charges may not be made governors or LEA may nevertheless request or invite parents to make 'voluntary contributions for the benefit of the school or other activities' (section 118(1)). The request or invitation must make it clear that there is no obligation to contribute and that pupils whose parents do not contribute will receive no different treatment from children of parents who do (s.118(2)).

Charging and remission policy: LEAs and governors may not make any permitted charges until they have prepared a statement of their charging and remission policy (section 110(1) and (2)). A permitted charge for board and lodging on a residential trip must be remitted in full if a pupil's parents are in receipt of income support or family credit (section 118(3)).

Questions

1. To what extent has the move towards central control of the school curriculum undermined the professional autonomy of the teacher?
2. How might the legal requirements concerning sex education affect the manner in which pupils might be informed about 'safe sex' in the context of AIDS?
3. Bob, a teacher at a comprehensive school, has written a letter to Carol, a former colleague who has recently been appointed to a post at another school. After the usual pleasantries, Bob writes:

   . . . and our head has recommended that the daily act of collective worship should include one Christian hymn and the Lord's prayer. As you know, Carol, 25 per cent of the pupils at Catchley are not of the Christian faith. I am not at all happy about carrying out the head's instructions.

   You went on that INSET course last year on Law and the Teacher. Do you think that it would be within the law to cut out the specifically Christian content? Would it need a governors' vote on the matter?

   Actually, I would prefer there to be silent contemplation or private prayer – would this be within the terms of the Education Reform Act?

   I would be grateful for your views.

   Yours sincerely,

   Bob.

   As Carol, reply to Bob.

Notes

1   Dent H C 1944 *The New Education Bill*, University of London Press, p. 30.

2   DES 1985 *Better Schools,* Cmnd 9469, HMSO, ch. 2. See especially paras 37 and 38.

3   See, for example, Becher T and Maclure S 1978 *The Politics of Curriculum Change,* Routledge & Kegan Paul; Salter B and Tapper T 1981 *Education, Politics and the State,* Routledge & Kegan Paul.

4   Lawton D. 1980 *The Politics of the School Curriculum*, Routledge & Kegan Paul, p. 1.

5   Griffith J 1990 'The Education Reform Act: abolishing the independent status of the universities'. *Education and the Law* 2(3): 97–108.

6   See Becher and Maclure, *op. cit.* pp. 40–4.

7   Plaskow M 1985 'A long view from the inside', in M Plaskow (ed.), *Life and Death of the Schools Council*, Falmer.

8   Department of Education and Science (DES) and Welsh Office 1987 *The National Curriculum 5–16, a Consultation Document,* DES, p. 5.

9   House of Commons Education, Science and the Arts Committee 1981 *Session 1981/82, Second Report, The Secondary School Curriculum and Examinations*, para. 9.16.

10 *R v Hereford and Worcester LEA ex parte William Jones* (1981), per Forbes J.

11 Note 9, above, para. 9.18.

12 DES/Welsh Office 1979 *Local Authority Arrangements for the School Curriculum,* HMSO, pp. 6–7.

13 DES/Welsh Office 1987 *The National Curriculum 5–16, A Consultation Document*, DES.

14 Maclure S, *Times Educational Supplement*, 29 April 1988.

15 DES 1989 *National Curriculum: From Policy to Practice*, HMSO.

16 Under Part I, Chapter I of the Act, which deals with the National Curriculum, a 'maintained' school is defined as a county or voluntary school, a maintained special school which is not established in a hospital and a grant-maintained school: section 25(1). A city technology college or college for the technology of the arts is not bound to follow the 'basic curriculum'.

17 The Education (National Curriculum) (Modern Foreign Languages) Order 1989, SI 1989, No. 825.

18 Education (National Curriculum) (Attainment Targets and Programmes of Study in *) Order . . . * Mathematics, SI 1989, No. 308 / Science, SI 1989, No. 309 / English, SI 1989, No. 907 and English (No. 2), SI 1990, No. 423 / Technology, SI 1990, No. 424 as amended by SI 1990 No.1531/ Welsh, SI 1990, No. 1082 / Geography (England) SI 1991, No. 678, (Wales) SI 1991, No. 751, / History (England) SI 1991, No 681, (Wales) SI 1991, No.752.

19 Section 4(4).

20 1989, HMSO, Annexes C1 and C2.

21 Education (School Curriculum and Related Information) Regulations 1989, SI 1989, No. 954, as amended – in force 1 Aug. 1989. These regulations amend the Education (School Information) Regulations 1981, SI 1981, No. 630.

22 ERA 1988, section 4(2)(c); see the Education   (National Curriculum)
    (Assessment Arrangements in English, Welsh, Mathematics and Science)
    (Wales) Order 1990 SI 1990 No. 1639.
23 *SEAC Recorder*, No.2, Summer 1989, p. 2 and 29 April 1991. Parents of
    a boy, a Leeds primary school pupil, went so far as to keep him away
    from school in the face of the head teacher's insistance that the child
    would have to take the tests if he attended: see *The Independent* 19 April
    1991. A Devon mother managed to avoid compulsory testing for her son
    by persuading the head teacher that exception from the National
    Curriculum (see pages 117–18 above) was warranted in the child's case:
    see *The Observer* 21 April 1991.
24 Note 15, above, para.6.9.
25 *The Times*, 1 June 1990.
26 ERA 1988, section 5; Education (Prescribed Public Examinations)
    Regulations 1989, SI 1989, No. 377, as amended.
27 See, further, DES Circular 1/89.
28 ERA, section 20. The NCC, Curriculum Council for Wales and the SEAC
    are to consist of 10–15 members, appointed by the Secretary of State
    from persons with relevant knowledge or experience in education: section
    14. A full list of their powers is in Schedule 2 to the Act.
29 Note 15, above, para. 10.2.
30 See note 13, para. 27.
31 The Education (National Curriculum) (Temporary Exceptions for
    Individual Pupils) Regulations 1989, SI 1989, No. 1181.
32 See draft DES circular, *The National Curriculum: Temporary Exceptions
    for Individual Pupils*, 1989, para.12.
33 Garrett R M 1985 'Disparities and constraints in Peruvian education', in
    Brock C and Lawlor H (eds) *Education in Latin America,* Croom Helm.
34 Muckle J 1988 *A Guide to the Soviet Curriculum*, Croom Helm, p. 5.
35 *Ibid.*
36 Clune W H 1986 'The deregulation critique of the federal role in
    education', in Kirp D L and Jensen D N (eds) *School Days, Rule Days*,
    Falmer, p. 187. *State* power is an important feature of the US education
    system, and it extends to textbook selection and the curriculum. State
    power is seen as 'a check on the discretion of local boards of education,
    administrators and teachers': Yudof M G *et al.* 1982 *Educational Policy
    and the Law* (2nd edn), McCutchan, p. 381.
37 Clune, *op. cit.* n. 36.
38 Poulter S 1990 'The religious education provisions of the Education
    Reform Act', *Education and the Law* 2(1):1–11.
39 Education Act 1944, section 26(1).
40 *Ibid.*, section 26(2).
41 Poulter, *op. cit.,* pp. 4–5.
42 Education Reform Act 1988, section 9(3) and (4).
43 Education Act 1944, section 26(3) and (4).
44 *Ibid.*, section 25(1).
45 *Ibid.*
46 Poulter S 1986 *English Law and Ethnic Minority Customs*, Butterworths,
    pp. 169–70.
47 DES Circular 3/89 *The Education Reform Act 1988: Religious Education
    and Collective Worship,* para. 31.
48 ERA 1988, section 7(1) and (2).

49 See Poulter 1990, *op. cit.*, p. 1.

50 *The Times*, 1 May 1990.

51 *Ibid.*, p. 5.

52 ERA 1988, section 7(3).

53 *Ibid.*, section 7(4)(a).

54 *Ibid.*, section 7(4)(b) and (c).

55 The functions of the local SACRE, which each LEA must set up, are (a) to advise the authority (i) on matters relating to collective worship in county schools and (ii) on the agreed RE syllabus, and (b) to consider applications to lift or modify the requirements concerning collective worship: ERA 1988, sections 11(1) and 12(1). They are to comprise governors (where an agreed syllabus is in force) and representatives of Christian and other principal religious traditions in the area, the Church of England (other than in Wales), teachers' associations and the LEA: section 12(3) and (4). There may also be co-opted members (section 11(3)), but only the representative members are entitled to vote, each group having a single vote (section 12(6)).

56 *Ibid.*, section 12(2).

57 *Education for All: The Report of the Committee of Inquiry into the Education of Children from Ethnic Minority Groups*, Cmnd 9453, HMSO.

58 Foreword to Commission for Racial Equality, *Code of Practice for the Elimination of Racial Discrimination in Education*, CRE (1989).

59 DES 1989 *National Curriculum from Policy to Practice*, HMSO, para. 3.8.

60 Taylor W H 1990 *'Multi-cultural education in the 'white highlands' after the 1988 Education Reform Act'*. *New Community* 16(3): 369–78.

61 Race Relations Act 1976, sections 1 and 3(1).

62 *Mandla v Dowell Lee (1983); Commission for Racial Equality v Dutton* (1989); *The Crown Suppliers (PSA) v Dawkins* (1991) *(Rastafarians)*.

63 Race Relations Act 1976, sections 17–19.

64 *Ibid.*, section 71.

65 1989 *Murder in the Playground*, Manchester City Council.

66 *Op. cit.*, para. 8.

67 Section 35.

68 CRE *Code of Practice, op. cit.*, para. 32.

69 Section 1(1)(b)(ii).

70 *Mandla v Dowell Lee* (1983) (HL).

71 *Hampson v DES* (1990) (CA) – this case was heard in the House of Lords on another point, discussed in Chapter 9.

72 Poulter 1986, *op. cit.*, p. 177.

73 Section 19.

74 Section 57.

75 For a solid critique, see Milman D and de Gama K 1989 'Sexual discrimination in education: one step forwards, two steps back?' *Journal of Social Welfare Law* 4–22.

76 Section 22, as amended.

77 *Equal Opportunities Commission v Birmingham City Council* (1989) per Lord Goff.

78 Equal Opportunities Commission 1988 *Formal Investigation Report. West Glamorgan Schools*, EOC.

79 See further, Pannick D 1985 *Sex Discrimination Law*, OUP, p. 304;
    Milman D and de Gama K, *op. cit.*, p. 7; HMI 1988 *Secondary Schools,
    An Appraisal*, HMSO, p. 43.
80 See Milman D and de Gama K, *op. cit.*, p. 22, and Orr P 1985 'Sex bias
    in schools: national perspectives', in Whyte J (ed.) *Girl Friendly
    Schooling*, Methuen, p. 21.
81 Sex Discrimination Act 1975, sections 62 and 66.
82 Section 25(4).
83 See the Education (No. 2) Act 1986, section 18(2)(a).
84 Science Attainment Target 3, level 6, applying to key stages 3 and 4,
    states that pupils should 'know about the physical and emotional changes
    that take place during adolescence', 'understand the process of conception
    in human beings' and 'understand the need to have a responsible attitude
    to sexual behaviour'.
85 See Education Reform Act 1988, section 19.
86 Case of *Kjeldsen, Busk Madsen and Pedersen* (1976).
87 DES Circular 11/87 *Sex Education at School*, para. 19.
88 *Ibid.*, para. 23.
89 Macnair M R T 1989 'Homosexuality in schools – Section 28 Local
    Government Act 1988'. *Education and the Law* 1(1): 35–9.

CHAPTER 7

Discipline

INTRODUCTION

The scale of concern recently about the level of indiscipline and disruption in many schools resulting from pupil misbehaviour has to some extent been unwarranted, possibly inflamed by scare stories in the media and a greater willingness on the part of the profession, during a period of low morale and frustration, to report incidences of disruption and physical attacks on teachers.[1] All the evidence suggests that schools are generally well-ordered places where acceptable behaviour is the norm. But whilst the concern might, therefore, have been largely misplaced, it has been useful in fostering a re-examination of the way schools and LEAs maintain discipline amongst pupils and in prompting fresh research into the nature of misbehaviour in schools. It has also focused attention on the law governing pupil discipline at a time when interest in analysing the extent to which the autonomy interests of children are upheld by the law is high.[2]

Various studies have identified what is considered to be best practice for the maintenance of good discipline and the avoidance of pupil alienation, and the main recommendations are referred to below. The most important recent investigation was carried out by a Committee of Enquiry chaired by Lord Elton. The *Elton Report* has produced a detailed set of recommendations following a comprehensive examination of the subject, informed by specially commissioned research carried out by a team from the University of Sheffield.[3] MPs had been pressing for an enquiry[4] following the publication of a damning report on the state of school discipline by the Professional Association of Teachers in 1987, which was given prominent coverage in the press. The Committee took just under 12 months to carry out its investigation. Its report was published in 1989. This chapter focuses in particular on the legal issues raised by this important investigation.

The terms of reference for the enquiry by Lord Elton and his committee were as follows:

In view of public concern about violence and indiscipline in schools and the problems faced by the teaching profession today, to consider what action can be taken by central government, local authorities, voluntary bodies owning schools, governing bodies of schools, head teachers, teachers and parents to secure the orderly atmosphere necesary in schools for effective teaching and learning to take place.

Thus the principal focus was to be on examining ways in which higher levels of discipline might be achieved rather than analysing the causes of indiscipline. (Nevertheless, it is clear from the report that the Committee took into account identified causes of indiscipline in schools in producing their recommendations.)

DISCIPLINE AND PUNISHMENT

Although they are quite distinct concepts, discipline and punishment are often regarded, quite erroneously, as synonymous. Hirst and Peters[5] explain that the confusion arises because one of the logically necessary conditions for the existence of punishment, that it must be inflicted on an offender as a consequence of a breach of rules, is closely linked to the idea that a breach of rules is a breach of discipline. The other necessary conditions, that punishment must involve pain or unpleasantness and must be inflicted by someone in authority, do not fit the concept of discipline so exactly – although clearly discipline is associated with authority. Discipline is thus 'a very general notion which is connected with conforming to rules', whereas punishment is 'a much more specific notion which is usually only appropriate where there has been a breach of rules'.[6]

Traditionally it has been common practice for schools to seek to maintain discipline and control misbehaviour via the exertion of authority and the employment of sanctions as punishments. Although there has been a growing amount of evidence that rewarding good behaviour can be far more effective in maintaining pupil discipline than punishing bad behaviour, and despite official encouragement for rewarding,[7] there has been found to be 'a continuing emphasis' on punishments.[8] HMI (Her Majesty's Inspectorate (of schools)) found that 'in many schools, . . . the guidelines for staff contain much on sanctions and punishments, and very little on praise and rewards'.[9]

Best practice, as advocated by the *Elton Report* and HMI, is to strike a clear and healthy balance between rewards and punishments. The Children's Legal Centre has urged teachers to be 'quick to reward and slow to punish'.[10] Schools can do much to improve discipline in schools without the use of sanctions – by motivating pupils (emphasising and rewarding achievement), improving the physical environment, giving pupils more say and more responsibility, involving parents, and so on. The government has argued that many schools consistently secure good order 'not simply by a regime of sanctions and rewards but more broadly by creating within the school . . . . positive attitudes to good behaviour'.[11]

But it seems to be widely accepted as inevitable that indiscipline will not be eradicated, no matter how positive or imaginative the school tries to be; hence the need to be able to apply sanctions and punishments, 'to register disapproval of unacceptable behaviour and as a last resort to protect the necessary authority of teachers and the stability of the school system'.[12] In cases of bullying (which is widespread, though often ignored by teachers,[13] and can be linked to racial or sexual harassment), theft or vandalism, pupils may be guilty of criminal conduct where social services or police intervention is warranted. The Elton Committee expressed particular concern about the impact on a school of bullying and racial harassment,[14] and recommended that head teachers and staff be alert to signs of such behaviour, deal firmly with it, and 'take action based on clear rules which are backed by appropriate sanctions and systems to protect and support victims'.[15]

BEHAVIOUR AND DISCIPLINE

The importance of good behaviour amongst pupils has been stated thus: 'Good behaviour is a necessary condition for effective teaching and learning to take place, and an important outcome of education which society rightly expects.'[16] Thus it is accepted that without good discipline in a school the standard of teaching and learning, and thus the achievements of both teachers and pupils, will suffer. Pupil behaviour has been described as 'a touchstone of the quality of the school system'.[17]

Although many of the official reports point to a need for a school to have a clear view, which they should communicate to pupils and parents, of what is acceptable and unacceptable behaviour, they do not attempt to define these concepts. Obviously, it would be difficult to prescribe in precise legal terms for universal application acceptable standards of pupil behaviour – although the law does, of course, define criminal behaviour (albeit often with some difficulty). The law simply leaves the determination of 'acceptable' standards of behaviour to the head teacher and governing body,[18] whilst imposing a duty on the head teacher to: secure the promotion within the school of self-discipline and proper regard for authority amongst pupils; encourage 'good behaviour' on the part of pupils; and otherwise regulate the conduct of pupils.[19] The Elton Committee recommended that the head teacher should take the lead in defining the aims of the school in relation to standards of behaviour, create the conditions for establishing the widest possible measure of agreement on these standards and how they will be achieved, and ensure that these standards are consistently applied throughout the school.[20] This is a delicate process, as the Committee acknowledged. If teachers are to be expected to put the policy into practice, head teachers must ensure that teachers' views are taken into account, as well as those of the governors – with whose general statement of principles on discipline within the school the head is legally obliged to comply. [21]

The views of teachers were amongst the matters looked into by the Sheffield University team when carrying out research for the Elton Committee. They found that the types of pupil behaviour in the secondary school classroom presenting teachers with the most difficulty ranged from talking out of turn, physical aggression towards the teacher, calculated idleness, verbal abuse, hindrance of other pupils, general rowdiness and so on. Around the school, the main problems were physical aggression and/or verbal abuse towards the teacher or fellow pupils, lack of concern for others, persistent infringement of school rules, general rowdiness and physical destructiveness.[22] The extent to which these problems will be tolerated, and the measures adopted for dealing with them, will vary from school to school, and it is accepted that it would be impossible to lay down precise rules about the steps to be taken. As we have seen, this is left to the discretion of the head teacher, acting on the guidance of the governors. In an extreme case, the LEA may intervene – if it considers that there has been a breakdown of discipline at the school. LEAs are empowered to take such steps as they consider are necessary to prevent the breakdown or continuing breakdown of discipline at a school,[23] a power which the Elton Committee urges them to invoke when the situation warrants it.[24] The 1986 Act states that the power is only exercisable where the education of pupils at the school is likely otherwise to be 'severely prejudiced'.[25] LEAs will probably be reluctant to use this power and rather uncertain as to the kinds of circumstances when it should be exercised.

AUTHORITY TO PUNISH

Traditionally it was supposed that the teacher's authority to inflict punishment on a pupil derived from the implied delegation of parental authority. The basis for this implied authority was, therefore, seen as the *in loco parentis* principle – the teacher acting in place of the parent and subject only to the same limits imposed by the law on the parent.[26] In the corporal punishment case of *Ryan v Fildes* (1938) Tucker J confirmed that:

when a parent sends his child to school, he delegates to teachers at the school the power to inflict reasonable and moderate punishment as required . . . and . . . he delegates to the teacher the taking of such steps as are necessary to maintain discipline with regard to the child committed to the teacher's care.

It has been suggested that, at least in schools maintained by LEAs, the teacher's authority to inflict corporal punishment is, in fact, independent of that of the parent.[27] In relation to punishment in general in schools, lawyers point to section 1 of the Children and Young Persons Act 1933 which, in prescribing offences of cruelty to persons aged under 16, concludes (in sub-section (7)) by stating that 'nothing in this section shall be construed as affecting the right of any parent, teacher, or other person having lawful control or charge of a young person to administer punishment to him'.

The Elton Committee suggested that there was some doubt about the application of the in loco parentis principle to the disciplining of pupils – for its application would mean that a parent's request to a school for a particular form of punishment not to be administered to his/her child would have to be granted. Although the European Court of Human Rights had declared that it would be a breach of the European Convention on Human Rights for a child to be given corporal punishment against the philosophical or religious convictions of his/her parent,[28] it was felt that the ruling did not revoke the teacher's independent authority to administer punishment.[29] The Committee concluded that the 'case law is probably sufficient to inhibit litigation by parents opposed to particular actions, such as putting a child in detention', but felt that the teacher's independent authority to impose sanctions was insufficiently explicit and should be made more definitive[30] (see below).

Although the existence of a teacher's *independent* authority to punish contrary to parents' wishes is inconsistent with the generally pervasive notion of parental choice in education, it would seem to be justifiable. As *Street on Torts* puts it, the basis of this authority and the defence it affords to torts such as false imprisonment 'is the need to maintain order in the particular organisation responsible for the training of the child'; parental wishes would merely be factors to be taken into account in deciding whether a punishment was reasonable.[31] Clearly the maintenance of discipline within a school is in all pupils' best interests if it helps produce an environment conducive to learning, and it seems appropriate to leave with teachers the decision of how to achieve that objective, acting on the guidance provided by HMI, the *Elton Report* and so on.

In any event, it was clear, when the Education (Corporal Punishment) Bill 1985 was being considered by Parliament following the ruling in *Campbell and Cosans*, that to give parents a choice over whether or not their children should receive corporal punishment was justifiable in principle but practically unworkable. Moreover, it would have undermined the important principle of consistency in the response to like cases which should underpin any punishment regime. Of course, not all parents would wish to dictate to the school how it should exercise discipline over their children. In a major study of poor families in the inner city, it was discovered that a large majority of parents saw the teacher as a person of authority whose action they were prepared to back up, especially if they saw it as strict.[32] One suspects that the position has been more complex where middle-class parents are concerned; such parents may well be more assertive, and keen to support discipline but perhaps more divided about how it should be achieved. In any event, social attitudes towards teacher authority appear to be changing. In the British Social Attitudes Survey of 1988, 90 per cent of people thought there to be less respect for teachers amongst parents and pupils than 10 years ago.

The Elton Committee noted changing attitudes towards professional providers of services both generally and specifically with regard to education, and expressed concern lest the increasing willingness among parents in the United States to pursue legal actions against the disciplining of their children be mirrored in Britain.[33] Such legal action in the United States is reported to be seen by teachers there as limiting their disciplinary authority to a significant extent.[34] The Elton Committee felt that teachers' authority in this country would be better protected by setting out the fundamental principles governing that authority in statute. They viewed the law as providing a basis for the teacher's authority to exert discipline within the school, but lamented the fact that the legal limits were derived from a collection of diverse sources, more especially case law or precedent under common law. The Report says that 'If, as we believe, society wants teachers to have effective authority over pupils, it should make the basis and nature of that authority clear in statute'.[35] Of course, to a limited extent it already *has* – via the Education (No. 2) Act 1986, which has banned corporal punishment in state schools. This Act has also established in law the authority (and responsibilities)[36] of the head teacher over disciplinary matters, and has imposed a system for dealing with exclusions from school. But there is some justification for the argument that, so far as in-classroom sanctions such as detention, confiscation and withdrawal of privileges are concerned, some consolidation of the law in a statutory form would be desirable. However, it is doubtful that establishing the teacher's authority in a statutory form would automatically, as the Elton Committee hoped, remove all scope for argument, since any rules would have to retain the flexibility which exists at present – inevitably leaving grey areas.

The provisions the Committee recommend for inclusion[37] involve little more than a restatement of the existing common law position:

1 The teacher has general authority over discipline for the purposes of securing the education and well-being of all pupils at the school.
2 The teachers' authority is not to be regarded as delegated by the parent. Instead, teachers have authority to discipline pupils by virtue of their position as teacher.
3 The teachers' authority extends to the enforcement of school rules (which a head teacher has authority to make under the articles of government of school and which may, unless they are unlawful –

for example because of sex or race discrimination – be regarded as the 'law of the land' so far as pupils and parents are concerned). The teacher may impose reasonable punishments which are consistent with the school's discipline policy and the law.

4   Teachers are entitled to discipline pupils in respect of conduct while out of school, such as on a school trip or bullying out of school where a pupil's conduct 'impinges on the school'. (This re-states the authority to punish for out of school misbehaviour established by the courts.[38])

THE USE OF SANCTIONS/PUNISHMENTS

Sanctions used by teachers take many forms. Less severe forms of sanction include rebuke, withholding of praise and demanding repetition of work; in more serious cases there may be referral to senior staff, detention, putting a pupil on report, writing to parents and calling them into school, referring the pupil to a special unit in the school and ultimately exclusion from school.

It is clear that in most cases limited sanctions such as disapproval of a particular form of conduct can be most effective.[39] The research carried out by the University of Sheffield team for the Elton enquiry found that a preponderance of teachers considered reasoning with pupils outside the classroom setting as the most effective strategy for dealing with difficult pupils.[40] Opinions were rather divided over the effectiveness of other strategies and sanctions such as setting extra work or detention. The Elton Committee concluded that the lack of uniformity suggested that the effectiveness or otherwise of a particular sanction depended both on the individual teacher and on the circumstances of the school.[41]

Within the framework established by the Education (No. 2) Act 1986 for the head teacher to be in overall control of discipline in a school (taking account of the governors' policy on discipline), the law is content to allow teachers much discretion in the enforcement of school rules and application of sanctions. Generally, the law has traditionally played a minimal role in controlling the use of sanctions at school. The banning of corporal punishment by statute (from 15 August 1987) and the new procedures governing reinstatement of excluded pupils must be regarded as exceptions to the prevailing *laissez-faire* approach by Parliament towards punishment of pupils.

The rulings of the courts have established limits on the power to punish, and the cases on corporal punishment are of continuing relevance in this respect. In the case of *R v Hopley* (1860), for example, Chief Justice Cockburn said that punishment inflicted on a pupil must be reasonable and moderate, not motivated by passion or rage, and must not be 'excessive in its nature or degree' or 'protracted beyond the child's powers of endurance'. Whilst this statement was made in a case arising out of an alleged assault on a pupil, its relevance surely extends to other punishments which are similarly controlled by the common law. For example, detaining a child would be false imprisonment but for the fact that the law permits a teacher to carry out a reasonable punishment. In those independent schools where corporal punishment may still be inflicted,[42] the teacher is able to avoid committing the torts of assault or battery when striking a pupil by ensuring that the punishment is moderate and not unreasonable.

So far there have been very few legal challenges to disciplinary action falling short of exclusion, apart from those concerning the use of corporal punishment which is now banned in the state sector. This may be a reflection of the willingness of parents to accept the authority of the teacher where only limited sanctions are employed. However, where exclusion from school is concerned it would be reasonable to suppose that parents are far more likely to question the decision in view of its implications. There is, since the Education (No. 2) Act 1986, a very important legal framework within which exclusions from school may take place, which allows parents and others to have their say in the decision-making process (see below). The establishment of relatively uniform statutory procedures is particularly important in view of the wide disparities between individual schools in their policies on the sanction of exclusion.[43]

PARTICULAR FORMS OF PUNISHMENT

Corporal punishment

Only about one-third of the state sector secondary school teachers questioned by the University of Sheffield team for the Elton Committee reported that in their school corporal punishment had not been in use prior to 1987 when it became illegal. Thus for the majority of teachers corporal punishment was available as a sanction against pupil misbehaviour until comparatively recently, although some LEAs, about 30 in all, had banned its use prior to then.[44] As stated earlier, the European Court of Human Rights ruled in the case of *Campbell and Cosans v United Kingdom* that to inflict corporal punishment on pupils when parents were opposed to such punishment on the grounds of their religion or philosophical convictions would be a breach of the European Convention.[45] Moreover, corporal punishment could amount to 'degrading treatment or punishment', contrary to Article 3 of the Convention.[46] Although the European Convention on Human Rights has not been incorporated into domestic law in the United Kingdom and is not enforceable via legal sanctions against signatories, the government was under political pressure following *Campbell and*

Cosans to change the law. Instead of banning corporal punishment outright, however, it sought merely to give effect to the Court's ruling. The Education (Corporal Punishment) Bill would, in effect, have given each parent the right to veto the use of corporal punishment against his/her child. As stated above, this would not have been workable.

The Education (No. 2) Act 1986 banned the use of corporal punishment in the state sector. At last the government recognised what many researchers had been saying for years: that corporal punishment did not address the causes of bad behaviour, caused resentment among older pupils in particular, and was 'inimical to the quality of relationships between teachers and pupils upon which good behaviour is based'.[47] There was also evidence that corporal punishment was counter-productive: the use of physical force by teachers tended to promote violent behaviour by pupils.[48] Regardless of what parents may think, and evidence suggests that many still support corporal punishment by teachers and seek to sanction its use in schools,[49] the banning of corporal punishment in state schools was a wise measure.

Section 47 of the Education (No. 2) Act 1986 has not criminalised corporal punishment by a teacher (although in some cases striking a pupil excessively was and still is an offence). Instead, it has removed from teachers a defence to civil proceedings. Thus corporal punishment is defined in the section with reference to the tort of battery. Corporal punishment amounts to anything done for the purposes of punishing the pupil, whether or not there are other reasons for doing it, which would amount to a battery.[50] The general rule is that a battery is committed where a person touches or strikes another, grabs hold of their sleeve or lapels and so on, without implied or express permission. There is implied permission to tap someone on the shoulder to attract their attention. The most common purpose for which this might be done would probably be to ask for directions. So far as teachers are concerned, it might be necessary to tap a pupil on the shoulder to point out that s/he has dropped something on the floor, or to grab hold of a pupil to prevent an assault by that pupil on another. It is doubtful whether in either of these situations the action taken is primarily concerned with punishment; but the first example could fall within the definition of corporal punishment in the Act, which requires the action to have been taken wholly or *partly* for the purposes of punishment. In any event, the Act makes it clear that it is not unlawful for a teacher to inflict corporal punishment (as defined in the Act) where it is necessary 'for reasons that include averting an immediate danger of personal injury to, or an immediate danger to the property of, any person (including the pupil concerned)'.[51] Using reasonable force to break up a fight would, either way, not be unlawful, whereas pushing a pupil back into line most probably would be.

Detention

The Elton enquiry research showed that the majority of teachers in secondary schools had used detention of individual pupils or groups of pupils but that teachers were divided as to the effectiveness of detention as a sanction.[52] Rutter *et al* found that detention had a neutral effect on pupil behaviour.[53]

The law permits detention of pupils by teachers; provided it is not excessive or unreasonable, in accordance with the test laid down in *R v Hopley* (1860) (above), it may be imposed without risk of liability for false imprisonment being incurred.[54] The Elton Committee concluded that a parent would not be able to prohibit a teacher from detaining his child for the purposes of punishment. However, despite the teacher's independent authority to discipline pupils, the test laid down in the case of *R v Rahman*[55] by the Lord Chief Justice Lord Lane for the limits to a parent's right to detain his/her child probably offers a guide to teachers. Lord Lane said it would be unlawful to detain a child 'for such period or periods or in such circumstances as to take it outside the realm of reasonable parental discipline'. Thus detention beyond a reasonable time would be unlawful; what is reasonable will depend on the circumstances, including the ages of the children concerned. Parental wishes, although not conclusive, would be relevant.[56]

Detention of a whole class may technically still be lawful, although it is becoming increasingly likely that a judge would have doubts about the reasonableness of this course of action where it is known that there may only be one or two culprits. The Elton Committee recommended avoidance of the punishment of whole groups,[57] and this is consistent with the view of a judge in one recent case, who said that 'Punishment should not be indiscriminate. A blanket punishment such as detention of a whole class must only be used as a last resort, otherwise people who are quite innocent may be detained incorrectly or unlawfully.'[58] The Children's Legal Centre has argued that the practice of what it calls 'mass detentions' should be prohibited altogether, because it is morally unjustifiable to punish a whole class for the actions of one or two of its members and likely to precipitate resentment among pupils.[59]

Exclusion

Exclusion of a pupil from school may be temporary (either for a fixed or indeterminate period) or permanent. In either case it is generally seen as a last resort. In the survey of secondary schools by Her Majesty's Inspectorate it was found that schools resorted to short- or longer-term exclusion of pupils 'only when absolutely necessary and then with reluctance'.[60] In the *Elton Report* survey, only 9 per cent of secondary school teachers had ever requested the suspension of a pupil.[61] Research shows that there is considerable variation in what schools regard as sufficient ground for exclusion and in exclusion rates in different schools.[62] Exclusion, which usually takes the initial form of suspension, is almost universally available for cases of severe disruption of lessons or verbal abuse of staff.[63] But it is also used in some cases for rather trivial offences.[64]

The law states that the power to exclude a pupil from a county, voluntary or maintained special school may be exercised only by the head teacher.[65] This should be taken as referring to the *office* of head teacher, so that where a person is acting in place of the head teacher (usually this will be the deputy head teacher), s/he will be able to exercise this power. Cases have established that the power of expulsion must be exercised 'reasonably' and that wrongful (that is, unjust) expulsion does not in itself constitute an actionable tort.[66]

The head teacher is required[67] to inform the parents of a pupil who is to be excluded (or the pupil him/herself if aged at least 18) of the period of, and reasons for, the exclusion. Reasons must also be given if the head teacher decides to make a temporary exclusion permanent. The head teacher must also inform the parents (or pupil, if aged 18-plus) of their right to make representations about the exclusion to the LEA and/or governors. In certain cases the head teacher is obliged to inform the LEA of his decision and the reasons for it. First, s/he must do so if the pupil is to be excluded for an aggregate period of more than five days in any term, or if the pupil's exclusion will mean that s/he misses an opportunity to take a public examination which s/he was going to take. Second, the LEA must be informed if the head teacher has decided to exclude permanently a pupil excluded for a fixed or indefinite period.

Reinstatement of an excluded pupil may be ordered by an LEA; but governors also have powers with regard to reinstatement. The Poundswick dispute in Manchester, when the LEA wished to reinstate pupils excluded for scrawling graffiti on a school wall, and the teachers, backed by the governors, objected because the graffiti allegedly contained personal insults to teachers, prompted a reappraisal of the respective powers of schools and LEAs over reinstatement. The position now depends on whether the period of exclusion which has been ordered is *permanent, indefinite* or *fixed term*. The undoubtedly complex provisions in the Education (No. 2) Act 1986, outlined below, apply to county, controlled and maintained special schools. (In voluntary aided schools the governors have many of the rights enjoyed by LEAs over reinstatement of pupils in other schools.)

If exclusion is to be *permanent*, the LEA's decision on whether to order the pupil's reinstatement is binding on the head teacher,[68] although the governors may appeal against an LEA's refusal to reinstate a permanently excluded pupil, using the same machinery which the LEA is required to establish for such appeals by parents (and pupils if aged 18 or over).[69] If the pupil has been excluded for an aggregate period of more than five days in any term or will miss an opportunity to take an examination as a result of his/her exclusion, the governors may order his reinstatement and the head has to comply.[70] (Note that the Act also establishes a general rule that where the LEA and governors both have a say in the matter, and their decisions conflict, whichever leads to the earlier return of the pupil should prevail.[71]) The *Elton Report* recommends that in order to ensure that there is central monitoring of the exercise by LEAs of their power to order reinstatement of a pupil permanently excluded by the head teacher with the backing of the governors, the LEA should be required to submit a report to the Secretary of State within 14 days after every such occasion. The *Report* also recommends that the head teacher be asked to supply a report both in the above situation and where the governing body has directed that a permanently excluded pupil be reinstated against the head teacher's wishes.[72]

If the pupil has not been excluded permanently, but has been excluded for an *indefinite* period, the governors can only order the head teacher to reinstate him/her if the aggregate period of exclusion would be more than five days in any term or if the pupil would miss an opportunity to take a public examination. If the governors choose not to reinstate, the LEA may order reinstatement.[73] The *Elton Report* recommends that if a pupil is to be readmitted to school after an indefinite period of exclusion, the school should ensure that before the pupil is allowed to return his/her parent signs an agreement in which the terms of the pupil's readmission have been spelt out.[74] This is clearly seen as a way of encouraging parental involvement in the reintegration of the pupil into school life.[75]

If the exclusion is for a *fixed period* which would bring the aggregate exclusion in any term to more than five days or would involve the pupil missing a public examination, the governors or LEA may order the reinstatement of the pupil and the head teacher would be bound to comply with the direction.[76]

The governing body may delegate decisions concerning reinstatement to a committee of three or more of their number, excluding the head teacher.[77]

The Elton Committee suggested that because of the concern in schools about the fact that LEAs will often be able to order reinstatement against the wishes of parents and governors, the Secretary of State should monitor the operation of the new arrangements for five years and consider any changes that appear necessary.[78]

DISCRIMINATION

Race

The Race Relations Act 1976 makes it illegal for an LEA or governors to discriminate on the grounds of colour, race, ethnic or national origins or nationality against a pupil – 'by excluding him from the establishment or subjecting him to any other detriment' (section 17(c)(ii)). In the context of employment, where the Act refers to dismissal 'or other detriment', it has been held that the phrase in quotation marks refers to an act of the same type as dismissal. In a case where an employer referred to a secretary using racist language, this was not a 'detriment' for this purpose.[79] It may be, therefore, that section 17(c)(ii) (above) refers to the more serious forms of sanction only, although detention or removal to a special unit would surely fall within its scope. Withdrawal of privileges would be covered by section 17(c)(i), which refers, *inter alia*, to denial of access to 'benefits, facilities or services' provided by the school.

It is difficult for an individual complainant to show that there has been discrimination against him/her on the grounds of race. However, where a discriminatory practice has been in operation for some time it may be easier for the Commission for Racial Equality to produce evidence in support of an allegation. For example, the Commission demonstrated that in Birmingham LEA's schools between 1974 and 1980 black children were four times more likely to have been suspended from school than whites, and that factors such as place of residence and single-parent family background could be discounted.[80] The Elton Committee urged schools not to stereotype pupils from certain racial groups as troublemakers.[81] Brief guidance on exclusions has been offered to schools by the Commission in its Code of Practice for Education.[82]

Gender

Section 22(c) of the Sex Discrimination Act 1975, like section 17(c) of the Race Relations Act 1976 (above), outlaws discrimination in exclusion 'or other detriment' or in denial of access to benefits, facilities or services provided by the school. Girls are under-represented in the exclusion statistics – which would imply that there is unlawful sex discrimination, until one takes account of the well-documented fact that the behaviour of girls and boys and girls at school differs. On the whole, boys tend to be more noticeably deviant and aggressive. McManus notes that 'aggression does not pay off for girls in the way some boys find it does for them',[83] with the result that many girls adapt to the social world of school in a different way. If girls deviate, they tend to do it in a way that causes far less disruption than boys, such as pretending to write when they are bored. The consequence is, therefore, that far fewer girls than boys are excluded from school.[84]

The Elton Committee urged teachers to take account of this difference in the way they exert discipline. They felt that the aggressive behaviour and attention-seeking which are more prevalent among males should not be reinforced by teacher responses.[85] It almost goes without saying that any disciplinary strategies adopted by teachers must involve an even-handed approach towards both sexes if they are to be lawful.

THE GOVERNMENT'S RESPONSE TO THE ELTON REPORT

The government has endorsed many of the Elton Committee's recommendations, most of which call for action by schools and LEAs rather than central government.[86] The government was urged to provide funds for the training of staff and additional support for dealing with the more difficult pupils. Provision has been made, via the LEA Training Grants and Education Support Grants Schemes.[87] Central government may also be expected to monitor the implementation of the Elton Committee's recommendations if not to provide the extra resources necessary for the extended role for (and numbers of) education welfare officers, teachers and LEA officers envisaged by the Report. Of particular interest to lawyers will be the Committee's recommendations concerning monitoring the operation of the exclusion and reinstatement provisions of the Education (No. 2) Act 1986 by the DES, for five years. Already, a National Exclusions Reporting System (whereby heads, governors and LEAs, as appropriate, provide information relating to permanent exclusions (but not details of individual pupils) to the Secretary of State) has been established. Lawyers, as well as teachers, will also be interested in the proposed establishment of the teacher's disciplinary authority in statute form. Realistically, though, there was little prospect of the government's making time for the introduction of such a provision, and in any event, the government has decided 'after very careful examination of the issues, that legislative action would not be appropriate'.[88] Also rejected has been the Elton Committee's proposal that parents might have civil liability imposed upon them in respect of their children's acts.

CONCLUSIONS

The Elton Committee managed to produce a comprehensive and widely supported report and a coherent set of recommendations in a relatively short period of time. But because Lord Elton's team was established as a Committee of Enquiry to look into a serious and immediate problem, it was precluded by its terms of reference from addressing the more fundamental questions concerning the conflict between teachers' autonomy and children's rights. Wringe has shown how, traditionally, any conflict of notional 'rights', as might arise, for example, between a pupil's freedom of expression in classroom discourse and a teacher's authority to control a lesson and behaviour during it, is irreconcilable and tends to be weighed in favour of the teacher almost every time.[89] The Elton Committee did, however, offer pupils an opportunity to benefit from a more child-centred approach to school discipline. Schools were urged to recognise the importance of ascertaining pupils' views both generally and more specifically in relation to the development of a behaviour policy by the school, and to instil a sense of 'belonging' amongst pupils. Even so, these measures, like the abolition of corporal punishment before them, are not primarily concerned with the rights of children. Instead, they are guided by institutional and functional considerations rather than moral principles. The fact that it was shown that corporal punishment in a school tended to exacerbate rather than diminish misbehaviour was the principal reason for reform. In any event, there are undoubtedly inherent difficulties in applying a child-centred approach to discipline in an institutional setting, although they are probably not insurmountable.

Another relevant factor here is the prevalence of parental rights in education (see Chapter 4). This stands in marked contrast to the emphasis on parental responsibility in recent child-care law developments, although it must be acknowledged that in extending parental rights in education the government has been keen to stress the duty of parents to involve themselves in their child's schooling in various (often 'consumerist') ways. Thus it has been observed that 'it remains unclear whether the abolition of corporal punishment in schools results from a spread of child-centred views or not: references to parents' rather than children's rights to decide school policies make such interpretation doubtful'.[90] Similarly, if parents are able to have their views upheld (as might occur on an appeal against a decision not to reinstate a permanently excluded pupil), 'it may not be clear whether it is primarily the child's right or the parents' rights over upbringing which is being upheld'.[91] Although it may not necessarily clarify the position, there should nevertheless be greater recognition of children's autonomy interests in the context of school discipline. To take one example, there is no provision for independent representation for pupils aged under 18 in respect of appeals concerning reinstatement following permanent exclusion. Such rights are now available in the family courts, and the lack of a child-centred approach in the law governing school discipline amounts to a clear anomaly·

Case study on discipline

At a primary school, Joan, a teacher of five years' experience, notices two 9-year-old pupils scuffling in the corridor. As she approaches them, she forms the impression that one of the pupils, Victor, is bullying the other, Robert.

Joan decides to intervene immediately to prevent injury to Robert. She manages to separate the boys forcibly, whereupon Victor kicks her shin.

Joan is angered by this. She knows Victor to be a troublemaker, and even remembers the boy's father's remarks at the last parents' evening, encouraging her to give Victor a 'good smack if he causes any trouble'. Instinctively, Joan reacts to Victor's kick by slapping the boy on the back of the leg. She orders Victor to accompany her to the head teacher's office. Victor refuses to move, and Joan pushes him, saying 'get moving'. Unfortunately, Joan catches Victor slightly off-balance and he falls against a wall, bruising his arm slightly.

When the two arrive at the head teacher's office, Joan explains the situation to the head, Lydia. Lydia telephones Victor's mother, Karen, immediately. She tells Karen that Victor is being excluded from school indefinitely for bullying and for kicking Joan.

The next day Karen telephones Lydia and threatens to tell the local newspaper and the national press about the 'assault on her boy by a teacher' if he is not reinstated immediately.

Consider the legal implications of the above events and advise Lydia.

Notes

1   More than 500 physical attacks on teachers in inner London in one year were reported (Poyner B and Warne C 1988 *Preventing Violence to Staff,* HMSO), although the extent of the problem has been disputed (see, e.g., *The Times,* 9 Nov. 1988). Recent evidence suggests that attacks on teachers are relatively rare: Lord Elton 1989 *Discipline in Schools, Report of the Committee of Enquiry Chaired by Lord Elton,* HMSO, p. 17.

2   See, for example, Jeffs T 1986 'Children's rights at school', in Franklin B (ed.) *The Rights of Children,* Blackwell; Bainham A 1988 *Children, Parents and State,* Sweet & Maxwell.

3   *Discipline in Schools, op. cit.*

4   E.g., Mr Cartwright, 126 HC Debs, col. 399w, 29 Jan. 1988; Mr Pawsey 127 HC Debs, col. 583w, 16 Feb. 1988.

5   Hirst P H and Peters R S 1970 *The Logic of Education,* Routledge & Kegan Paul, pp. 128–9.

6   Peters R S 1972 *Ethics and Education,* George Allen & Unwin, pp. 267–8.

7   HMI 1987 *Education Observed 5: Good Behaviour and Discipline in Schools,* DES, para.37; HMI 1988 *Secondary Schools – an Appraisal by HMI,* HMSO, para. 283.

8   HMI 1988, *op. cit.;* Elton, *op. cit.,* pp. 239–40.

9   HMI, *Education Observed 5, op. cit.,* para. 37.
10 Rosenbaum M 1989 'The Children's Legal Centre: evidence to the Elton Committee', in Jones N (ed.) *School Management and Pupil Behaviour,* Falmer, p. 11.
11 DES 1985 *Better Schools,* Cmnd 9469, HMSO, para.186.
12 HMI, *Education Observed 5, op. cit.,* para. 40.
13. Tattum D P and Lane D A (eds) 1989 *Bullying in Schools,* Trentham Books.
14 On racial tension in schools, see Macdonald I 1989 *Murder in the Playground* (Report of enquiry into death at Burnage High School Manchester), Manchester City Council.
15 Elton, *op. cit.,* para. 66.
16 *Education Observed 5, op. cit.,* para. 1.
17 DES, *Better Schools, op, cit.,* para. 88.
18 Education (No. 2) Act 1986, section 22(a) and (d).
19 *Ibid.,* section 22(a).
20 Elton, *op. cit.,* R17.
21 Education (No. 2) Act 1986, section 22(b)(i).
22 Elton, *op. cit.,* pp. 237–8.
23 Education (No. 2) Act 1986, section 28(1).
24 *Op. cit.,* R120.
25 Section 28(3).
26 See *Fitzgerald v Northcote* (1865).
27 Scutter A K 1978 'Schoolteachers' position as to corporal punishment – 1'. *Solicitors' Journal* 122:671–3.
28 *Campbell and Cosans v United Kingdom* (1982).
29 Elton, *op. cit.,* para. 72.
30 *Ibid.*
31 Brazier M 1988 *Street on Torts* (8th edn), Butterworth p. 87.
32 Wilson H and Herbert G W 1978 *Parents and Children in the Inner City,* Routledge & Kegan Paul, pp. 159–60.
33 Cases have, for example, upheld the constitutional rights of children not to be excluded from school as a simply disciplinary measure: see *Harvard Educational Review* 43(4) (1973) and 44(1) (1974).
34 Elton, *op. cit.,* para. 71.
35 *Ibid.,* para. 72.
36 See also the *Teacher's Pay and Conditions Document 1990.*
37 *Ibid.,* para. 74.
38 *Cleary v Booth* (1893); *R v Newport (Salop) Justices ex parte Wright* (1929).
39 DES, *Education Observed 5, op. cit.,* para. 41.
40 *Elton Report, op. cit.,* p. 240.
41 *Ibid.,* p. 241.
42 Corporal punishment may be inflicted in independent schools with the exception of direct grant schools, schools maintained by the Ministry of Defence, city technology colleges and city colleges for the technology of the arts: Education (Abolition of Corporal Punishment) (Independent Schools) Regulations 1987, SI 1987, No. 1183, as amended. Even in those schools where it may still be inflicted, it cannot be given to pupils whose fees are being paid for by an LEA or a Scottish education authority or Northern Ireland Education Board: Education (No. 2) Act 1986, section 47(6)(b) and (7), and Education (Abolition of Corporal

Punishment) (Independent Schools) (Prescribed Categories of Persons) Regulations 1989, SI 1989, No. 1825.

43   McManus M 1989 *Troublesome Behaviour in the Classroom,* Routledge, pp. 17–34.

44   In many cases LEAs were responding to the cogently argued case presented by STOPP – the Society of Teachers Opposed to Physical Punishment. Manchester LEA ran into difficulty when it sought to ban the use of corporal punishment in the voluntary aided sector – see *R v Manchester City Council ex parte Fulford* (1984).

45   See Pogany I 1982 'Education: The Rights of Children and Parents Under the European Convention on Human Rights'. *New Law Journal* 132:344–7. It may be noted that the Elton Committee also recommended the avoidance of *any* form of humiliating punishment (p. 101). Jeffs points out that humiliation may, for example, arise out of being forced to take PE in underwear after forgetting to bring kit into school (*op. cit.,* p. 63).

46   *Warwick v UK* (1986).

47   HMI, *Education Observed 5, op. cit.,* para. 45.

48   Rutter M *et al.* 1979 *Fifteen Thousand Hours: Secondary Schools and their Effects on Children,* Open Books.

49   See Partington J and Wragg T 1989 *Schools and Parents,* Cassell, p. 30; see also Sutherland M 1988 *Theory of Education,* Longman, p. 72, and Brompton S 1985 'Parents say "yes" to keeping the cane'. *The Times,* 27 Feb. 1985.

50   Section 47(2).

51   Section 47(3).

52   *Op. cit.,* p. 240.

53   (1979) *op. cit.*

54   See *Fitzgerald v Northcote* (1865).

55   (1985).

56   See *Terrington v Lancashire County Council* (1986) Blackpool County Court, 26 June.

57   *Elton Report, op cit.,* R26 and p. 101.

58   *Terrington v Lancashire County Council* (1986), *op. cit.*

59   Rosenbaum, *op. cit.,* p. 116.

60   HMI 1988 *Secondary Schools: An Appraisal by HMI, op. cit.,* para. 73.

61   *Op. cit.,* p. 240.

62   HMI, *Education Observed 5, op. cit.,* para. 47. McManus (*op. cit.,* ch. 2) looks at the factors contributing to variation in exclusion rates.

63   The research conducted for the Elton Committee found verbal attacks relatively common in contrast to physical attacks, which were extremely rare. See also Rosenbaum, *op. cit.,* p. 108.

64   *Ibid.,* p. 117.

65   Education (No. 2) Act 1986, section 22(f).

66   *Hutt and Another v The Governors of Haileybury College and Others* (1888); *Hunt v Damon* (1930).

67   All the duties referred to in this paragraph are contained in section 23 of the Education (No. 2) Act 1986.

68   Education (No. 2) Act 1986, section 24(a).

69   Education (No. 2) Act 1986, section 26(1). Appeal lies to an appeal committee, constituted in the same way as the committees that hear school admissions appeals (see page 65).

70 *Ibid.*, section 24(b.)
71 *Ibid.*, section 24(g).
72 Elton, *op. cit.*, R138.
73 *Ibid.*, section 24(b), (c) and (f).
74 Elton, *op. cit.*, R 65.
75 *Ibid.*, p. 14.
76 *Ibid.*, section 24(b).
77 Education (School Government) Regulations 1989, SI 1989, No. 1503, regs 25(4) and 26(6).
78 *Ibid.*, p. 17 and R137.1 and .2.
79 *De Souza v Automobile Association* (1986).
80 Commission for Racial Equality 1985 *Birmingham Local Education Authority and Schools Referral and Suspension of Pupils, Report of a Formal Investigation*. CRE.
81 Elton, *op. cit.* R91 and p. 159.
82 Commission for Racial Equality 1989 *Code of Practice for the Elimination of Racial Discrimination in Education*, especially paras 38–41.
83 McManus, *op. cit.*, p. 12.
84 *Ibid.*, p. 11.
85 Elton, *op. cit.*, R89.
86 DES Press Releases 75/89 (13 March 1989) and 141/90 (2 May 1990).
87 See DES Circular 20/89 *Local Authority Training Grants Scheme: Financial Year 1990–91*, Annex A; The Education (Training Grants) Regulations 1987 SI No 96, as amended by Amendment Regulations 1990 SI No 221; Education Support Grant Regulations 1984, as amended by 1989 SI No. 2446.
88 DES Press Release 141/90, 2 May 1990.
89 Wringe C 1981 *Children's Rights*, Routledge & Kegan Paul, pp. 18–19.
90 Sutherland M 1988 *Theory of Education*, Longman, p. 71.
91 Bainham A 1988 *op. cit.*, n2, p. 187.

CHAPTER 8

The care of pupils

INTRODUCTION

Responsibility for the physical care of pupils is one of the most important duties resting with schools. The potential for injury to pupils from the actions of their fellow pupils or from the increasingly run-down state of many school premises is great. Moreover, the increasing range of sporting activities offered to pupils and the growing emphasis in many areas of the curriculum on learning through practical work rather than simply from textbooks have undoubtedly increased the potential risks to pupil safety.

For the most part teachers are aware of these risks and take steps to guard against them. They can draw on the guidance issued by the DES, LEAs, teachers' associations and the Health and Safety Executive to fulfil the standard of care expected of them by the law. Often, however, it is only when a particularly serious incident involving pupils is reported in the media that teachers reassess their approach to safety in school activities. The incident at Land's End a few years ago, when several pupils were swept into the sea, and in the Austrian Alps, when four other pupils slid to their deaths down a snow-covered mountain, must have caused great concern amongst the teaching profession. However, provided teachers obey certain basic rules about supervision and safety they need not sacrifice the undoubted educational value of visits and other activities through fear of mishap and consequential liability.

It is necessary to offer a brief exposition of the general principles of law relevant to health and safety at school, although this is not an easy task. The law derives from a variety of sources – common law and statute – and takes the form of civil or criminal law. Much of it is of wide application, in that it applies to most places where people work or where activities take place. Moreover, the common law areas in particular, especially negligence, are still developing. Therefore, what might realistically be attempted is to raise awareness of the nature of legal responsibility in this field and to demonstrate the applicability of the law to particular situations or activities in which teachers and pupils are likely to be involved. Readers will note the cautious or even evasive approach adopted to questions of liability – these will depend on the facts in any particular case, and often it is impossible to be definite about when a court would, for example, uphold a claim of negligence.

In emphasising, in this chapter, the physical care of pupils, where legal issues can be critical, there is no wish to deny the importance of the *emotional or pastoral care* of pupils. The fact that teachers are required by their contracts of employment to give guidance on 'social matters' does emphasise this wider aspect of care associated with the teacher's role. Problems such as teenage pregnancy, child abuse or drug abuse, or other less serious personal problems, can all affect pupils, and teachers may have an important caring role to play, even if it is not one clearly defined in law.

The particular aspect of care with which this chapter deals is pupil safety, an area of enormous practical importance.

NEGLIGENCE

The chief area of concern rests with liability for negligence. Negligence is a tort, a civil wrong in respect of which a court may order a person held liable to remedy his/her wrong. In negligence cases the remedy generally takes the form of monetary compensation, or 'damages'. These may be determined by a court or agreed in an out-of-court settlement – but sanctioned by the court where the person injured is a child. A teacher who is held liable for negligence for causing injury to a pupil (or fellow member of staff or member of the public) in the course of his/her duties may find that insurance (such as is offered by professional associations) covers payment of compensation. Also, there is a general principle that where a teacher (or indeed any other employee) is negligent in the course of his/her duties, the employer may be vicariously liable. There is not the scope here to discuss this principle in any detail, for there is a considerable amount of case law on the question of whether a person is or is not acting in the course of his/her employment. Given the detailed list of duties in a teacher's contract, laid down in *Teachers' Pay and Conditions Order*, it is far easier to say whether an act was within the scope of employment, although the mere fact that a function is performed voluntarily does not necessarily take it outside the scope of employment. If, on the other hand, a teacher disobeys an employer's instruction and injury to a pupil results, the teacher may well be acting outside the scope of his/her employment. Therefore, if a teacher employed at a split-site school is forbidden to give lifts between sites to pupils and does so in a negligent manner, resulting in injury to the pupil, his/her employers will most probably not be vicariously liable.[1]

Where the situation does give rise to vicarious liability, both the teacher and his/her employer may be held liable. In many cases the injured party (known in a legal action as the 'plaintiff') may decide to sue the employer because the latter's financial resources available to satisfy any judgment will obviously be far greater than those of the teacher. Strictly speaking, an employer who is required to compensate his employee's victim may claim a contribution from the employee. It is unusual for this to happen in the case of teacher negligence.

The question of *who* is the employer for the purposes of vicarious liability is clearly very important. So far as schools are concerned, despite the increased powers given to governing bodies over staff selection and dismissal by the Education (No. 2) Act 1986 and ERA 1988, the position for the purposes of vicarious liability is that the LEA is still the employer (except in aided, special agreement and grant-maintained schools, where the governors would be the employer for this purpose).

Having established *who* may be responsible for a teacher's negligent act (or omission), the question of *when* negligence occurs must be considered. It has been said that 'it is not for every careless act that a man may be held responsible in law, nor even for every careless act that causes damage'.[2] A person will only be negligent if he is under a duty of care to a person (the plaintiff) and has broken that duty, with the result that consequential damage has been suffered by the plaintiff. A teacher is clearly under a duty of care towards his/her pupils.[3] The reason is that whichever of the tests the courts have applied to establish the existence of such a duty – whether the classic 'neighbour principle' laid down by Lord Atkin in 1932[4] and applied widely,[5] or the three-part test favoured more recently by the Court of Appeal and House of Lords[6] – the teacher would be expected to guard against foreseeable harms to which pupils might otherwise be subjected.

An injury which no reasonable amount of care would have prevented and which was not reasonably foreseeable will not give rise to negligence. So, for example, although pupils must be supervised during a games lesson in the playground, a teacher would not be liable if, on a calm day a freak gust of wind suddenly knocked a pupil to the ground. Obviously, if pupils were kept indoors all day they could not be blown over in this way. But it would be absurd to expect that level of care, and tantamount to a derogation of the school's duty to educate the pupil. In one recent case the judge said that in order to offer a broad education a school has to involve pupils in a variety of indoor and outdoor activities, many of which undoubtedly carry risks. The school is 'under a duty to exercise reasonable care' for the health and safety of its pupils, and provided it does so its duty is fulfilled.[7]

This, of course, begs the question: what is 'reasonable care' in the school context? The classic statement of Baron Alderson in *Blyth v Birmingham Waterworks* frequently forms the starting point for discussion of the standard of care which the law expects: 'Negligence is the omission to do something which a reasonable man, guided upon those considerations which ordinarily regulate the conduct of human affairs, would do, or doing something which a prudent and reasonable man would not do.' The 'reasonable man' test implies an objective standard of care. But clearly one would expect a teacher to be better able to supervise the activities of a group of young children than a hairdresser or surgeon! Thus the objective test of reasonableness must be applied in a special way, put neatly in *Winfield* thus: 'Where anyone practises a profession . . . the law expects him to show the amount of competence associated with the proper discharge of the duties of that profession'; if that amount of competence is lacking and someone is injured in consequence, he is 'not behaving reasonably'.[8]

The standard expected of teachers, or of any other professionals, is set by the courts. Although the courts will have regard for general and approved practice within the profession as a whole, they will not let this override their own view of what is appropriate. Thus if a practice, whilst generally approved, carries an intrinsically greater risk of harm than pupils should be subjected to, a court may still find negligence – as in *Fryer v Salford Corporation* (1937), where Slesser L J felt that a cooker used in domestic science should have had a guard even though it was not educational practice at the time to have one installed. But normally, general and approved practice will weigh heavily in the court's judgment – as it did in *Wright v Cheshire County Council* (1952), when a child was injured during gymnastics, and *Rich v London County Council* (1953), when a child was injured by a piece of coke taken from an uncovered pile in the playground.

Sometimes a practice will not be 'generally' approved in the sense that most members of the profession subscribe to it. If there is more than one school of thought within the profession as to how an activity should be conducted (as in *Chilvers v London County Council* (1916), where it was accepted that various methods of judo instruction were considered appropriate by instructors), the court will only regard a practice as generally approved if it is subscribed to by 'a responsible body of professional men' with the relevant skills. In other words, the method of instruction, and so on, must be well supported within the profession, even if a significant body of opinion favours an alternative method.

Within any profession, the level of experience possessed by individuals will vary enormously. What bearing, if any, will this have on the question of whether there has been a breach of the duty of care? In particular, would the law expect a higher standard of care from an experienced teacher than from a new recruit to the profession? The courts have held that it is the standard which may be expected of a person holding the *post* in question which is important.[9] This implies that no allowance would be made for age or experience amongst teachers, all of whom would be expected to possess the necessary skill to supervise a class properly.

A further factor which has been taken into consideration in assessing the standard of care expected of a teacher has been whether the teacher has exercised the care, in looking after pupils, that a 'reasonably careful and prudent parent' would show towards his/her children. The basis for this test is the *in loco parentis* principle, that the teacher acts in place of a parent in having the care of children. The careful and prudent parent test was articulated in *Williams v Eady* (1893) and was applied subsequently in various cases. But by the 1960s the courts began to acknowledge the limitations to the test, and in particular the inappropriateness of judging the standard of care expected of a teacher in school, where s/he may have a class of 30 pupils to control, against that expected from a parent having to look after a far smaller number in the context of the home.[10] In *Beaumont v Surrey County Council* (1968) the court, in a case where a pupil had discovered a piece of discarded heavy duty elastic in a bin in the playground and had struck another pupil in the face during larking about, regarded the careful and prudent parent test as unhelpful in the context of playground supervision. Geoffrey Lane J (as he then was) said that the head teacher was expected to take 'all reasonable and proper steps' – namely, those which could reasonably be expected of a competent head teacher – to prevent injury to pupils. In similar vein, Croom-Johnson LJ in a more recent case said that 'the duty of care which the school owes to its pupils is not simply that of the prudent parent . . . it goes beyond mere parental duty, because [the school] may have special knowledge about some matters which the parent does not or cannot have. The average parent cannot know of the unusual dangers which may arise.'[11]

The courts will also take account of the particular purpose for which the activity in which the injury occurs is taking place. The fact that school activities have an educational purpose means that the courts will balance the need to exercise care against the educational object to be achieved. The fact that it is 'fundamental to the relationship between school and pupil that the school undertakes to educate him in as wide a sense as it reasonably can' means that the school may be justified in subjecting the pupil to ordinary risks, provided that it exercises proper care.[12] Part of the educational process involves encouraging pupils to take increasing responsibility for their own actions, and this has been acknowledged in various judgments.[13] The age of the child will clearly be a relevant factor here. If a teacher entrusts a pupil or group of pupils with a degree of independence, s/he must have regard not only for the propensity of children for mischief in certain situations (such as during playtime)[14] but also the age of the pupils. Older children may themselves be held negligent, or, if the teacher is partly to blame, contributorily negligent (as in *Barnes v Bromley LBC* (1983), when an unsuitable implement shattered when used by a pupil in an inappropriate manner causing him injury). Age was the only material distinguishing feature between the facts of *Butt v Cambridgeshire and Ely County Council* (1970), in which a teacher of 9- and 10-year-old pupils was not liable when a pupil poked sharp-pointed scissors into the eye of another pupil, and *Black v Kent*

County Council (1983), where the Court of Appeal awarded damages to a 7-year-old pupil who was similarly injured (this time by the scissors he himself was using). Older pupils may also be expected to guard themselves against risks of which the teacher has warned them[15] (adequately – that is, referring to the specific dangers)[16], whereas younger pupils may not be trusted to do so, depending on the circumstances.

As the courts will also take account of the degree of risk involved in assessing whether there has been a breach of the objective standard by which the duty of care is measured, the question of the degree of risk to which pupils may legitimately be subjected becomes relevant. It appears that there are two elements to be considered in relation to the degree or magnitude of the risk – the likelihood of injury and the potential seriousness of the injury that is risked.[17] It is in many ways difficult to separate these two elements in the school context. The use of equipment in the workshop (as in *Barnes v Bromley LBC*, above) and the gathering of pupils around a cooker to witness the fruits of their labours (*Fryer v Salford Corporation* (1937)) were both intrinsically dangerous activities where the degree of risk of injury was higher than in most other school activities *and* where the potential injuries would have been serious. When injury resulted, from the tool splintering because of its age and condition (*Barnes*) and the cooker not being fitted with a guard (*Fryer*), there was liability for negligence.

An extra element of risk had been present in *Van Oppen v Clerk to the Bedford Charity Trustees* (1989). The plaintiff was aged 16½ and taking part in a school game of rugby football. A legitimate tackle left him permanently paralysed. The accident had occurred in 1980. The year before, the school had received recommendations from the association of school medical officers (MOSA) concerning accident insurance cover for pupils, but had, at the time of the accident, not yet made a decision about which sort of insurance was needed nor about how it was to be obtained. The plaintiff claimed damages for negligence on various grounds:

1   The school had not warned of the risks inherent in the game of rugby;
2   The school's coaching of rugby had been carried out negligently;
3   The school had not advised the boy's parents to take out accident insurance cover;
4   The school had not informed the parents that they had not arranged such cover;
5   The school had failed to take out insurance cover for accidents to pupils playing rugby.

The claim failed on all these counts in the High Court. Counts 3–5 were pursued further in the Court of Appeal but were rejected by the

Court. The Court held that regardless of the desirability of the school providing both the advice and/or the cover that had been lacking, their duty to take care for the safety and welfare of their pupils did not extend as far as protecting the *economic* welfare of pupils in this way, nor, in Balcombe LJ's view, would it be fair and reasonable that it did so. Thus the first part of the case had also failed, because in the coaching of rugby the school had not fallen short of the standard of care which was expected. In the High Court Boreham J said that the staff who had been coaching had been 'well aware of the inherent risks in playing rugby football' and of the need to give proper instructions in the correct techniques. The standard of supervision had been high and the game had been played in the disciplined manner instilled by the school. The second stage of the case turned on the extent of the school's duty rather than the standard of care.

A further case which illustrates some these issues is *Affutu-Nartoy v Clarke and ILEA* (1984) (note that both the teacher and the ILEA were joined as parties). A teacher participated in a game of rugby with teenage boys he was instructing. His tackle on one boy was so fierce (even though within the rules of the game) that it was dangerous and unlawful. Clearly the objective of demonstrating the way to tackle did not justify the means employed, in view of the risk involved. The injury to a boy was foreseeable and could have been prevented by the exercise of reasonable care.

If the magnitude of the risk is greater because the plaintiff suffers from a particular disability, then that disability becomes relevant in determining whether there is liability – provided the defendant knew or ought to have known about it.[18] In *Moore v Hampshire County Council* (1981) a 12-year-old girl, who had a congenital dislocation of the hip, persuaded her PE teacher that she had been allowed to take PE, which was not in fact the case. The teacher knew that the girl had previously not been allowed to take part in PE. The girl fractured her ankle. Even if the girl had been allowed to join the class (and the teacher should have checked with the girl's mother first before allowing her to take part), careful supervision of her would have been needed, especially in the first instance, but it had not been offered. The Court of Appeal upheld the girl's claim.

It might be helpful to summarise the principles which have been identified thus far, before applying them to particular situations:

1   Teachers owe a *duty of care* towards pupils.
2   The employer (LEA or governors) may be held *vicariously liable* if the teacher's negligence arose in the course of his or her employment.
3   *Negligence* arises where the duty of care is broken and consequential damage results.
4   The duty of care is broken when the teacher fails to exercise *reasonable care*.

5   In assessing the standard of care which might be expected of a
teacher the court will take account of *general and approved
practice* in the teaching profession, the need to *balance the risk*
attached to a particular activity *against the object to be achieved*,
and the fact that a teacher acts *in loco parentis*.

In perhaps the majority of cases where pupils are injured at school
or in off-site school activities, allegations of negligence are based on a
failure of supervision. But in order for a claim of negligence to be
upheld, it has to be shown that, amongst other things, greater
supervision would have prevented the injury from occurring *and* that
the school might reasonably have been expected to take the necessary
steps to ensure that greater supervision was available. Two important
cases have concerned a failure of supervision prior to the start of
school. In the first of these, *Ward v Hertfordshire County Council*
(1969), children were playing in the playground prior to the start of
the school day. The playground had flint walls with jagged edges.
Children tended to race in the playground. According to the head
teacher, this had happened for a number of years, without serious
mishap. An 8-year-old boy crashed into a wall during a race and was
seriously injured. The children had been unsupervised. In the Court of
Appeal, their Lordships did not consider there had been any duty
resting with the school to stop children from racing. Therefore, even if
teachers had been present in the playground to supervise the children
(felt unnecessary by the court), they could not have prevented the
injury. In the words of Lord Denning: 'It often happens that children
run from one side of the playground to the other. It is impossible so to
supervise them that they never fall down and hurt themselves.' Lord
Justice Salmon said that the fact that there was no teacher in the
playground at the time of the incident in question was 'irrelevant,
because even if there had been, I can see no reason why he should
have prevented the children racing or playing'. Thus there was no
failure of reasonable care on the part of the school. His Lordship said
that pupils will always fall down in playgrounds and graze their knees
or elbows. In his Lordship's view it would be 'wrong to try to protect
them against minor injuries of that kind by forbidding them the
ordinary pleasures which school children so much enjoy'.

In *Mays v Essex County Council* (1975) the children were engaging
in a more dangerous pastime – sliding on ice. One boy fell and
suffered brain damage as a result of the impact. The incident occurred
a few minutes before the start of the school day. The LEA had decided
to instruct all of its schools to have a teacher on playground duty for
15 minutes prior to the start of school, but at the time of the incident
the school in question had not received the authority's instructions.
The head teacher had, however, already asked parents (via a circular)
not to send their children, some of whom arrived half an hour before
the start of school, too early. The judge adopted a similar approach to

that taken by the Court of Appeal in *Ward*. Describing orderly sliding on the ice as an 'innocent and healthy amusement', His Honour said that it would not have been incumbent on a teacher present to have prevented the activity. In any event, the pupils had been allowed on to school premises early not because the school was voluntarily accepting responsibility for them but rather as a charitable gesture (for example, it would have prevented pupils from having to congregate outside the school and would have helped parents who were rushing to work). The head teacher's circular to parents had demonstrated to them that the school was not accepting responsibility for pupils. There was no requirement to supervise the pupils.

The fact that the playground had icy patches which were left untreated was not considered to give rise to negligence. It is submitted that this case could well be decided differently today on this point, especially when there is a 'common duty of care' under the Occupier's Liability Act 1957 to avoid foreseeable injuries occurring to visitors to premises. This Act is discussed below, but it may be noted that in a case decided under the forerunner to the 1957 Act there was liability in respect of a school's failure to clear frozen snow from a school step (*Woodward v Mayor of Hastings* (1944)). Moreover, the comment by the judge in *Mays*, that 'life is full of dangers which children must learn to recognise, and . . . avoid. The playground is the place to learn,' shows a complacency which one hopes that the courts would be unlikely to demonstrate today.

Although there is some doubt about the extent of the school's duty to supervise pupils in the playground prior to the start of the school day, it is clear that during break-times supervision must be provided, whether by teachers or (especially at lunch-times when most teachers are not required by their employment contracts to work) ancillary staff. If supervision is inadequate, there may be liability in respect of any injuries which could have been prevented and ought reasonably to have been foreseen. Thus, in the case of *Beaumont v Surrey County Council* (1968), referred to earlier (p. 162), the lack of supervision in the playground resulted in the horseplay with the heavy-duty piece of elastic, which had been discovered by a pupil, not being prevented or interrupted. But the degree of supervision required during break-times is less than during periods of instruction. The fact that a boy aged 10 had been able to leave school premises at lunch-time and return with a bow and arrow which he fired, injuring a 6-year-old girl, was not felt to give rise to negligence by the school through lack of supervision (*Ricketts v Erith Borough Council* (1943)). In another case an injury occurred during a lunch-time which the children spent indoors due to wet weather. A 15-year-old boy was hit in the eye by a piece of chalk thrown by a classmate. Only one teacher had been on duty; he had had to supervise more than 200 pupils who were in various classrooms. The judge distinguished the facts from those in *Beaumont*, which he said had concerned a foreseeable injury which had not been prevented.

His Honour said that the injury from the chalk was not reasonably foreseeable and that to hold otherwise would be tantamount to imposing an absolute duty on LEAs and schools. Furthermore, even if there had been greater supervision, this would not have prevented the horseplay (*Pettican v Enfield LBC* (1970)).

The fact that the judge in *Pettican* felt inclined to come to a different conclusion from that reached in *Beaumont* illustrates the difficulty in offering a clear statement as to the level of care which is expected. As the judge said, 'the duty is to take such care as is reasonable in the circumstances of the case'. As circumstances do differ from one case to the next there is an element of unpredictability about each case. The decision in *Pettican* contrasts with a more recent case where a judge awarded damages to a pupil whose sight in one eye had been lost when a paper clip had been flicked at him by another pupil. The incident occurred indoors, during a wet lunch-time. One dinner lady had been supervising two classrooms. The judge said that this level of supervision had been inadequate.[19]

In some respects the duty to supervise continues for a short period after children are let out of school. The school must ensure that a safe system for delivering younger pupils to their parents is in operation. If children are let out early, parents must, therefore, be notified in advance or the consequences can be serious. In *Barnes v Hampshire County Council* (1969) the children were let out just one minute early, but that was long enough for one child, whose parent had not yet arrived to collect him, to wander into the street and be injured in the road. The LEA was liable because the injury was foreseeable. In *Good v ILEA* (1981) there was a system in operation in the school whereby children who were not collected at the end of the school day at 4 p.m. could go to a play centre across the school grounds to wait for their parents. Two children went instead to a pile of sand which was to be used in the construction of a swimming pool on the site. All the pupils had been warned by the school to keep away from the area in question, which had been roped off. These two children played with the sand and one threw sand containing a sharp object into the other's eye, causing an injury. The question of whether the school had been negligent in failing to ensure that the children were supervised throughout their journey to the play centre was central. The court held that the system of supervising the departure of pupils from school, either to be collected by their parents or else to go to the play centre, was satisfactory and consonant with the school's duty of care. A similar view was taken to that expressed in *Pettican* (above), that it was unreasonable as well as unrealistic to expect constant supervision of pupils to be provided.

During the course of the school day, and especially during lesson time, supervision might be expected to be more thorough. Even so, there may be moments, or even longer periods, when a teacher has to leave a class. What seems to determine the approach of the courts towards the question of adequate supervision is, above all else, whether there is a reasonably foreseeable risk of injury which could be avoided. One has to balance cases like *Barnes v Hampshire*, when the young child was let out of school early and there was a clear risk to him from the dangers of a busy road, with cases like *Pettican*, where 15-year-olds were left largely to their own devices during a wet lunch-time spent indoors. In between are a whole variety of cases where the question of liability will almost always be less than clear-cut.

One such case was *Carmarthenshire County Council v Lewis* (1955), which progressed all the way to the House of Lords before being resolved. A 4-year-old child was one of two children who were to accompany a teacher on a walk. Before they were to set off, the teacher had left the two children unattended in the classroom while she went to the lavatory. Her return was delayed by the fact she had had to attend to another child who was injured. During the 10 minutes which elapsed between her departure and return to the classroom, one of the two children had wandered out of the school, through the school gate, into the street and on to the road. A lorry driver who had swerved his vehicle to avoid hitting the child ran into a telegraph pole and was killed. His widow sued the LEA. The House of Lords held that irrespective of the lack of negligence on the teacher's part, the LEA was liable in not taking reasonable precautions to ensure that pupils of this age could not wander so easily on to the road. We cannot leave this case without noting that the question of the teacher's negligence proved extremely contentious. Unlike the House of Lords, both the trial court and the Court of Appeal had felt that she had been negligent. Where a teacher has to leave very young pupils s/he should arrange for someone else to watch them while s/he is away or else take them with him/her.

Where pupils are outside school there may still be a duty to supervise; indeed, one could say that the need for supervision is, if anything, greater because of the dangers that lurk beyond the school gate. The LEA's or school's duty to supervise therefore extends to transport to or from school (if provided by them),[20] where a similar test for the standard of care to that applied to pupils in school will operate.[21] Supervision is also very important on school trips. School trips have, in fact, resulted in very little case law although they have produced some of the most disturbing incidents. Often, because of the publicity which can attend these incidents, the legal disputes are resolved via negotiation and out-of-court settlement, not least to prevent further probing by the media into circumstances surrounding vulnerable members of society. Nevertheless, public concern when visits end in pupil fatalities (as in the Land's End and Austrian Alps incidents in the 1980s) is perfectly legitimate. The Austrian Alps incident sounded alarm bells amongst the profession and resulted in revised codes of guidance from teachers' and local authorities' associations.

It is a pity that there has not been widespread circulation of the Court of Appeal decision in a 1985 case, *Porter v City of Bradford Metropolitan Council*, which rams home the importance of exercising strict supervision and of anticipating the consequences of possibly dangerous distraction on the part of certain pupils. The facts were that a geology teacher took a party of 12 pupils, aged 15 and 16, on a field trip to Shipley Glen. During the first stage of the walk, the teacher noticed a boy rolling large stones down a slope towards a number of other pupils and told him to stop. As the trip progressed, it became clear that not all the pupils had a keen interest in geology. The teacher took those who appeared to be interested further up the glen and out of sight and sound of the remainder of the party. This remainder included the boy who had been rolling large stones. He now started to drop stones from a bridge, one of which landed on a girl and fractured her skull. The boy had been misbehaving for some 15 minutes before this incident occurred. Had the teacher been negligent? In the High Court, Bennett J felt that he had. As the teacher had already become aware of the boy's mischievous bent, he ought to have foreseen the danger and taken steps to avert it – by supervising this boy. The Court of Appeal upheld the judge's decision. Lord Justice Stephenson said that the teacher should have kept all the pupils together and stayed within sight and sound of them; the learned judge did, however, 'sympathise with him and appreciate the difficulty of his task'.

THE OCCUPIER'S LIABILITY ACT 1957

Another area giving rise to possible civil liability, specifically concerned with damage resulting from the state of premises, is occupier's liability, which is covered by the Occupier's Liability Act 1957. With many school premises in a poor state of repair – see discussion of the Education (School Premises) Regulations below – this legislation is important, although more concerned with providing a means of redress in individual cases than with the promotion of safety standards and good maintenance practice (which is more the province of the School Premises Regulations and Health and Safety at Work Etc. Act 1974, below).

The 'common duty of care' which, under the 1957 Act, an occupier owes to visitors,[22] corresponds closely to the duty of care at common law in negligence, which was discussed earlier. The 'common duty of care' is defined as a duty to take such care as is reasonable in the circumstances to see that the visitor can be reasonably safe in using the premises for the purpose for which s/he is entitled to be on them.[23] A 'visitor' is anyone with express or implied permission to be on the premises – in the school setting this would include pupils,[24] parents,[25] school governors, persons visiting on business such as educational welfare officers, the postman/woman, the milkman/woman, someone delivering office supplies or fuel, and so on. There may be more than one 'occupier' – the Act states that the occupier is the person in control of premises; that is, the governors and/or the LEA. School premises are covered by the Act, both the exterior (such as a path or step)[26] and interior (such as the floor of the school hall, which in one case was too highly polished and caused a child to slip).[27]

Among the factors to be considered in determining the standard of care which the occupier owes to a visitor is that 'an occupier must be prepared for children to be less careful than adults'.[28] A reasonable expectation that the child will be accompanied by an adult or that the parent will in some other way exercise a degree of care for their child's safety would probably be taken into account in assessing the extent of the duty owed.[29] This provision parallels the common law position in relation to the age of the child being a relevant factor in assessing the standard of care (above), with younger children assumed to be less responsible and careful.[30] Age will also be relevant to the question of whether a warning given by an occupier to a visitor is sufficient to absolve the occupier from liability. The law holds that if a proper warning (that is, one that points out the actual risk involved and could reasonably be acted upon)[31] is given to a visitor who chooses to accept the risk willingly, the occupier should not be held liable.[32] But the courts are unlikely to regard young pupils as being able to accept willingly risks of personal danger.

If the danger to which the visitor was exposed was caused not by the occupier but by a contractor, the occupier can escape liability if he acted reasonably in hiring a contractor for the job, made reasonable efforts to engage a contractor who was competent, and checked that the work was properly done.[33] In some cases the character of the work makes it difficult for the occupier to know if the work has been carried out properly, although where the work is very complex it may be necessary for the occupier to hire an architect or other professional to assess the work.[34] However, in *Woodward* (above note 24), where snow had not been cleared from a school step by a cleaner, the occupier was held liable when someone slipped; du Parcq J said that 'The craft of the charwoman may have its mysteries, but there is no esoteric quality in the nature of the work which the cleaning of a snow-covered step demands'. Thus the occupier should have checked that the contractor (on the assumption that the cleaner was a contractor, not an employee) had rendered the step safe in some way.

THE HEALTH AND SAFETY AT WORK ETC. ACT 1974

The Health and Safety at Work Etc. Act 1974 aims to protect the health, safety and welfare of employees and others in the work-place and to protect persons not at work from threats to their health and safety caused by persons at work. The Act imposes duties on employers towards their employees and others[35] and on employees towards their fellow workers and others.[36] Manufacturers and suppliers of equipment intended for use at work owe a duty to ensure that the equipment is properly designed, constructed and tested and that accurate information as to its safe use is provided.[37]

Teachers are clearly employees for this purpose, and pupils are 'others'; but who are the employers? For the most part financial delegation under LMS will not alter the position which has persisted since the enactment of the 1974 legislation: the LEA is the employer, other than where aided schools are concerned, where the governors are the employer. LMS will leave governors in either category with responsibilities in respect of health and safety provision arising out of their expenditure of delegated budgets (purchasing and maintaining equipment).[38] In so far as they are controllers of school premises, governors have to ensure that the premises and any plant or equipment on them are safe for persons other than their employees.[39]

Particularly clearly-stated duties in the Act are owed by employers to their employees. The Act requires an employer to prepare and bring to employees' attention a statement of his/her health and safety policy[40] and to ensure the health, safety and welfare at work of all his employees, so far as 'reasonably practicable'.[41] Where the risk of harm is very small and would present a wholly disproportionate burden on the employer (in money, time or trouble), it would not be 'reasonably practicable' to remove it.[42] Balancing the need for safety against the cost, and so on, can be 'a delicate judicial task'.[43]

The Act says that in fulfilling his/her duty the employer must have regard for a number of factors – relating to everything from safe storage systems to the provision of information and staff training. Some of these duties have been made more specific by regulations made under the Act by the Secretary of State.[44] For example, there is now a duty to display in the work-place an approved poster which explains most of the main duties under the Act and provides certain other information.[45] Regulations also make provision for staff safety representatives and safety committees.[46]

The duty owed to persons other than employees, which in a school includes pupils, is spelt out in less detail although is similar in scope.[47] Pupils are also protected by the duties resting on teachers, as employees, to take reasonable care for their own safety and that of others likely to be affected by their acts or omissions, and to co-operate with their employer as regards the latter's fulfilment of his/her duties under the Act.[48] Note that pupils on work experience are not treated as employees, although young people undergoing Youth Training are.[49]

The Act also makes it an offence for anyone to tamper with or misuse safety equipment.[50] Children aged under 10 are irrebuttably presumed to be incapable of forming criminal intent, and so would have to be dealt with solely under a school's disciplinary procedures (unless there are other factors which might make care proceedings in the child's interests).

The Act is enforced by inspectors on behalf of the Health and Safety Executive. Inspectors have a wide range of enforcement powers, including entry on to premises and the right to seize dangerous items, measure, photograph, take samples, and so on. The Act imposes criminal liability, and over 1,500 prosecutions take place each year in England and Wales. However, prosecutions involving schools are rare. This may seem surprising in view of the poor state of some school buildings at the present time, but it has to be remembered that conditions in school premises fall within the remit of both LEA and Her Majesty's Inspectors and that there are, in any event, alternatives to prosecution (see below). Where a breach of the Act has occurred, the courts have powers to fine and in serious and repeated cases to imprison. Inspectors generally prefer to rely on the 'improvement notice' or 'prohibition notice', which they may issue, to secure the necessary compliance with the law. An improvement notice requires specific action to be taken to remedy the problem; a prohibition notice, used in cases where there is a clear risk of injury or threat to health, prohibits the use of a room or piece of equipment, and so on, until the problem has been rectified.

SCHOOL PREMISES – SPECIFIC PROVISIONS

The Education (School Premises) Regulations 1981[51] apply to all maintained schools, including those which are grant- maintained. The regulations lay down minimum standards for school premises. If an injury to a child results from a failure to meet the required standard, civil proceedings for breach of statutory duty may be brought. In *Refell v Surrey County Council* (1964) a 12-year-old girl put up her hand to stop a swing door that was swinging towards her and her hand went through a one-eighth of an inch thick glass panel on the door. Veale J held that there had been a breach of the regulations,[52] which imposed an 'absolute duty' to assure the reasonable safety of pupils, and, because the damage was foreseeable (the glass being too thin), common law negligence as well. Two earlier cases in which damages were also awarded breach of statutory duty were *Ching v Surrey County Council* (1910) and *Morris v Carnarvon County Council* (1910). In the first of these cases, there was a hole in the school playground which caused a pupil to fall and be injured. The authority was held liable and damages were awarded. In the second case, a classroom had a heavy swing door with a powerful spring. When a girl was leaving the room the door swung very quickly and closed on her fingers. The Court of Appeal held that there was a breach of duty in that the authority should have discovered and remedied the deficiency in the door. It should be noted that in both *Morris* and *Refell* there was no disrepair as such, but rather a deficiency in the required standard of premises.

School buildings and grounds must be adequate to provide classroom, playing field, recreation and other facilities of the required standard. The standard relates not merely to the construction of facilities (for example, one-third of infants school recreation areas must be paved) but also to their size. A formula, which contains reference to the ages of pupils using the facilities, is used to determine the maximum capacity of classrooms, gymnasia, and so on. Reference is also made to corridor and storage space, private study facilities for the over-16s, wash-basins and sanitary fittings, changing rooms and showers, sick rooms, lighting, heating and acoustics. The regulations also require buildings to be reasonably resistant to fire, rain, snow, wind and rising damp and to provide a safe means of escape from fire. Staff facilities are also covered by the regulations.

It will be seen that regulation of standards is extensive; but there are limitations. For example, there is a shortage of specialist teaching accommodation in many schools, with the result that teaching of art, modern languages and science can be taking place in ordinary classrooms,[53] without the school or LEA being in breach of the law. Also, many classrooms are drab and poorly decorated,[54] which problems are also beyond the scope of these regulations. More generally, it appears that many school buildings and grounds are not meeting the required standards. A host of reports have highlighted the problem. For example, the HMIs found that 'not all schools had sufficient accommodation to give sixth form students their own social area',[55] although such provision is expressly required by the School Premises Regulations.[56] The HMIs recently found that in one-third of the secondary schools it surveyed general maintenance was 'poor': 'Peeling paint, flaking plaster and leaking roofs were the most common problems.'[57] A National Association of Inspectors and Educational Advisers conference was reportedly told in 1989 by a past president that he felt 'quite ashamed that so many of our children are being taught in such sub-standard accommodation. If the same standards that are applied to houses were applied to schools, hundreds of them would be closed down.'[58] A report of a survey of work in physical education in secondary schools by Her Majesty's Inspectorate noted that many playing fields and gymnasia were in a very poor and sometimes dangerous state.[59] The backlog of necessary repairs has been rising, partly because of budgetary pressures on LEAs which mean that repairs are given less priority, but also because many school buildings are old and expensive to maintain. The National Audit Office is expected shortly to publish a report offering the most comprehensive picture so far of the state of the country's schools; all the evidence so far suggests that it will make depressing reading.[60]

It would appear that it is only in determining the amount of space required in special school buildings that account must be taken of the special educational needs of the pupils.[61] If such is indeed the limitation, it would seem to be at variance with the principle of integration promoted by the Education Act 1981.[62] When giving advice in connection with an assessment of a child's special educational needs under section 5 of the 1981 Act, advisers are expected to refer, where relevant, to access and facilities for non-ambulant pupils.[63] But it seems that the costs of integration, and in particular the need for physical adaptation of premises, have not been adequately catered for.[64]

However, looking at disability more generally, it may be noted that there is a requirement in the Chronically Sick and Disabled Persons Act 1970, as amended, for there to be access for the disabled to and within school buildings; there must also toilet and car parking facilities for the disabled.[65] Notices of such facilities must be displayed.[66] At present these requirements need only be met if, in the circumstances, provision is 'both practicable and reasonable'. However, there is a statutory power to remove this condition and simply require 'appropriate provision' to be made.[67] Where provision is made under the 1970 Act, it must conform to the standard laid down in *Access for the Physically Disabled to Educational Buildings*.[68]

A further provision concerned specifically with safety on school premises, although not in respect of the condition of the premises themselves, is section 40 of the Local Government (Miscellaneous Provisions) Act 1982, which makes it a summary offence for anyone to cause a nuisance or disturbance on school premises. Although principally designed to enable troublesome strangers to be removed by the police or other person authorised by the LEA, the section would also appear to enable parents who are causing a nuisance to be ejected.

Case studies

The task here is not to find the 'right' answer. As we have seen, it is not always possible to predict the outcome of a case, and in any event further information about a case might be needed before the true legal position becomes clear. However, it should be possible to identify relevant legal principles, apply them to the facts, and speculate about possible liability.

1. Diane, head teacher of a comprehensive school, is asked by Alan, an enthusiastic probationer, if she would agree to a group of 10-year-old pupils performing a BMX cycle display as the prelude to the annual sports day at the school in July. Alan argues that there would be greater parental support for the event were the display to occur. The children will be using their own bikes.

Consider whether there might be any legal pitfalls of which it would be useful for Alan and Diane to be aware.

2. Elaine is escorting a class of 9- and 10-year-olds from the home economics room when she suddenly remembers that she has left the electric cooker switched on. 'Wait here and be still,' she shouts as she dashes back to the room, leaving the class standing in the corridor. Colin, a particularly obstreperous boy, notices that the door to the store cupboard nearby, which is usually kept locked, is slightly ajar. He takes out a pot of glue, removes the lid, pours glue down classmate Timothy's neck, and then throws the pot away. The pot hits Fiona in the mouth, injuring her. Elaine returns within two minutes, horrified at the tumult in the corridor.

Consider the legal implications of these events.

3. Ian, Head of Geography at Carefree Comprehensive School, and David, a probationary teacher, have organised a day trip to the Lake District for a GCSE geography group, to take place in May. The trip is not compulsory, but Ian has sought to generate interest in it, so that take-up is sufficient to make it viable, by emphasising the 'fun' of walking the hills. The children have received verbal instructions to bring 'strong walking shoes or boots, and definitely not training shoes'. Also, a letter has been sent home to parents stressing the need for suitable footwear and waterproof anoraks or jackets.

When the coach arrives at Langdale, the 22 children change into their walking shoes. One girl, Heather, has brought only plimsolls. Ian, knowing the girl comes from a large, poor family, and not wishing to embarrass her, says nothing to her about her footwear.

As the children set off up the hill, Ian quietly advises Heather to be careful in view of her unsuitable footwear. Ian remonstrates with two boys, Ashley and Michael, for showing off by walking across large boulders several metres from the main path. 'But sir', says Michael, 'you said we could have fun.'

When the party reach a suitable place, they stop and have their packed lunch. Then Ian and David discuss the features of the landscape with a group of keen pupils who are doing sketches. Meanwhile, Ashley and Michael sneak away to look at some ruins about 200 metres away. Ashley climbs a wall but slips and falls, injuring his arm. They have been away from the main party for only about 10 minutes.

Later, as the group near the completion of their descent of the hill, Heather runs down the final, grassy slope, anxious to secure a seat on the bench at the foot of the hill. She slips and sprains her ankle.

Discuss any legal issues arising from the above.

Notes

1 *Twine v Bean's Express Ltd* (1946); Rogers W V H 1989 *Winfield and Jolowicz on Tort*. (13th edn), Sweet & Maxwell, pp. 72–3.
2 Rogers, *op. cit.*, p. 72.
3 See Brazier M 1988 *Street on Torts* (8th edn), Butterworth, p. 160.
4 *Donoghue v Stevenson* (1932).
5 See, for example, *Home Office v Dorset Yacht Co* (1970).
6 *Caparo Industries plc v Dickman* (1990).
7 Ralph Gibson LJ in *Van Oppen v Clerk to the Bedford Charity Trustees* (1989) (QBD), cited with approval in the Court of Appeal in that case by Balcombe LJ.
8 Rogers, *op. cit.*, p. 114.
9 *Wilsher v Essex Area Health Authority* (1988).
10 *Lyes v Middlesex County Council* (1962); see also *Van Oppen v Clerk to the Bedford Charity Trustees* (1989).
11 *Van Oppen, op. cit.*, p. 414.
12 *Ibid.*, in the High Court (1989) at 291 per Ralph Gibson LJ.
13 *Hudson v Governors of Rotherham Grammar School* (1938); *Jeffrey v London County Council* (1954); *Simkiss v Rhondda Borough Council* (1983).
14 *Beaumont v Surrey County Council, op. cit.*
15 *Crouch v Essex County Council* (1966).
16 *Noonan v ILEA* (1974).
17 Rogers, *op. cit.*, p. 119.
18 *Ibid.*, p. 120.
19 Sir Basil Nield J – *Times Educational Supplement*, 13 Nov. 1981.
20 *Shrimpton v Hertfordshire County Council* (1911); *Jacques v Oxfordshire County Council* (1967).
21 *Ellis v Sayers Confectioners Ltd* (1963).
22 Occupier's Liability Act 1957, section 1(1).
23 *Ibid.*, section 2(2).
24 *Woodward v Mayor of Hastings* (1944); *Ward v Hertfordshire County Council* (1969).
25 *Griffiths v Smith* (1941).
26 *Murphy v Bradford Metropolitan Council* (1991);*Woodward v Mayor of Hastings* (1944).
27 *Gillmore v London County Council* (1938).
28 Occupier's Liability Act 1957, section 2(3)(a).
29 *Bates v Parker* (1954); *Phipps v Rochester Corporation* (1955).
30 See *Williams v Cardiff Corporation* (1950).
31 Occupier's Liability Act 1957, Section 2(4)(a).
32 *Ibid.*, section 2(5).
33 *Ibid.*, section 2(4)(b).
34 See Rogers, *op. cit.*, p. 219.
35 Health and Safety at Work etc. Act 1974, sections 2 and 3.
36 *Ibid.*, section 7.
37 *Ibid.*, section 6.
38 See DES Circular 7/88, para. 189.
39 *Op. cit.*, section 4.
40 *Ibid.*, section 2(3).
41 *Ibid.*, section 2(1).

42 See *Edwards v National Coal Board* (1949) and *West Bromwich Building Society v Townsend* (1983).

43 Lord Wedderburn 1986 *The Worker and the Law*, (3rd edn), Penguin, p. 417.

44 Health and Safety at work etc. Act 1974, section 15.

45 The Health and Safety Information for Employees Regulations 1989, SI 1989, No. 682.

46 Safety Representatives and Safety Committees Regulations 1977, SI 1977, No. 500. Health and Safety at Work etc. Act 1974, section 2(4) and (7).

47 *Ibid.,* section 3.

48 *Ibid.,* section 7.

49 Health and Safety (Youth Training Scheme) Regulations 1983, SI 1983 No 1919; Health and Safety (Training for Employment) Regulations 1988, SI 1988, No. 1222.

50 Section 8.

51 Made under section 10 of the Education Act 1944.

52 At that time the relevant regulations were the Standards for School Premises Regulations 1959.

53 HMI 1988 *Secondary Schools: An Appraisal by HMI*, HMSO, para.324–4.

54 *Ibid.,* para. 325.

55 *Ibid.,* para. 322; Elton, *op. cit.,* p. 277.

56 Note 52, Regulation 9.

57 Note 53, para. 325.

58 Mr Peter Mann, quoted in *The Times*, 25 Sept. 1989.

59 HMI 1990 *A Survey of Work in Physical Education in 16 Secondary Schools*, DES.

60 For a detailed review of the state of school buildings and an analysis of the causes of their poor state, see *Times Educational Supplement*, 2 March 1990, pp. 14–17.

61 Regulation 8(2).

62 See page 82 above.

63 DES Circular 22/89, Annex 1.

64 House of Commons Education, Science and the Arts Committee 1987 *Session 1986–87, Special Educational Needs: Implementation of the Education Act 1981*, vol. 1, HC, 201–1, para. 23.

65 1970 Act, section 8.

66 Disabled Persons Act 1981, section 5.

67 *Ibid.,* section 6, which requires a statutory instrument to bring it into effect.

68 Published by the Secretary of State for Social Services as Design Note 18.

CHAPTER 9

Teachers as employees

INTRODUCTION

The regulation of teachers' employment contracts has increased in recent years. Teachers' terms and conditions of employment are now found in a complex combination of statute, regulations, orders and common law. Recent statutory provisions govern the appointment, discipline and dismissal of staff, as well as their pay and conditions of service. These are in addition to the framework of employment law rights which apply to all employees. This chapter looks at both the general and specific legal aspects of employing teachers.

The main statutes which will be considered in this chapter are the Education (No.2) Act 1986 and the Education Reform Act 1988, as well as various Regulations issued under those Statutes. For example, s.218 of the ERA empowers the Secretary of State for Education to make Regulations regarding qualifications of teachers.[1] There are also Regulations[2] issued under s.222 of the ERA. This empowers the Minister to modify existing statutory provisions relating to employment protection rights. These modifications are discussed in detail where appropriate.

The E (No.2) Act sets out procedures relating to the employment of teachers in county, controlled, and special agreement schools (maintained schools) *without* a delegated budget. Control over staffing in those schools lies with the Local Education Authority (LEA), although the governing bodies of those schools have the right to be consulted.

The ERA established local management of schools (LMS) – maintained schools *with* a delegated budget. This will include the vast majority of schools by 1993. In those schools, the governing body has control over staffing, in consultation with the LEA. However, the LEA is still the employer.

The ERA also introduced grant-maintained schools, where governing bodies are guaranteed complete control over staffing (teaching and non-teaching). Staff in those schools are transferred to the governing body along with the other 'property' of the school. The responsibilities of being an employer are also transferred.

Clearly, governors in grant-maintained schools and schools under LMS will need to be aware of statutory employment rights and duties affecting their staff. They will need to work closely with the LEAs, and the LEAs will continue to provide advice to governing bodies, particularly in maintained schools with delegated budgets, where ultimate responsibility for staff still lies with the LEA.

This chapter also deals with the terms and conditions of employment of teaching staff, and how they are established. The relevant statute is the Teachers' Pay and Conditions Act 1987 together with Orders made subsequent to it. There have been great changes. The negotiating machinery of the Burnham Committee was abolished in 1987, and replaced by an Interim Advisory Body. The School Teachers' Pay and Conditions Bill 1991 provides for the reintroduction of a national negotiating body, with provision for LEAs to 'opt–out' of the national agreement. We consider the position of trade unions in the negotiating machinery, and look at the future of collective bargaining.

RECRUITMENT OF STAFF

The powers of appointment laid down by statute are central to recruitment of staff. But it is also necessary to consider who actually employs staff in schools. The contract of employment is central to any employment relationship, so it is necessary to ascertain the parties to the contract.

There are other statutory requirements which affect recruitment – relating to qualifications, advertising for staff and discrimination.

Who is the employer?

It is important to ascertain who the employer is, as it determines who has ultimate responsibility for the staff. If, for example, an employee acts negligently in the course of their employment, the employer could be vicariously liable for damages (see chapter eight). If a sacked teacher successfully claims unfair dismissal, the employer will be liable to pay compensation.

Despite the changes in control over staffing, in most cases the Local Education Authority remains the employer. The employer of teaching and non-teaching staff in county, controlled, special agreement and special maintained schools is the LEA, whether or not the school has a delegated budget.

In voluntary aided schools the governors are, as previously, treated as employers, except in certain circumstances where the LEA is deemed to be the employer (see page 194).

The staff of a school which becomes grant-maintained transfer to the governors, who have control over staffing and also the responsibilities of being the employer.

Conflicts could easily arise, particularly in schools under LMS where, for example, the governing body is responsible for dismissal of staff, but the LEA is liable to pay compensation if the dismissal is unfair. The LEA cannot prevent the dismissal, so clearly there needs to be close co-operation between the two bodies. Moreover, this division in responsibilities could leave the teacher who is dismissed wondering who they should complain against in an industrial tribunal. This is dicussed below at page 194.

Staffing levels

LEAs are under a general duty to ensure adequate staffing levels in schools (s.8 Education Act 1944). Furthermore, s.218(1)(d) of the ERA empowers the Secretary of State to make provision in respect of teaching staff. The Education (Teachers) Regulations 1989 provide that:

'At any school . . . there shall be employed a staff of teachers suitable and sufficient in numbers for the purpose of securing the provision of education appropriate to the ages, abilities, aptitudes and needs of the pupils having regard to any arrangements for the utilisation of the services of teachers employed otherwise than at the school.' (Reg. 6(1))

The staff must include a head teacher (Reg.6(2)) and teachers must be suitably qualified (Reg.6(3)).

In grant-maintained schools and schools with a delegated budget, it will be the governors who decide on the staffing levels. Clearly they will need to do this in consultation with the head teacher.

In maintained schools without a delegated budget, the LEA must determine a 'complement of teaching and non-teaching posts'.[3] The LEA's powers over the appointment and dismissal of staff extend only to the complement.

Appointment of staff

The procedures to be followed in the appointment and dismissal of teaching and non-teaching staff are laid down by statute, and they vary depending on the type of school. However, staffing in all schools is subject to orders and regulations made by the Secretary of State and to the statutory obligations which affect all employees.

– county, controlled, special agreement and special maintained schools without a delegated budget

In these schools, LEAs still maintain control. The procedures which apply are contained in the E (No.2) Act.

If a vacancy occurs, the authority must first decide whether or not to retain the post as part of the complement. If they decide to fill the post it must be advertised in accordance with s.38(3)(a) (see page 188), unless the LEA wishes to appoint a person already employed by them, or who has been appointed to take up employment at a future date. In that case, the governing body has the power to determine the specification for the post, in consultation with the head teacher. And the LEA must 'have regard to' the specification (s.38(4)(c)).

Where the post is advertised, the school governors interview candidates and recommend who to appoint (s.38(3)(b)). However the LEA is not bound to accept the governing body's recommendation.

The governing body can delegate its functions to one or more governors, the head teacher or a combination of the two acting together. In any case, the head teacher, and a person appointed by the LEA, have the right to attend meetings, but only for the purpose of giving advice. It is envisaged that governing bodies will make use of such advice, seeking the advice of head teachers on the suitability of candidates. LEA representatives will be available to advise on statutory requirements, such as the anti-discrimination legislation.

The procedures do not apply to the appointment of temporary staff. The LEA simply appoints the person they want. 'Temporary' is not defined and the temporary or permanent nature of an appointment may be called into question. However, it is likely that courts or tribunals will be guided by the definition in the ERA, which states that temporary means an appointment for up to four months duration (in schools with a delegated budget).

Heads and deputy heads

The appointment of head teachers is dealt with in s.37 E (No.2) Act. The governing body has a greater say in the appointment of head teachers (and where the articles of government specify, deputy heads[4]) than for other teaching staff, though the LEA are again entitled to decline to appoint the governing body's recommended candidate. However, the LEA cannot appoint a person unless they are recommended by a selection panel.

The selection panel is composed according to s.36. It must have the same number of governing body appointees as LEA appointed members, and no less than three of each. Meetings of the selection panel can be requisitioned at any time by the LEA, so long as they give reasonable notice. Once constituted, the panel regulates its own proceedings, subject to Education (School Government) Regulation 1989 Part IV. However, the selection panel cannot operate without the full complement of members. In *R v Birmingham City Council ex parte McKenna* (1991) the High Court held that the statue is specific. A panel must be properly constituted in accordance with the statutory provisions, and a meeting with less than a full complement was not a selection panel. Furthermore, provision is made for the replacement of a panel member and this procedure must be followed, otherwise the panel's selection will be invalidated. Decisions of the panel must be by a majority of the members, but there is no provision for a casting vote.

The LEA's Chief Education Officer, or his or her nominee, has the right to attend all meetings of the panel, including the interview, but only to give advice.

The selection panel's duty is to interview candidates and to make a recommendation for appointment. If there is a failure to agree on an appropriate candidate, the selection panel must repeat the process, interviewing other applicants or asking the authority to re-advertise the post. The process must similarly be repeated if the LEA decline to appoint the recommended candidate. There is clearly the possibility of an impasse. LEA appointees and governing body appointees may have differing views as to the appropriate person wanted, and if they fail to agree, the LEA cannot make an appointment.

If the selection panel fails to agree on the applicants to be interviewed, the governing body members of the panel, and the other members of the panel, can each nominate up to two candidates for interview.

Pending the appointment of a head teacher, the LEA must appoint an acting head in consultation with the governing body. However, the above procedures do not apply.

Deputy head teachers are appointed according to the articles of government, by one of two procedures. Either using a selection panel as above, with the difference that the head teacher has the right to attend meetings of the panel. The head teacher is probably best qualified to know who is best for the job, and the panel would be advised to have regard to his or her advice.

Alternatively, the articles can provide for the appointment to be made in the same way as for other teaching staff, following the procedures laid down in s.38.

The LEA is not required to appoint an acting deputy head, as they are for an acting head. However, this would not preclude a provision in the articles for such an appointment.

None of these procedures applies to the temporary appointment of a head or deputy, pending the return to work of the holder of the post, or while the necessary procedures to fill the post permanently are being carried out.

– county, controlled and special agreement schools with a delegated budget.

When the 1988 Act introduced local management of schools, amendments were also made to the procedures for the appointment of staff. Where schools have a delegated budget, the provisions of the 1986 Act no longer apply and governors have power over staffing appointments, in consultation with the LEA. The relevant provisions are found in Schedule 3 to the 1988 Act.

In these schools, the procedure relating to appointment of teaching staff is similar to that for schools without delegated budgets, except that it is carried out by the governing body. They are under a duty to advertise the post, interview candidates and make a recommendation to the LEA. The major difference is that the LEA *must* accept the governing body's recommendation.

Before advertising, the governing body must send a copy of the specification for the post to the authority, who may nominate for appointment a person who is already employed by them or who has been appointed to take up employment in the future, or a person employed at an aided school maintained by the authority, with the consent of the governing body of the aided school.

The post need not be advertised where the governing body accept for appointment the LEA's nominee or they decide to recommend a person who is already employed at the school.

The procedures do not have to be followed for a temporary appointment. In these provisions, temporary is defined as a period of four months, or at least where the governing body believes that the period of the appointment will not exceed four months. The body can recommend a person for appointment for whatever duration they specify, and the LEA is under a duty to appoint that person on those terms.

Heads and deputy heads

The procedures here are similar to those which apply to the appointment of head teachers in schools without a delegated budget, although again the governors have more control. The governing body must follow the procedures relating to advertising the post and setting up a selection panel. However, only governors are nominated to sit on the panel, of whom there must be at least three. The LEA has no say in the appointment – they must simply implement the governing body's recommendation. They can refuse to appoint the recommended person only if that person does not meet the required qualifications.[5]

– grant maintained schools

In these schools, the governors, as employers, have great freedom. The LEA plays no part in staffing. The appointment of staff is entirely in the hands of the governing body, subject, of course, to statutory provisions concerning recruitment (in particular, sex and race discrimination). Governing bodies of grant-maintained schools must also comply with the same Regulations as LEA maintained schools in relation to employment. Therefore, they must ensure there are sufficient numbers of teaching staff[6] and that they are suitably qualified.[7]

Grant maintained schools are also bound by the same pay and conditions as apply in LEA maintained schools, although the School

Teachers Pay and Conditions (No.2) Bill allows grant maintained
schools to opt out of the statutory terms and conditions, following the
establishment of a pay review body (see page 209).

There are no specific requirements for advertising and selection
procedures, but governing bodies will be required to act in good faith
and for proper purposes in making decisions, the same as the LEAs.[8]
To ensure that they can be seen to be exercising their powers properly,
and to avoid breach of the discrimination legislation, governing bodies
should establish procedures for recruitment and selection.

– aided schools

Appointment of staff in these schools is still governed by the
Education Act 1944. Section 24 provides that appointment and
dismissal of teachers is regulated by the articles of government,
subject to certain requirements contained in sub-section (2):

1   the LEA determines the staffing level;
2   the governing body makes appointments, but the LEA can
    prohibit appointments if so stated in the articles of government, or
    if determined by order of the Secretary of State;
3   the LEA can give directions on educational qualifications.

However, these provisions do not apply if an aided school has a
delegated budget. In that case, the role of the governing body is
similar to that in maintained schools with a delegated budget.

Qualifications

Whoever has responsibility for appointing teaching staff can appoint
only persons who are suitably qualified. The required qualifications
are laid down in the Education (Teachers) Regulations 1989.[9] They
were introduced by the Secretary of State on 1.8.90, under s.218 of the
ERA, and came into force on 1.9.90.

The Regulations open up the teaching profession by providing ways
to qualify to teach other than the traditional Postgraduate Certificate in
Education or Bachelor of Education. It is envisaged that in the
majority of cases qualified teacher status (QTS) will be gained through
the traditional route, but it now possible to qualify by way of a period
of 'in-house' training as a 'licensed teacher'.

Following a transitional period (which allowed applications for
QTS to be made under the 1982 Regulations up until 1.11.90) the only
way to obtain QTS is by the following routes:

1   successful completion of an approved course for the degree of Bachelor of Education, the Certificate in Education, and Post-Graduate Certificate in Education or a comparable academic award;

2   successful completion of a course of initial training for teachers in schools in Scotland or Northern Ireland or by being recognised as a qualified school teacher in either of those countries;

3   by successful completion of mutually recognised higher education diplomas in EC countries;[10]

4   by satisfactory completion of a period of service as a licensed teacher.

Licensed teacher status

One of the biggest problems facing education is the shortage of teachers. By introducing licensed teacher status, the government is seeking to attract more people into the profession by offering a way in for those without formal qualifications. This route is available to:

1   overseas trained teachers, other than EC nationals;

2   persons who meet the following requirements[11]:

●   English and Mathematics at Grade C GCSE, or an equivalent qualification (as listed in Appendix 1 to DES Circular 7/89, though this list is not exhaustive); and

●   at least two years' full time higher education, as defined in Regulation 3(2), or the part time equivalent; and

●   be at least 24[11a] years old (except for overseas students).

To attain QTS, the 'trainee teacher' must first obtain a licence or, in the case of overseas trained teachers, an authorisation[11b] from the Secretary of State. However, individuals cannot apply for a licence. The LEA or governing body, whichever is appropriate, must make the application. Thus, this route applies only to those who have already been selected for training. In making the application, the LEA or governing body must have regard not only to the suitability of the candidate but also to their own ability to provide the relevant training and experience necessary for the teacher to attain qualified status.

The governing bodies of grant-maintained schools, in their proposals for grant-maintained status, must explain what arrangements would be made for the induction and in-service training of teachers.[12]

In schools without delegated budgets the LEA must make the application. It will usually be for a named school, but in the case of overseas trained teachers with one year's training experience, employed as supply or peripatetic teachers, it can apply to a named authority. Normally teachers will be expected to remain with the school or LEA who recommend them for licensed teacher status.

In schools with delegated budgets, the governing body can apply for a licence, but only with the consent of the LEA who will be responsible for forwarding the application. In grant-maintained schools and non-maintained special schools, the governing body must apply directly to the Secretary of State. Clearly in that case, the licence will apply to a particular school.

Responsibilities of LEAs and governing bodies

These provisions put the onus for training and assessment of unqualified teachers (or those qualified overseas) upon the LEAs and governing bodies.

When submitting an application for a licence, the LEA or governing body must give particulars of the training to be given and the means to be used to assess the licensee's competence.

It is envisaged that LEAs and governing bodies who intend appointing licensed teachers regularly will submit a general policy statement to the Secretary of State, prior to making individual applications, following DES advice. The statement should ideally cover policies on appointment, training, assessment, monitoring and support for licensed teachers.[13]

However, general policy is not enough. The training programme must be tailored to fit individual needs. The training requirements of an applicant with no teaching experience will differ from those of an overseas trained applicant with relevant practical experience.

Guidance as to the qualities required to attain QTS is included in DES Circular 18/89 (Appendix 2) and it is up to LEAs or governing bodies to arrange the assessment of licensees in order to ensure the relevant training is provided to meet the competencies specified.

Training period

Licences are issued initially for two years and generally QTS will not be granted before the licensed teacher has completed two years' full time experience as a licensed teacher or, if working part time, after the period specified in the licence. The licence can be extended for one year, if the LEA or governing body consider that they cannot recommend a teacher for QTS after two years, but may be able to do so in a further year's time.

In certain circumstances, licensed teachers may acquire QTS earlier than the two year period. This applies to overseas-trained teachers, teachers from independent schools or further or higher education institutions or Armed Service Education Officers or Instructors, who have previous teaching experience. They must complete one year as a licensed teacher, except overseas-trained teachers who may qualify after one term.

Application for qualified teacher status

At the end of the licence period, again it is not the individual who applies for QTS, but the appropriate authority. In schools without delegated budgets it is the LEA. Where the school has a delegated budget, the governing body must apply, with the consent of the LEA. Governing bodies of grant maintained schools have sole responsibility.

In their application, the LEA or governing body should include 'brief details of the programme of in-service training undertaken as a licensed teacher (this may simply be by reference to the original application for licence).'[14]

If the LEA or governing body consider that no recommendation can be made for QTS, the Secretary of State must be informed. A record will be kept of those who fail to qualify after a period as a licensed teacher, but there is nothing to indicate that a different LEA or governing body cannot subsequently apply for a licence for the failed trainee.

This raises the question of how LEAs and governing bodies know that the licensed teachers have achieved the required standard. Clearly head teachers will have to play a major part in the assessment of trainees. But, is this satisfactory? Head teachers' duties already include appraisal of staff. With this, and other management duties introduced by legislation, the workload of head teachers has greatly increased, leaving them with little time to monitor and assess licensed teachers.

In submitting the application for licensed teacher status, the relevant body has to submit details of the method of assessment. There is, however, no way of ensuring the same standard is being achieved throughout the system. This could be a particular problem in grant maintained schools, where governors are concerned only with what happens in their own school. At least LEAs can ensure a common standard in schools within their area.

There are obvious disadvantages for LEAs and governing bodies in employing licensed teachers. It will involve extra work as they will have to plan individual training programmes. It will also involve extra cost and effort. However, funds are available from the DES, under the Local Education Authority Training Grant Scheme.[15]

On the other hand, school governors may decide it is cheaper to employ unqualified or newly qualified teachers. And cost will be an important consideration for grant-maintained schools and schools with a delegated budget. Funds allocated for staffing do not take account of where teachers are on the salary scale. Obviously, if a school has a staff profile of older, more experienced teachers, the staffing costs will be greater. The governors may well decide it is advantageous to appoint someone at the lower end of the scale.

Other qualifications

The Regulations also contain provisions relating to health. A person can be refused employment on grounds of ill-health.

Furthermore, a teacher can be barred from employment by the Secretary of State in three circumstances:

1   medical grounds;
2   grounds of misconduct (for example, criminal conduct which makes a person unsuitable to teach children);
3   educational grounds (for example, where a teacher has previously been dismissed for poor performance).

Teachers of visually or hearing impaired children

Qualification for teachers of a class of pupils who are visually or hearing impaired or both, are set out in the Regulations. These teachers are required to have approved qualifications, unless employed to teach a craft, trade or domestic subject. However, there is provision for the temporary employment of teachers who intend to acquire the approved qualification.[16]

Probationary period

The Regulations provide for a probationary period[17] for newly qualified teachers, except for licensed teachers who are granted QTS and who have gained experience comparable to that of probationary teachers.

Under the Regulations, the LEA or governing body must take the decision as to whether a teacher has successfully completed a probationary period. The normal period for probation is one year, although the LEA or governing body have power to waive the requirement or to substitute a shorter period.

The LEA or governing body may decide that the teacher has failed the probationary period. In that case, the teacher is found to be not fitted to their current post, but they are eligible to serve a new period of probation in another post.

Advertisements

There is a statutory requirement to advertise vacancies for teaching posts and headships in maintained schools, with or without a delegated budget.

In relation to heads and, in some cases, deputy heads, the LEA[18] or the governing body,[19] as appropriate, is under a duty to advertise the post nationally in appropriate publications. If the vacancy is for other teaching staff, the LEA[20] or governing body[21] are obliged to advertise the vacancy 'in a manner likely in their opinion to bring it to the notice of persons (including employees of theirs) who are qualified to fill the post'.

Clearly, posts must be widely advertised and probably in publications which are commonly regarded as a likely source of such vacancies. In *R. v Derbyshire County Council ex parte Times Supplements and others* (1990), a case of judicial review, Watkins LJ said that:

'no sensible education committee or county council could properly have concluded that abandoning its policy of advertising in the TES and switching national advertising to the Guardian would lead to the county council reaching a higher number of qualified teachers looking for jobs and certainly not any higher number such as to justify the extra expense involved in advertising in the Guardian'.

In this case, the Council's decision not to advertise in the TES was held to be an abuse of power, in bad faith and for an improper purpose, because the decision was not for valid educational reasons.

It would be interesting what the courts would make of a governing body (in a school with a delegated budget) which departed from the advertising policy of the LEA. Unless they had sound educational reasons for doing so, it may be found to be in breach of the statutory duty to advertise contained in the 1988 Act.

Discrimination

Advertisements are also covered by the Sex Discrimination Act 1975 (SDA) and the Race Relations Act 1976 (RRA). Sections 38 and 29 of the SDA and RRA respectively provide that it is unlawful to publish an advert which indicates an intention to discriminate on grounds of sex or marital status (SDA) or on racial grounds (RRA).

The use of a job description in an advertisement which has a sexual connotation is taken to indicate an intention to discriminate.[22] Thus advertising for a school*master* or head*mistress* would be a criminal offence, unless it was made clear that the job was open to both women and men.

It is lawful to show an intention to discriminate in favour of a particular sex or racial group, where the discrimination itself is lawful because sex or race is a 'genuine occupational qualification'.[23] For example, if the job entails the provision of personal services promoting welfare, which can 'most effectively be provided' by a person of a particular race.[24] This could apply to the employment of, say, a student counsellor.

Sections 29 and 38 are enforceable only by the Equal Opportunities Commission (EOC) or Commission for Racial Equality (CRE), not individual applicants. The anti-discrimination legislation does, however, provide important individual employment rights, including non-discrimination selection, which will be discussed in detail below (see page 202).

Rehabilitation of Offenders

The Rehabilitation of Offenders Act 1974 provides that certain criminal convictions are 'spent' after a specified period of time. Once spent, the individual is not obliged to disclose the conviction when applying for a job, even if expressly asked the question.

However, some professions are exempt, where the existence of a spent conviction can justify dismissal or refusal to employ. Teaching is one of the professions listed, so that rehabilitation does not give an unrestricted right of employment. If applicants are asked about previous convictions, they must be disclosed.[25]

Non-teaching staff are not affected, and do not have to disclose spent convictions.

TERMINATION OF EMPLOYMENT

In this section we examine the discipline, dismissal and premature retirement of staff. The most significant point about the statutory provisions discussed is the division of power between governing bodies and the LEAs. In locally managed schools, the governing bodies make the decisions, but the LEA pays.

It is arguable that there has been an attempt to treat public sector employment as if it is the private sector. The result is an anomolous position which resembles nothing in the private sector.[26]

Discipline of staff

The E (No.2) Act and ERA deal with the issue of discipline. Both provide the power to suspend staff, with pay. In maintained schools without a delegated budget, the LEA's existing disciplinary rules and procedures continue to apply, although E (No 2) Act gives powers of discipline and dismissal to the governing body. However, the LEA has ultimate power, as they may direct the governing body to end the suspension, so long as the person suspended is part of the complement.

Where the school has a delegated budget, the ERA states that the governing body or head teacher can suspend a member of staff, but only the governing body can end the suspension. The ERA requires governing bodies to establish disciplinary and grievance rules and procedures. The issue of discipline is a sensitive one, and it would be advisable for governing bodies to follow existing good practice adopted by the LEA.

In grant-maintained schools, discipline of staff rests with the governors, with no specific statutory requirements except that the articles of government must establish disciplinary rules and procedures and grievance procedures.

The governors will, of course, be bound by statutory obligations which apply to all employees. They are also bound by the contracts of employment of staff transferred to the grant-maintained school. This may include disciplinary and grievance procedures established by the LEA, though they will not necessarily be contractual.

Dismissal of staff

The power to dismiss staff, like appointment and discipline, varies according to category of school.

– county, controlled and special agreement schools **without** a delegated budget

LEAs have the power to dismiss teaching and non-teaching staff, if they are part of the 'staff complement' (s.41 E (No.2) Act). There is a duty to consult the governing body and head teacher of the school, but the LEA's decision prevails. The LEA is also responsible for any payments relating to the dismissal; for example, in accordance with the LEA's policy or as required by statute (unfair dismissal, redundancy payment).

– county, controlled and special agreement schools **with** a delegated budget

In these schools, the LEA has no control over the decision to dismiss staff, but can still be left with the responsibility of footing the bill for any payments relating to the dismissal.

The governing bodies of schools with delegated budgets determine when a teacher's employment should be terminated (Para.8, Schedule 3, ERA). They must inform the LEA in writing of their reasons for bringing the employment to an end, and the LEA must implement that decision.

If the teacher concerned is not employed solely at the school involved, as in the case of supply and peripatetic teachers, the LEA must remove the teacher from that school. Where the teacher is employed solely at the school, and has not resigned within 14 days of the notification to the LEA, the LEA must dismiss that employee, either with or without notice.

The governing body must give the person to be dismissed an opportunity to make representations, and the right to appeal against the decision to terminate the contract. The head teacher or chief education officer (or their representative) have the right to attend all meetings to discuss the dismissal. Their duty is to give advice, which the governing body must consider.[27] Bearing in mind the statutory rights relating to unfair dismissal (discussed below) governing bodies are likely to need this advice.

The LEA has no control – they must dismiss when required to do so and cannot dismiss in any other circumstances, except where a teacher is not suitably qualified.[28]

Furthermore, the governing body may decide that a payment should be made to compensate the employee for dismissal or to secure resignation (s.46 ERA). They also determine the amount to be paid, unless the payment is required by law, either under contract or by statute. The LEA can make a payment only in accordance with the governing body's decision, regardless of the LEA's own policies. So if, for example, the LEA has an enhanced redundancy payments' scheme, the governing body is not bound by it, unless it is part of the teacher's contract.

If a member of staff is dismissed with notice they are entitled to normal pay for the notice period. If the LEA makes payment beyond the notice period (maybe implementing their policy) the cost cannot be deducted from the school's budget.

Any other costs incurred in respect of dismissal cannot be deducted from the school's budget. Compensation for unfair dismissal, and any legal fees incurred, would be an additional cost for the LEA, even though they have no control over dismissal and play only an advisory role. They can deduct the costs, or part of them, if they have a *good reason* for doing so. It will be for the courts to decide what is a good reason, but it seems that LEA policy will not count as a good reason. Certainly, a 'no redundancy policy' does not fall within that category (s.46(6) ERA). However, it is arguable that if the governing body ignore the LEA's advice that a dismissal would be unfair, it would be a good reason to deduct any compensation from the school's budget. The result, of course, would be that the staff and pupils of the school would suffer. Governing bodies are going to need careful guidance on employment practice.

– grant maintained schools

Here, as we have seen, the governors are solely responsible for staffing, including dismissal. It is worth noting again that the governors will be bound by the contracts of employment of staff transferred to the school. There are no specific provisions relating to dismissal, except that in their proposals for grant-maintained status, the governors must include disciplinary rules and procedures. These will be relevant in relation to claims for unfair dismissal (see pages 193–4).

– aided schools

Similarly to grant-maintained schools, the governors of aided schools have responsibility for staff. However, the LEA may *require* a member of staff to be dismissed. In that case, the LEA is deemed to be the employer for the purposes of unfair dismissal (s.80 Employment Protection (Consolidation) Act 1978).

Premature retirement

Premature retirement is retirement before the normal retiring age, which is the age at which teachers are required to retire under their contract of employment (generally between 60 and 65), on grounds of redundancy or in the interests of 'the efficient discharge of the employer's functions'. It is not permitted below the age of 50, unless it is due to infirmity.

The provisions relating to premature retirement are found in the Teachers (Compensation for Redundancy and Premature Retirement) Regulations 1989.[29] The DES has produced technical guidance on the operation of these regulations.[30] Here we consider the division in power between LEAs and governing bodies. There are two decisions to be made in relation to premature retirement. First, whether in principle a person should be offered premature retirement, and secondly whether they should be credited with extra years' service, thus enhancing their pension entitlement.

Conflict may arise in maintained schools with delegated budgets where the governing body is the 'deciding authority' on both the above questions, but the LEA is the 'compensating authority'; that is, they have to make the payments, which cannot be deducted from the school's budget (s.46(5) ERA). If the LEA has a 'good reason' it can deduct the costs. For example, if the number of years credited by the governing body is in excess of the LEAs own practice. The governing body, to avoid cost to the school, will need to consult the LEA before making their decision.

Teachers' contracts, agreed with the LEA prior to a budget being delegated to the school, may include provisions on premature retirement. If so, the governing body will be bound to honour those legal obligations.

STATUTORY EMPLOYMENT RIGHTS

In this section, we look at employment rights which affect all employees, but in the context of teaching staff. It is not possible here to go into the same detail as an employment law textbook, so specific points are highlighted where Regulations affect these rights or cases have arisen concerning teachers.

In order to rely on statutory rights, in most cases there are certain qualifications and exclusions. Most employment protection rights (with the exception of the discrimination legislation) apply only to those employed under a contract of employment.[31] There is also, generally, a qualifying period of service, eg for unfair dismissal it is two years. These qualifications present no bar to teachers who are employed on a full-time permanent basis, but for temporary and part-time teachers and those on fixed term contracts it is not so straightforward.

Unfair dismissal

Whoever has responsibiity for dismissal will be subject to the statutory rights on unfair dismissal.[32] Section 54 of the Employment Protection (Consolidation) Act 1978 states that employees have the right not to be unfairly dismissed. They can complain to an industrial tribunal[33] which has the power to grant the remedies of compensation and/or re-employment.[34]

First, the employee must establish that they have been dismissed. This is defined[35] as termination by the employer (with or without notice), non-renewal of a fixed term contract and resignation by the employee in circumstances where they would be entitled to leave without notice. That has been held to mean where the employer is in breach of the contract[36] and includes the situation where the employers' conduct has become so intolerable that no reasonable person can be expected to carrying on working. Although a contractual test is applied, the tribunals have interpreted it widely, and covers the situation where an employee 'can take no more'. So if, for example, the head teacher in a school acted in a way which continually undermined a member of staff, particularly in front of others, and as a result the teacher left, the teacher may be able to claim unfair dismissal even though they resigned.

Complaint against whom?

If a teacher wishes to bring a complaint, against whom should it lie? We have seen that in maintained schools (with or without a delegated budget) the employer is the LEA, even though it may be the governors who decide whether or not to dismiss. And in some circumstances it may be the head teacher's action which leads to the claim for unfair dismissal. So who is the respondent?

In schools without a delegated budget nothing has changed. The LEA is the employer, decides upon dismissal and is party to proceedings in the tribunal. But in schools with a delegated budget, by Regulations[37] issued under s.222 ERA, the governing body is treated as the employer where an employee is dismissed. The claim in the tribunal will be against the governing body, and the statutory provisions apply as if the governing body had dismissed, and the reason for dismissal is the reason given by the governing body.

This does not seem to cover the situation where the teacher resigns and claims constructive dismissal. However, the DES advice[38] is that the provision applies where the governing body *fails* to take action (for example, fails to stop action by a head teacher which causes a member of staff to leave). Also, the governing body is responsible for acts done on its behalf, and again this would be applied to action by the head teacher. Clearly, it is difficult to establish a 'reason for dismissal' if a person has resigned – but there is the opportunity to put forward potentially fair reasons for the acts which led to the teacher's departure.

Reasons for dismissal

Under the statute, there are certain specified reasons which may render dismissal fair. The employer must put forward the reason for dismissal and, as seen above, in most cases the onus will be on the governing body. We consider these potentially fair reasons in relation to teachers.

As well as being for a potentially fair reason, the dismissal must be implemented fairly. The employer must follow a fair procedure. This was clearly established by the House of Lords in *Polkey v A E Dayton Services Ltd* (1987). In some areas, the procedures to be followed are laid down in Regulations.

Capability

A dismissal may be fair if it is on grounds of lack of ability to perform the work or lack of qualifications.[39] In relation to teaching staff, the qualifications required are clearly laid down in the Education (Teachers) Regulations 1989. The LEA has power to dismiss (or refuse to appoint) in any maintained school if the teacher lacks those qualifications.[40] So, for example, where a licensed teacher does not meet the required standard, and no application is made for QTS on their behalf, they may be dismissed for a potentially fair reason – lack of qualifications. However, the dismissal must also be procedurally fair. For example, there must have been the opportunity to reach that standard, i.e. an appropriate training course.[41]

If dismissal is due to poor performance, staff need to be told why their work is not up to standard, and be given the opportunity to improve, with training if appropriate. This suggests some form of staff appraisal and development, and teachers' contracts include the duty to participate in national procedures. There is provision for the Secretary of State to introduce Regulations on staff appraisal, and these are expected to come into force in September 1991. In the meantime, LEAs and governing bodies will have to consult head teachers about performance of staff for the purposes of dismissal.

Ill-health is also covered by capability. Health standards are covered by Education (Teachers) Regulations which set out the procedure not only for appointment of staff but also for their further employment. An industrial tribunal would expect medical evidence to be sought before an employee is dismissed on grounds of ill-health.[42] The Regulations require a medical examination to be carried out, and it is arguable that unless the procedure laid down in Regulation 9 is followed, dismissal will be unfair.

Conduct

Dismissal for misconduct is potentially fair. If it involves gross misconduct (eg theft of employer's property, violence at work) it can be fair to dismiss for a first offence. Less serious offences generally call for warnings before dismissal is imposed.[43]

Dismissal for disobeying reasonable orders from the employer can be fair. What is reasonable will depend on the contract of employment. But in the case of teachers the limit to those orders may be difficult to ascertain as their contracts require them to carry out 'such particular duties which may be assigned' to them, in accordance with such directions of the head teacher 'which may reasonably be given'[44] (see page 207).

Again, dismissal will be fair only if a fair procedure is followed. Sechedule 3 to the 1988 Act states that LEAs must have disciplinary rules and procedures. The procedures should give staff an opportunity to answer allegations and the right to an oral hearing. They should also have the opportunity to appeal against decisions of the governing body. The appeal should be to a person or body who was not involved in the decision to dismiss (natural justice would require this anyway). The DES recommends[45] that the governing body should appoint a panel with responsibility for appeals and that they should not be involved in decisions on dismissals.

Although the 1988 Act applies only to schools with a delegated budget, fair procedures will have to be followed by LEAs in all schools and tribunals will expect the procedures set out in Schedule 3 to be applied, at the very least.

The ACAS Code on Disciplinary Rules and Procedures states that conduct outside of work should lead to dismissal only if it affects a person's suitability to carry out their work. As teachers have contact with and influence on children, this might be quite widely interpreted, but the tribunal will consider each case on its merits.[46]

In *Norfolk County Council v Bernard* (1979), a drama teacher was dismissed following conviction for a criminal offence relating to the possession of cannabis. The tribunal in this case stated that an offence committed outside employment might justify dismissal if it 'seriously and genuinely affects the employee's relationship with his fellow employees' or 'if the nature of the offence . . . made the employee a danger to others, particularly children'.

It was held that the dismissal was unfair, because the Council had failed to take account of support from staff and parents, and the teacher's previous good conduct.

The tribunal will consider the reasonableness of the employer's decision to dismiss in the light of the risk involved. It seems that if it is arguable that there is a potential risk, it is open to the tribunal to find the dismissal fair.

In *Wiseman v Salford City Council* (1981) a drama teacher was twice charged with gross indecency in a public lavatory. He was dismissed as it was believed that there was a potential risk in his continuing to work with young people. The EAT rejected the argument that it was self-evident that the teacher was not a risk to teenage boys. As the subject was 'highly controversial' it was open to the tribunal to find the employer's action reasonable and the dismissal fair.

Redundancy

Dismissal on ground of redundancy is potentially fair. It will, however, be unfair if a person is 'unfairly selected' for redundancy. Redundancy selection must be in accordance with an agreed procedure or normal practice. LEAs will be able to continue to follow existing procedures. It would be advisable for governing bodies to follow those procedures also, particularly if agreed with the recognised trade union.

Statutory restriction

It is potentially fair to dismiss an employee if continuing to employ them would be unlawful; for example, if an overseas teacher did not have a required work permit.

Some other substantial reason

This is a catch all section, which states that a reason 'which justifies dismissal' will be potentially fair. Tribunals have recognised various reasons as some other substantial reason. It most often arises in the context of re-organisation of staff on economic grounds resulting in, say, a change in hours or a reduction in pay. A change-over to LMS or grant-maintained status may well result in a change of duties of staff (subject to the 1990 Document). Refusal to accept proposed changes may be a fair reason for dismissal.

However, the changes must be genuinely on grounds of economic efficiency and must be implemented in a fair way. This would require consultation with the staff, and their trade union where appropriate.

Natural justice and judicial review

Tribunals decide whether a dismissal is fair and reasonable. In doing so, they will apply rules of 'natural justice'. A person must have the opportunity to answer the case against them, to be heard by an impartial body and to be given the opportunity to appeal.

Furthermore, the actions of LEAs and governing bodies, as 'public bodies', may be subject to judicial review.[47] R. v Derbyshire County Council has already been discussed (see pages 188–9) where, on judicial review, the council was found to have acted in bad faith and for an improper purpose.

Judicial review may also apply to dismissal. In a recent case, a teacher was found to be wrongly dismissed because the disciplinary panel acted in breach of natural justice. They used 'extraneous matter' which was not relevant to the complaint against the teacher. Consequently, the disciplinary procedures were held by the High Court to be null and void.[48]

Redundancy payments

Under the EP(C)A a person is redundant where the requirements for the work which they are employed to do, or at the place where they are employed to do it, have ceased or diminished. In which case, they are entitled to a redundancy payment.

A redundancy payment is calculated by multiplying the number of years service by a week's pay (or ½ or 1½ weeks' pay, depending on age), subject to a maximum set by Order of the Secretary of State for Employment. However, a teacher's employer is allowed to disregard the limits set, and to pay compensation for redundancy on the basis of the teacher's full earnings.[49]

In schools without delegated budgets, the LEA as employer decides and pays. In schools with a delegated budget, the governing body decides whether or not to exercise discretion under Reg. 5. But it is the LEA who pays the enhanced payment. The ERA provides that this cost is not to be met from the school's budget, unless the LEA have a good reason for deducting the costs. Departing from LEA practice may be such a reason.

Where the governing body has responsibility for redundancies, they must ensure that they meet the statutory consultation requirements in s.99 of the EPA 1975, ensuring also that they consult recognised trade unions where appropriate. Furthermore, they must offer alternative employment if possible. They will be able to do this only in consultation with the LEA, as only the LEA will know of possible vacancies in other schools. The transfer of staff between schools has been made more difficult with LMS, as each governing body will be concerned only with staffing at their own school whereas the LEA could take a broader view of staffing requirements in schools throughout their area.

If an employee refuses an offer of suitable alternative employment, they will lose their entitlement to a redundancy payment. The alternative position must be offered before the existing contract ends, and must start within four weeks of the end of the contract. So, it is important for the governing body to consult the LEA at an early stage.

If work offered is similar it will generally be suitable, i.e. involving similar duties, pay and status. It seems it will not be suitable if it involves a change in status, even if the same salary is paid.

In *Tayor v Kent County Council* (1969), a head teacher whose job disappeared when two schools amalgamated, was offered a post in a mobile pool of teachers who could be required to work in any capacity. Mr Taylor refused the offer, even though his salary was guaranteed. It was held that expecting a head teacher of Mr Taylor's age and experience to accept such reduced status was 'quite unsuitable'.

Written reason for dismissal

An employee with two years' continuous service who has been dismissed is entitled to a written reason for dismissal from their employer (s.53 EP(C)A). In the case of schools maintained by the LEA, the LEA is obliged to provide the reason. The statute has been modified in relation to schools with a delegated budget, so that the reason given by the governing body in their notification to the LEA is deemed to be the reason for dismissal. However, the LEA is still responsible for providing the written reason.

In grant-maintained schools, the governing body as the employer will have to provide the reason when requested.

Notice periods

Normally, entitlement to notice will be as contained in the contract of employment. However, contractual notice cannot be less than the statutory period. Section 49 EP(C)A states that an employee is entitled to one week's notice after one month's service, two weeks' notice after two years' service, and an additional week for each year of service after that, up to 12 years.

Continuity of employment

Most statutory employment rights require a period of qualifying service. For example, to claim unfair dismissal or a redundancy payment, the employee must have two years' continuous service with the same employer.

In most cases, this will not be a problem. If an employee is employed full-time on a permanent contract, terminable by notice, they can acquire the requisite continuous service. Here we consider situations outside the 'norm' – part-time, fixed term and temporary contracts.

Continuous service is calculated under schedule 13 to the EP(C)A. The usual method of calculation is by looking at the employee's contract. If they are employed under a contract which normally requires them to work 16 hours or more a week, the weeks will count as continuous, even during the vacation.

200 The Legal Context of Teaching

So, in deciding an employee's hours, the tribunal will look at what is normally required under the contract. They will not count up the number of hours worked each week and apply the average.

In *Harber v PNL* (1990), following a change in his teaching arrangements, Mr Harber was paid for eight hours a week although in some weeks he actually worked less than eight hours. It was held that in calculating whether Mr Harber had the requisite continuous employment, the tribunal should not look at the hours actually worked but the hours the contract normally involved, which was eight.

Change of employer

Normally, continuous employment applies to only one employer. However, there is provision in Schedule 13 for preserving continuity. Paragraph 18A applies to employment by LEAs and governing bodies, so that service at different schools will not break continuity of employment.

Furthermore, when staff transfer to a grant-maintained school and their employer changes, s.75 of the ERA provides that employment with the LEA and the governing body is to be continuous.

Fixed term contracts

Teachers are often employed on fixed term contracts for a teaching year, but with no contract during the vacation. In that case continuity would be broken as there is no contract normally requiring them to work 16 hours or more. But, despite the gaps in employment, a teacher employed on a series of fixed term contracts can acquire the qualifying period. In *Ford v Warwickshire County Council* (1983) the House of Lords held that the vacation periods can count as a 'temporary cessation of work'[50] and so count as continuous employment.

In that case, Mrs Ford, who has been employed for eight years on a series of fixed term contracts was entitled to a redundancy payment.

The same argument would apply to employment under a 'temporary contract', although the gap between contracts must be short, relative to the periods of employment on either side of the break in the contract.

Non-renewal of a fixed term contract counts as dismissal for the purposes of unfair dismissal and redundancy. A teacher on a fixed term contract may still be entitled to a redundancy payment, even though the redundancy was anticipated, so long as they have the relevant qualifying service.[51]

Part-time contracts

There is no statutory definition of a part-time worker, but in order to build up continuous service an employee must have a contract for at least 16 hours each week (or eight hours if they have been working for five years or more).

A teacher may have a number of concurrent contracts to work, say, in different schools for a few hours at each. In calculating their hours, they cannot add together the number of hours worked under each contract. In *Lewis v Surrey County Council* (1988) the House of Lords held that contracts must be regarded separately, so long as they are genuinely separate and not an attempt by the employer to avoid their statutory obligations. Where a teacher is employed under more than one contract with different schools (each with a delegated budget), it is most unlikely that the hours under the contracts can be added together, even though the employer (the LEA) is the same under each contract.

Anti-discrimination legislation

The ERA expressly requires the governing body of grant-maintained schools to comply with the Race Relations Act and Sex Discrimination Act. The anti-discrimination legislation applies to teaching and non-teaching staff in all schools. The SDA and RRA give individuals the right not to be discriminated against in relation to recruitment, opportunities for promotion, training and other benefits, and dismissal or any other detriment.[52] No qualifying service is needed to acquire rights under these statutes.

Discrimination can be direct. This occurs where a person is treated less favourably on grounds of sex, race or marital status (s.1(1)(a) SDA and RRA). It is generally easily recognisable but can be difficult to prove. Some help is available to the complainant, who has the burden of proving that they have been discriminated against. If on the face of it, a person has been discriminated against, it will be for the employer to show there was some other reason for refusing a person employment or promotion or for their dismissal.

One area which has given rise to a number of cases recently is that of sexual and racial harassment. Harassment is not expressly covered by the legislation, but has been held to fall within the definition of direct discrimination.

One such case is *Porcelli v Strathclyde Regional Council* (1985). Mrs Porcelli was employed in a Strathclyde school as a laboratory technician. Two male colleagues subjected Mrs Porcelli to a campaign of sexual harassment (brushing against her, suggestive remarks) in an attempt to make her leave. She was forced to apply for a transfer, and claimed unlawful discrimination. It was held that sexual harassment was 'less favourable treatment' on grounds of sex (direct discrimination). It was treatment of a sexual nature 'to which a man would not be vulnerable'.

Discrimination can also be indirect – where a condition is imposed which, although applied to all employees, has a disproportionate effect on members of one sex or of a particular racial group. For example, a requirement that candidates be aged between 17½ and 26 was held to amount to 'indirect' discrimination, in *Price v Civil Service Commission* (1978). The age limit was found to have a disproportionate effect upon women because, due to child care responsibilities, a considerably smaller number of women than men could comply with it.

A requirement or condition relating to qualifications may have a discriminatory effect on grounds of race. This was the issue in the recent House of Lords decision in *Hampson v DES* (1990).

Mrs Hampson, a Hong Kong Chinese, had completed teacher training in Hong Kong. She claimed she had been discriminated against when she was refused qualified teacher status in the UK. Under the 1982 Regulations (predecessor to the 1989 Regulations), the Secretary of State could determine whether a teacher had completed training 'approved as comparable' to an approved UK course.

The DES argued that in refusing to grant Mrs Hampson QTS they were protected by s.41(1)(b) of the RRA as they were acting 'in pursuance of any instrument made under any enactment by a Minister of the Crown'. But the House of Lords held that an act could be 'in pursuance of' an instrument only if it is specified in a statute, order or instrument. In this case it was not. The Order gave the Secretary of State power to determine comparable qualifications. In exercising that power, he or she cannot apply discriminatory criteria.

Indirect discrimination can also arise in the way duties are assigned to teachers, particularly in relation to extra-curricula activities where teachers are expected to perform their duties outside school hours. This could have a disproportionate effect on women with child care responsibilities, as occurred in *Briggs v North Eastern Education and Library Board* (1990).

Mrs Briggs, an assistant science teacher, assisted in badminton coaching sessions after school hours. When she was promoted, 'extra curricula school games' were included in her contract. Mrs Briggs continued with the badminton sessions, until she adopted a daughter. She informed the head teacher that she would no longer be available for after school activities. She continued to run the additional badminton classes at lunch time. When her salary was reduced, she claimed unlawful discrimination.

It was held that the employers had imposed a requirement to carry out duties outside working hours, even though it was part of Mrs Briggs' contract, and that it had a disproportionate effect upon women, due to child care responsibilities. However, the court went on to find that although the requirement had a discriminatory effect, it was justifiable. The court applied an 'objective' test (also upheld in Hampson) which requires a tribunal to balance the discriminatory effect against the reasonable needs of the employer. In this case, it was in the interests of the school and the benefit of the pupils that badminton practice be held after school hours.

Genuine Occupation Qualifications

It is lawful to discriminate if the sex or race of the person is a genuine occupational qualification (g.o.q.). As discussed above (see page 189), one such g.o.q. is where the holder of the job provides personal services promoting their welfare and those services can most effectively be provided by a person of a particular race or sex.

This exception was given a wide meaning in *Tottenham Green Under Fives' Centre v Marshall* (1989). Even if the services can be provided by persons from any racial group, it will still be lawful to discriminate if they can *most effectively* be provided by someone from a particular racial group. In deciding the question of effectiveness the tribunal has to balance the need to guard against discrimination and the desirability of promoting racial integration. In this case, the tribunal found that there was no special need for a person of Afro-Caribbean origin to work in a nursery where a balance was maintained in the ethnic background of the children.

In *London Borough of Lambeth v Commission for Racial Equality* (1990) the meaning of 'personal' services was considered. It was decided that 'personal' involves direct contact between the giver and the recipient. Where, as in this case, the posts are managerial, it is less likely that such personal service will be provided.

Equal Pay

There has been a statutory requirement to pay equal pay for like work since 1975. Teachers were among the first groups of workers to introduce the same grades and salary scales for women and men. However, there is potential for unequal pay in respect of the grade or point on the scale at which women and men are appointed.

A case which arose recently in relation to University lecturers illustrates the point. In *Benneviste v University of Southampton* (1989), Dr Benneviste was appointed as a lecturer at the University, but at a salary level below that which was normal for a person of her age and qualifications. When she claimed equal pay with four male colleagues who were doing the same work it was argued that her contract was no less favourable. She was paid on the same contractual scale as they were, and she, like them, had no contractual entitlement to be appointed at any particular point on the scale (an argument which could be applied to school teachers).

However, the Court of Appeal held that there was a term in Dr Benneviste's contract which was less favourable than her colleagues' – she was paid less for doing the same work. The Court accepted that the University had discretion as to where on the scale a person should be placed, but that must reflect criteria such as ability, skills and experience. There was no question of that here, and she was entitled to equal pay.

The Act states that a woman is entitled to equal pay for work which is the same or of equal value to that which a man does. It applies to teaching and non-teaching staff, and may also be used to compare salaries of staff employed by the same employer but at different establishments. This may cause problems for LEAs who, as the employer of staff in maintained schools with a delegated budget, are responsible for paying salaries, but the governing body of each school decides the salary level. If a disparity in pay emerges between sexes at different schools, complaints may be made to an industrial tribunal. If successful, pay inequalities will have to be remedied, and the LEA will have to decide how increased salary costs are to be funded.

Other statutory employment rights

Conditions of service of teachers and other staff are affected by numerous statutory rights; for example, maternity leave, paid time off for ante-natal care and union duties, guarantee pay, rights under the Wages Act.

It is not appropriate to discuss these in detail here. Reference should be made to specialist works on employment law.[53]

However, many statutory rights are also found in the contracts of employment of teachers and other staff. These contractual provisions cannot take away statutory rights but they can improve upon them. Thus staff need to familiarise themselves with the conditions in their contracts.

TEACHERS' PAY AND CONDITIONS

The determination of the remuneration and conditions of employment of teachers is a controversial issue. The School Teachers' Pay and Conditions Document (the Document) sets out current pay and conditions. The document is introduced by an Order of the Secretary of State. The method of determining the pay and conditions has been the subject of much debate and change.

The Teachers' Pay and Conditions Act 1987 gave the Secretary of State the power to make an order relating to pay and conditions. Section 3(6) and that Act provides that:

1 the remuneration of teachers is determined according to the pay scales set out in the document, and
2 in relation to conditions of employment, the provisions in the document take effect as terms of the contracts of employment of teachers, and
3 the provisions of a teacher's contract of employment shall have effect only so far as consistent with those provisions.

Thus, the level of pay and the main conditions of employment are laid down by statute.

The 1987 Act repealed the Remuneration of Teachers Act 1965 and terminated the arrangements for determining pay and conditions contained in that Act. It abolished the Burnham Committee – the joint trade union and employers' negotiating body.

In its place, the Interim Advisory Committee on School Teachers' Pay and Conditions was established[54] to report to the Secretary of State on matters relating to remuneration and other conditions referred to them and to make recommendations on any changes.

The constitution and proceedings of the Committee are set out in Schedule 1 to the 1987 Act. It provides for appointment, resignation, termination of office and remuneration of members of the Committee. It must include members who have relevant knowledge or experience of education.

There is a requirement to allow associations of local education authorities, those representing governing bodies, and trade unions, to make representations and give evidence on matters before the Committee. Local Education Authorities should also be consulted if it appears to the Committee 'to be desirable'.[55]

However, the School Teachers' Pay and Conditions (No 2) Bill proposes to repeal the 1987 Act. It is proposed (at the time of writing) to replace the Interim body with a permanent review body. Clause 4 of the Bill states that, following a report and recommendation from the review body, the Secretary of State is empowered to make a pay and conditions order. The powers contained in the Bill are similar to those in the 1987 Act, although the powers are extended to grant maintained schools.

Powers of the Secretary of State

The Order made by the Secretary of State may include different provisions for different cases. By virtue of s.3(5) the Order may, in relation to pay:

(a) confer discretion on the local education authority with respect to any matter;

(b) make provision as to the aggregate amount of allowances payable to teachers in a school;

(c) set lower and upper limits on the number or proportion of teachers in a school to be paid on specified scales or who are at any specified time to be paid any specified allowance;

(d) provide for the designation of schools in relation to which special provisions apply;

(e) provide for the determination of any questions arising as to the interpretation or application of the provisions set out or referred to in the order;

(f) make retrospective provision, but not so as to require the reduction of a teacher's pay in respect of a past period;

(g) provide that to the extent specified in the order matters may be settled by agreement between, or in a manner agreed between, teachers and local education authorities.

Pursuant to these powers, the Secretary of State has introduced a number of Orders, and dramatic changes have been made to the teachers' pay structures. These remain in force until amended by a subsequent order. It remains to be seen whether the proposed review body will recommend further changes to the structure.

From 1 October 1987, a single main scale with 11 points was introduced for all teachers, other than heads or deputies. Also introduced were five incentive allowances, payable in addition to the main scale.

An incentive allowance may be paid to teachers only where the LEA or governing body is satisfied that the teacher fulfils at least one of four criteria; i.e. that the teacher:

(a) undertakes responsibilities beyond those common to the majority of teachers;

(b) has demonstrated outstanding ability as a classroom teacher;

(c) is employed to teach subjects in which there is a shortage of teachers;

(d) is employed in a post which is difficult to fill.

In 1990 provision was made for greater discretion by the 'relevant body' – the governing body or the LEA depending on the type of school. It provided for 'incremental enhancement' and 'local scales', with effect from 1 January 1991.[56]

Incremental enhancement gives the LEA or the governing body (for schools with a delegated budget or grant-maintained) the discretion to enhance the pay of teachers on points 1 to 10 of the scale, by £249, £501, £750 or £999 a year, so long as it does not exceed the next incremental point. Additional payments can be made at any time, but they will not automatically be carried forward to the next year. They must be reviewed annually by the relevant body on 1 September. In fact, every teacher who has not reached point 11 should be reviewed at 1 September each year, against criteria adopted by the LEA or governing body, whichever is relevant. No guidance is given as to the criteria, though it is suggested[57] that LEAs should offer guidance to governing bodies. They are not, however, bound to accept that advice.

Although no criteria are given, the DES does state that whether or not an award was made in the previous year should not determine the outcome of the review. The criteria to be adopted are left to the relevant body to decide. However, it is likely that these awards will be connected with staff appraisal.

The introduction of local scales gives LEAs and governing bodies further flexibility. From 1 January 1991, the relevant body can introduce a local extended scale for teachers on point 11. They can use increments over and above the point 11 salary, subject to a maximum. However, where LEAs or governing bodies adopt an extended scale, teachers will not automatically progress to it. Again, there is discretion and it is envisaged that criteria similar to those for incremental enhancement will be used.

The intention of the Interim Advisory Committee, endorsed by the Secretary of State, in giving LEAs and governing bodies the discretion to award these allowances, in addition to incentive allowances, was to allow flexibility. The relevant body will be able to decide upon a framework of additional payments to suit the circumstances of individual schools.

There is no limit on the proportion of teachers who can be paid enhanced payments (unlike incentive allowances) subject, of course, to the funds available to the LEAs or governing bodies of grant-maintained schools.

Conditions of employment

Prior to 1987, teachers' duties under their contracts of employment were not clearly defined. This was highlighted in the cases which appeared in the courts during the teachers' dispute in 1984–85.

For example, in *Sim v Rotherham MBC* (1986) the High Court found that teachers had no express contractual duty to provide cover for absent colleagues. However, it held that professional people had duties relevant to their profession. Cover arrangements, it was said, were part of the administrative directions of the head teacher and that teachers were obliged to carry out additional duties if reasonably requested.

The School Teachers' Pay and Conditions Document attempts to clarify the extent of teachers' professional duties. However, there is still room for uncertainty as the Document states the duties are 'included' in teachers' contracts.

Teachers are under a general duty to carry out the professional duties of a school teacher 'under the reasonable direction of the head teacher'[58] of the school where they are employed or, where they are not assigned to any one school, the head teacher of the school where they are for the time being working as a teacher. The Document then goes on to list the duties which are included in the professional duties of a school teacher. It covers teaching, other activities and cover for absent colleagues.[59]

The duties also include participation in arrangements, within an agreed national framework, for the appraisal of teachers' performance.[60]

The number of hours a teacher is required to work is fixed at 1265 a year, spread over 195 days.[61] However, how the hours are allocated is left to the head teacher. Furthermore, the Document provides that teachers shall work 'such additional hours as may be needed to enable him to discharge effectively his professional duties including, in particular, the marking of pupils' work, the writing of reports on pupils and the preparation of lessons, teaching material and teaching programmes'. The amount of additional time is not defined but 'shall depend upon the work needed to discharge the teacher's duties'.

Other conditions of employment are those contained in the contract of employment between the teacher and the LEA (or governing body in grant-maintained schools). In most LEA maintained schools, the terms of the contract are found in the so-called 'Burgundy Book' – terms and conditions negotiated nationally by the teachers' unions. There may, however, be local variations where the LEA and union have agreed that local conditions should prevail.

The contractual terms are subject to the statutory employment rights – although these can be improved upon by agreement, the contract cannot take away those rights.

Conditions of employment of head teachers

Head teachers have to carry out their professional duties in accordance with the provisions of the Education Acts 1944 to 1988, any order and regulations made under those Acts and the articles of government of their school.

Head teachers are responsible for the internal organisation, management and control of the school. They must carry out their duties in consultation, where appropriate, with the LEA, the governing body, the staff of the school and the parents of its pupils.

The professional duties of head teachers are set out in the Document.[62] These include provisions relating to: managing staff; liaison with trade unions; appraisal, training and development of staff and providing information about staff to management (for example where dismissal is contemplated).

Industrial action

Teachers have taken industrial action in forms other than all-out strike. However, most types of action result in breach of the contract of employment. Consequently, employers are entitled to make deductions from pay for non-performance of contractual duties. In *Sim v Rotherham MBC* (1986), teachers had pay deducted when, as part of a programme of industrial action, they refused to provide cover for absent colleagues. It was held that the employers were entitled to deduct an amount for the period when cover was refused.

Similarly, in *Royle v Trafford Borough Council* (1984), a teacher took part in industrial action by refusing to accept an additional five pupils into his class of 31. He was entitled to be paid because he carried on with his duties, but the High Court allowed a deduction of 5/36ths as a nominal amount representing breach of his contractual duties.

However, if teachers are willing to work, but are unable to do so because their school has closed due to industrial action, it seems that their employers are obliged to pay them. In *R v Liverpool City Corporation* (1985), a case of judicial review, the High Court quashed a decision by the City Council not to pay teachers who had been available for work but unable to do so due to the the closure of their school.

The problem facing teachers in the future is that their pay and conditions are determined by statute. Any form of industrial action will inevitably result in a breach of statutory duty for which there is no protection in law for either individuals or trade unions. Furthermore, the establishment of a review body by the 1991 Bill depends upon a commitment to the end of industrial action. Although the government has not required unions to sign a 'no-strike' agreement the Secretary of State has made it clear that the government were 'proceeding on condition of no industrial action, and obviously circumstances would change so far as the government are concerned if industrial action was taken or threatened'.

Collective bargaining

National negotiations between the education authorities and teachers' trade unions were abolished by the 1987 Act, in relation to those matters determined by statute. However, other conditions (eg maternity provisions) are still subject to negotiation with recognised trade unions but this is more likely to occur on a local level. LEAs have continued to recognise unions locally, and where a union is recognised by the LEA, the governing body is obliged to regard the union as recognised in relation to their school.

The government stated its intention to restore negotiating rights to the teachers' union, and introduced a Bill to that effect. New negotiating machinery was proposed, similar to the Burnham Committee, but with provision for LEAs or governing bodies to 'opt out' of the national agreement.

This proposal has now been rejected in favour of a review body, as set out in the School Teachers' Pay and Conditions (No 2) Bill.

The Bill provides for a review body similar to those which apply to other professions, eg doctors and nurses. The Body is to be appointed by the Prime Minister. Governing bodies of grant maintained schools (but not LEAs) will be able to 'opt out' of the statutory terms and conditions and to make their own provision in relation to the conditions of teachers employed by them. It does not, apparently, apply to rates of pay. The governing body will be required to 'consult' the teachers employed at the school.

The future of collective bargaining looks bleak. The present government is clearly opposed to the restoration of national bargaining rights, and furthermore, intends to take away any industrial muscle left to the teachers by inhibiting industrial action.

Case studies

1. Anne-Marie, who is French, recently qualified to teach pupils aged 11–16, in France. She has a degree (or the French equivalent) in English, and wants to be able to practice her language. Consequently, she took up the opportunity to work in London, and is now employed by a London Authority as a supply teacher.

   When she was offered the post, her letter of appointment stated that she would be paid at point two on the scale. When she received her first salary, she found that her salary is at scale U2 (unqualified teacher rate). Advise Anne-Marie whether or not she is entitled to the higher salary.

2. Ben teaches English and Politics at a sixth form college. The college is maintained by the LEA, but it has a delegated budget.

   Ben was recently arrested while taking part in a demonstration against the Poll Tax. He was charged with causing a breach of the peace. He did not inform the head teacher at the college of his arrest, until he had to request time off to attend court in order to answer the charge.

   The head teacher is concerned about a member of her staff appearing in court on such a charge. She decided that any publicity would be bad for the school's reputation and that she had no choice but to suspend Ben, with pay, pending advice from the governing body.

   At its next meeting, three weeks later, the governing body discussed the position. The head teacher was at the meeting to explain her decision. In the meantime, Ben had been found guilty, and given an unconditional discharge.

   Some members of the governing body hold the view that Ben should be dismissed because of the 'undesirable influence he would have on the pupils, particularly as he teaches politics'. The governors voted on the issue, and by a narrow majority it was agreed that Ben should be removed from the school.

   The LEA were notified of the decision. The Chief Education Officer advised the governors against the dismissal, until there had been an investigation into Ben's involvement in the demonstration. However, the governing body insisted that the decision be implemented.

Ben now wishes to claim unfair dismissal. Advise Ben on the legal issues, and consider the implications for the governing body and the LEA.

3. The governing body of the Queen Elizabeth's High School has recently introduced some changes in employment policy, now that the school is under local management. Exercising their powers in relation to appointment of staff, they adopted a policy of appointing staff at a salary no higher than point seven on the scale.

Clare recently returned to teaching, two years after the birth of her child. Despite her age and previous teaching experience, she was offered the post at point seven on the salary scale. Clare accepted the appointment, even though she realised she should have been higher up the scale. She needed a post near to her home because of her child care arrangements.

Clare soon discovered that she was paid less than her male colleagues, some of whom had less experience than she had. She spoke to the head teacher, and asked him to raise this with the appropriate authority, saying 'surely I'm entitled to equal pay to the men in this day and age'.

The head teacher agreed to do this, but he is not convinced that it has anything to do with equality. In the meantime, there has been a re-allocation of duties amongst staff in the school. Clare has been asked to take netball practice two days a week after school hours. Clare pointed out that she had made it clear at her interview that she had child care responsibilities which prevented her from teaching after school hours. The head teacher, however, was adamant, saying that all teachers were expected to take part in extra curricular activities and that if Clare refused to take the netball practice, her contract would be terminated.

Consider the legal implications of these events.

Notes and References

1 Education (Teachers) Regulations 1989.
2 Education (Modification of Enactments Relating to Employment Order 1989; SI 1989/901.
   S.34 Education (No.2) Act 1986.
4 *Ibid.*, S.39.
5 Education (Teachers) Regulations 1989; SI 1989/1319.
6 *Ibid.*, Reg. 6(1).
7 *Ibid.*, Part IV.
8 *R v Derbyshire County Council ex parte Times Supplements Ltd.* – discussed pp. 188–9.
9 Op. cit., note 5.

10 EC Directive 89/48 (1989 OJ No. L 19/16) – all member States recognise higher education diplomas of other member States if awarded on completion of three years' full time professional education training, or the part-time equivalent.
11 Para. 5 of Schedule 4 to Regulations, *op. cit.*
11a Reduced from 26 years from 1 September 1991 by the Education (Teachers) (Amendment) Regulations 1991 SI 1991/1134.
11b *Ibid.*
12 S.6(7)(f)(iii) ERA.
13 Para. 26, DES Circular 18/89; 16.8.89.
14 Para. 31, ibid.
15 M Leonard 1988 *The 1988 Education Act: A Tactical Guide for Schools,* Blackwell Education.
16 Reg. 18 Education (Teachers) Regulations op. cit.
17 *Ibid.,* Schedule 6, see also paras. 43–46 DES Circular 18/89.
18 Section 37(1)(c) E (No.2) (1986) Act.
19 Para. 1(7) Schedule 3 ERA (1988).
20 Section 38(3)(a) E (No.2) (1986) Act.
21 Para. 2(7) Schedule 3 ERA 1988.
22 Section 38(3) SDA 1975.
23 Section 7 SDA; Section 5 RRA 1976.
24 *London Borough of Lambeth v Commission for Racial Equality* (discussed page 203).
25 G R Barrell J A Partington (1985) *Teachers and the Law* 197–200, Methuen.
26 S Fredman G Morris 19 ILJ 148–150.
27 Para. 8(9) Schedule 3 ERA 1988.
28 In accordance with Education (Teachers) Regulations 1989 op. cit.
29 SI 1989 No. 298.
30 See DES Circular 7/89, 22.3.89.
31 Section 153 Employment Protection (Consolidation) Act 1978.
32 For detailed discussion see Bowers *A Practical Approach to Employment Law* 3rd Ed. Financial Training Publications, 1990.
33 Section 67 Employment Protection (Consolidation) Act 1978.
34 *Ibid.,* Section 68.
35 *Ibid.,* Section 55.
36 *Western Excavating Ltd v Sharp* (1978).
37 Education (Modifications of Enactment relating to Employment) Order 1989; SI 1989 No. 901.
38 DES Circular 13/89; 9.6.89.
39 Section 57(2), EP(C)A 1978.
40 Para. 2, Schedule 3 ERA 1988.
41 see p. 186.
42 *East Lindsey DC v Daubney* (1977).
43 ACAS Code of Practice on Disciplinary Rules and Procedures.
44 School Teachers' Pay and Conditions Document 1990, see page 207.
45 DES Circular 7/88, Para. 159.
46 Farrell, Partington op. cit. 152 – 156.
47 Industrial Relations Legal Information Bulletin 332, 1.7.87.
48 Industrial Relations Legal Information Bulletin 406, 1.8.90.
49 Reg 5, Teachers (Compensation for Redundancy and Premature Retirement) Regulations 1989.

50 Employment Protection (Consolidation) Act 1978 Para. 9, Schedule 13 EP(C)A.
51 *Lee v Nottinghamshire County Council* 1980.
52 Section 6 SDA 1975; Section 4 RRA 1976.
53 For detailed discussion see Bowers J (1990) *A Practical Approach to Employment Law* (3rd edn), Blackstone; Wedderburn Lord (1989) *Worker and the Law.* (3rd edn.), Penguin; Smith I T and Wood Sir J (1990) *Industrial Law* (4th edn.) Butterworths.
54 Section 2 Teachers' Pay and Conditions Act 1987.
55 *Ibid.*, Section 2(5).
56 See Appendix II School Teachers' Pay and Conditions Document 1990.
57 DES Circular 6/90; 21.6.90.
58 Document *op. cit.*, Para. 33.
59 *Ibid.*, Para. 35(1) and (2).
60 *Ibid.*, Para. 35(3).
61 *Ibid.*, Para. 36.
62 *Ibid.*, Paras. 27–31.
63 Schedule 1 to the 1991 Bill.

SCHEDULE OF CASES

Affutu-Nartoy v Clarke and ILEA (1984) *The Times*, 9 Feb.
Associated Provincial Picture Houses Ltd v Wednesbury Corporation [1948] 1
    KB 223.

Barnes v Bromley London Borough Council (1983) *The Times*, 16 Nov.
Barnes v Hampshire County Council [1969] 1 WLR 1563.
Bates v Parker [1954] 1 All ER 768.
Beaumont v Surrey County Council (1968) 66 LGR 580.
Benneviste v University of Southampton (1989) IRLR 122.
Black v Kent County Council (1983) *The Times*, 23 May.
Bostock v Kay (1989) *The Times*, 20 April.
Bradbury v Enfield London Borough Council [1967] 3 All ER 434.
Briggs v North Eastern Education and Library Board (1990) IRLR 181.
Bromley London Borough Council v GLC [1983] 1 AC 768.
Brunyate v ILEA [1989] 2 All ER 417.
Butt v Cambridgeshire and Ely County Council (1970) 68 LGR 81.

Campbell v Tameside Metropolitan Borough Council [1982] 2 All ER 791.
Campbell and Cosans v UK [1982] 4 EHRR 293.
Caparo Industries plc v Dickman [1990] 1 All ER 568.
Carmarthenshire County Council v Lewis [1955] AC 549; 1 All ER 565.
Chilvers v London County Council (1916) 80 JP 246.
Ching v Surrey County Council [1910] 1 KB 736.
Cleary v Booth [1893] 1 QB 465.
Commission for Racial Equality v Dutton (1989) IRLR 8.
Coney v Choyce [1975] 1 WLR 422.
Council of Civil Service Unions v Minister for the Civil Service [1985] AC
    374; [1984] 3 All ER 935.
Crouch v Essex County Council (1966) 64 LGR 240.
Crown Suppliers (PSA) v Dawkins (1991) *The Times* 29 April (EAT).
Cumings v Birkenhead Corporation [1972] Ch. 12; [1971] 1 WLR 1458.

D, Re (1988) 86 LGR 442.
D v NSPCC [1976] 1 ALL ER 1088.
De Souza v Automobile Association (1986) IRLR 103.
Donoghue v Stevenson [1932] AC 562.

East Lindsey DC v Daubney (1977) IRLR 181.
Edwards v National Coal Board [1949] 1 KB 704.
Ellis v Sayers Confectioners Ltd (1963) 61 LGR 299.

Equal Opportunities Commission v Birmingham City Council [1989] 1 All ER 769.
Evans v Lloyd [1962] 1 All ER 239.

Factortame Ltd v Secretary of State for Transport [1989] 2 All ER 692 HL.
Fitzgerald v Northcote (1865) 4 F & F 656.
Ford v Warwickshire County Council (1983) IRLR 126.
Fryer v Salford Corporation [1937] 1 All ER 617.

Gaskin v United Kingdom [1990] 12 EHRR 36.
George v Devon County Council [1988] 3 All ER 1002.
Gillick v West Norfolk and Wisbech Area Health Authority [1985] 3 All ER 402.
Gillmore v London County Coucil [1938] All ER 31.
Good v ILEA (1980) 10 *Fam Law* 213.
Griffiths v Smith [1941] AC 170.

Hampson v Department of Education and Science (1989) IRLR 69.
Hampson v DES (1990) IRLR 302.
Harber v PNL (1990) IRLR 198.
Harvey v Strathclyde Regional Councill (1989) *Public Law* 160.
Home Office v Dorset Yacht Co [1970] AC 1004.
Hudson v Governors of Rotherham Grammar School (1938) LCT 303.
Hunt v Damon (1930) 46 TLR 579.
Hutt and Anr v Governors of Haileybury College (1888) 4 TLR 623.

Jacques v Oxfordshire County Council (1967) 66 LGR 440.
Jarman v Mid-Glamorgan Education Authority (1985) 82 *LS Gaz.* 1249.
Jeffrey v London County Council (1954) 52 LGR 521.
Jenkins v Howells [1949] 2 KB 218; 1 All ER 942.

Kejedlsen, Busk Masden and Pedersen (1976) 7 Dec, Series A No. 23.

Lee v Department of Education and Science (1968) 66 LGR 211.
Lee v Nottinghamshire County Council *The Times* 28 April 1980.
Legg v ILEA [1972] 3 All ER 177.
Lewis v Surrey County Council (1987) IRLR 509.
London Borough of Lambeth v Commission for Racial Equality (1990) IRLR 231.
Lyes v Middlesex County Council (1962) 61 LGR 443.

McCarthy's Ltd v Smith [1979] 3 All ER 325.
Mandla v Dowell Lee [1983] 1 All ER 1062.
Mays v Essex County Council (1975) *The Times*, 11 Oct.
Meade v Haringey London Borough Council [1979] 2 All ER 1016; 1 WLR 637.
Moore v Hampshire County Council (1981) 80 LGR 481.
Morris v Carnarvon County Council [1910] 1 KB 858.
Murphy v Bradford Metropolitan Council (1991) *The Times*, 11Feb.

Nichol v Gateshead MBC (1989) 87 LGR 435.
Noble v ILEA (1984) 83 LGR 291.

Noonan v ILEA (1974) *The Times*, 14 Dec.
Norfolk County Council v Bernard (1979) IRLR 220.
Nyasi v Ryman (1988) 367 IRLIB 15 (EAT).

Pettican v Enfield London Borough Council (1970) *The Times*, 22 Oct.
Phipps v Rochester Corporation [1955] 1 QB 450.
Polkey v A E Dayton Services Ltd (1987) IRLR 503.
Porcelli v Strathclyde Regional Council (1985) ICR 177.
Porter v City of Bradford Metropolitan Council (1985) 14 Jan. *Lexis*.
Price v Civil Service Commission (1978) IRLR 3.

Reffell v Surrey County Council (1964) 1 All ER 743; 62 LGR 186.
R v Birmingham City Council ex parte McKenna (1991) *The Times* 16 May.
R v Bradford on Avon Rural District Council ex parte Thornton (1908) 99 LT 89.
R v Brent London Borough Council ex parte Assegai (1987) *The Times*, 18 June; 151 LG Rev 891.
R v Brent London Borough Council ex parte Gunning (1985) 84 LGR 211.
R v Bromley London Borough Council ex parte C (1991) *The Times* 6 June (DC).
R v Camden London Borough Council ex parte S (1990) *The Times* 7 Nov.
R v Chief Constable of Gwent (1989) 139 NLJ 1754.
R v City of Birmingham DC ex parte 0 [1983] 1 ALL ER 497.
R v Commissioner for Local Administration ex parte Croydon London Borough Council [1989] 1 All ER, 1033.
R v Derbyshire County Council ex parte Times Supplements Ltd and others (1990).
R v GLC ex parte London Borough of Bromley [1982] 1 All ER 729.
R v Governors of Haberdashers' Aske's School ex parte ILEA *(See* Brunyate v ILEA (1989).
R v Governors of Small Heath School ex parte Birmingham City Council (1989) *The Times* 14 Aug.; *The Guardian*, 19 Sept.
R v Greenwich LBC ex parte Governors of John Ball Primary School (1989) *The Times*, 16 Nov.
R v Hampshire Education Authority ex parte J (1985) 84 LGR 547.
R v Hampstead BC ex parte Woodward (1917) 116 LT 213.
R v Hereford and Worcester LEA ex parte Wm Jones [1981] 1 WLR 768.
R v Hertfordshire County Council ex parte George (1988) *Lexis* CO/856/87.
R v Hopley (1860) 2 F & F 202.
R v ILEA ex parte Ali and Murshid (1990) *The Times* 21 February; *The Guardian* 8 March.
R v ILEA ex parte Bradby (1980).
R v Kirklees Metropolitan Borough Council ex parte Molloy (1988) 86 LGR 115; (1987) *The Times*, 17 Aug.
R v Lancashire County Council ex parte CM (1989) 2FLR 279.
R v Liverpool City Council ex parte Ferguson; Same v Same ex parte Grantham (1985) IRLR 501.
R v London Borough of Sutton ex parte Hamlet (1986).
R v Manchester City Council ex parte Fulford (1984) 81 LGR 292.
R v Mid-Glamorgan County Council ex parte Grieg (1988) *Lexis*.
R v Newham London Borough Council ex parte D (1991). *The Times* 27 May.
R v Newport (Salop) Justices ex parte Wright [1929] 2 KB 416.

R v Northamptonshire County Council ex parte Gray (1986) *The Times*, 10 June.

R v Oxfordshire Education Authority ex parte W (1986) *The Times*, 12 Nov.

R v Rahman (1985) *The Times*, 5 June.

R v Royal Borough of Kingston upon Thames ex parte Kingwell (1991) *The Times* 6 June (DC).

R v Secretary of State for Education and Science ex parte Avon County Council [1990] 88 LGR 716 QBD.

R v Secretary of State for Education and Science ex parte Avon County Council (No. 2) (1990) 88 LGR 737 (CA).

R v Secretary of State for Education and Science ex parte Birmingham City Council (1985) 83 LGR 79.

R v Secretary of State for Education and Science ex parte Chance (1982) 26 July (unreported).

R v Secretary of State for Education and Science ex parte Collins (1983) 20 June (unreported).

R v Secretary of State for Education and Science ex parte E (a minor) 1991, *The Independent* 24 January (DC); *The Times* 9 May (CA).

R v Secretary of State for Education and Science ex parte Keating (1986) 84 LGR 469; (1985) *The Times*, 3 Dec.

R v Secretary of State for Education and Science ex parte Lashford (1988) 1 FLR 72.

R v Secretary of State for Education and Science ex parte Talmud Torah Machzichei Hadass School Trust (1985) *The Times*, 12 April.

R v Secretary of State for the Environment ex parte Ward [1984] 2 All ER 556.

R v Secretary of State for Wales ex parte Hawkins (1982) 28 May (unreported).

R v Secretary of State for Wales ex parte Russell (1983) 28 June (unreported).

R v South Glamorgan Appeals Committee ex parte Evans (1984) 10 May, Lexis CO/197/84.

R v Surrey County Council ex parte H (1985) 83 LGR 219.

R v Tameside Metropolitan Borough Council ex parte Governors of Audenshaw H.S. *The Times*, 27 June (DC).

R v Trustee of the Roman Catholic Diocese of Westminster ex parte Andrews (1989) *The Times* 18 Aug. (CA); *sub nom* Mars (1987) 86 LGR 507.

R v Warwickshire County Council ex parte Dill-Russell (1990) *The Times*, 5 July (DC) and 7 December (CA).

Reffell v Surrey County Council [1964] 1 All ER 743; 62 LGR 186.

Rich v London County Council [1953] 1 WLR 895.

Ricketts v Erith Borough Council (1943) 42 LGR 471.

Rogers v Essex County Council [1986] 3 All ER 321.

Royle v Trafford Borough Council (1984) IRLR 184.

S (A Minor) (Care Order: Education), Re [1977] 3 All ER 572.

Secretary of State for Education and Science v Tameside Metropolitan Borough Council [1977] AC 1014.

Shrimpton v Hertfordshire County Council (1911) 104 LT 145.

Sim v Rotherham Metropolitan Borough Council (1986) IRLR 391.

Simkiss v Rhondda Borough Council (1983) 81 LGR 460.

Smerkinich v Newport Corporation (1912) 76 JP 454.

Smith v ILEA [1978] 1 All ER 411.
Spiers v Warrington Corporation [1954] 1 QB 61.

Taylor v Kent County Council [1969] All ER 970.
Terrington v Lancashire County Council (1986) 26 June (unreported).
Tottenham Green Under Fives' Centre v Marshall (1989) IRLR 147.
Twine v Bean's Express Ltd [1946] 1 All ER 202.

Van Oppen v Clerk to the Bedford Charity Trustees [1989] 3 All ER 389 (CA); 1 All ER 273.

Ward v Hertfordshire County Council (1969) 114 *Sol. J* 87.
Warwick v UK (1986) A 9471/81.
Watt v Kesteven County Council [1955] 1 All ER 473.
West Bromich Building Society v Townsend (1983) ICR 257.
Western Excavating v Sharp (1978) IRLR 27.
Williams v Cardiff Corporation [1950] 1 All ER 250.
Williams v Eady (1893) 10 TLR 41.
Wilsher v Essex Area Health Authority [1988] 1 All ER 871 (HL); [1986] 3 All ER 801.
Woodward v Mayor of Hastings [1944] 2 All ER 505.
Wright v Cheshire County Council [1952] 2 All ER 789.
Wood v London Borough of Ealing (1967) Ch. 346.

BIBLIOGRAPHY

Adler M, *et al* 1989 *Parental Choice and Educational Policy* Edinburgh
University Press.
AMMA, 1985 *Confidence and Confidentiality* AMMA.
Anderson D, 1990 'An Islamic lesson for the school masters' *Sunday Times*
29 April 1990.
Audit Commission, 1989 *Losing an Empire, Finding a Role – the LEA of the
Future*, HMSO.
Bainham A, *Children, Parents and the State* Sweet and Maxwell.
Barrell G R and Partington J A, 1985 *Teachers and the Law* Methuen.
Beattie N, 1985 *Professional Parents* Falmer.
Becher T and Maclure S, 1978 *The Politics of Curriculum Change* Routledge
and Kegan Paul.
Berg I, 1980 'Absence from school and the law' in Hersov L and Berg I (eds)
Out of School Hodder and Stoughton.
Berg I, *et al* 1987 'School attendance, visits by EWOs and appearances in
juvenile court' *Educational Research* 29: 19–24.
Blanchard T, *et al* 1989 *Managing Finance in Schools* Cassell.
Blyth E and Milner J, 1988 'Non-attendance and the Law: The Confused Role
of the Social Services and Education Departments' in Reid K (ed)
Combating School Absenteeism Hodder and Stoughton.
Bowers J, 1990 *A Practical Approach to Employment Law* (3rd edn)
Financial Training.
Bradney A, 1989 'The Dewsbury Affair and the Education Reform Act 1988'
Education & the Law 1(2): 51–7.
Brazier M, 1988 *Street on Torts* (8th edn) Butterworths.
Brompton S, 1985 'Parents say ''yes'' to keeping the cane' *The Times* 27
February.
Brown D, 1988 'The attitudes of parents to education and the school
attendance of their children' in Reid K (ed) *Combating School
Absenteeism* Hodder and Stoughton.
Brown I, 1990 'Truancy, delinquency and the Leeds adjournment system'
Education & the Law 2(2): 47–53.
Buck T, 1985 'School admission appeals' *Journal of Social Welfare Law*
227–51.
Bull D, 1980 'School admissions: a new appeals procedure' *Journal of Social
Welfare Law* 209–33.
Bull D, 1985 'Monitoring education apeals: local ombudsmen lead the way'
Journal of Social Welfare Law: 189–226.
Cane P, 1981 'Ultra vires breach of statutory duty' *Public Law* 11–18.
Clune W H, 1986 'The deregulation critique of the federal role in education'
in Kirp D L and Jensen D N (eds) *School days, Rule Days* Falmer.

Commission for Racial Equality, 1983 *Secondary School Allocations in Reading. Report of a Formal Investigation* Commission for Racial Equality.

Commission for Racial Equality, 1985 *Birmingham Local Education Authority and Schools' Referral and Suspension of Pupils, Report of a Formal Investigation* Commission for Racial Equality.

Commission for Racial Equality, 1989 *Code of Practice for the Elimination of Racial Discrimination in Education* Commission for Racial Equality.

Coopers and Lybrand Associates, 1987 *Local Management of Schools: Report to the DES* Coopers and Lybrand.

Cumper P, 1989 'Muslims knocking at the classroom door' *New Law Journal* 139: 1067–71.

Cumper P, 1990 'Muslim schools: the implications of the Education Reform Act 1988' *New Community* 16(3): 379–89.

Dent H C, 1944 *The New Education Bill* University of London Press.

Dent H C, 1969 *The Education Act 1944*, University of London Press.

Department of Health, 1989 *An Introduction to the Children Act 1989* HMSO.

DES, 1984 *Parental Influence at School* Cmnd 9242 HMSO.

DES, 1985 *Better Schools* Cmnd 9469 HMSO.

DES, 1986 Circular 8/86 *The Education (No 2) Act 1986* DES.

DES, 1987 Circular 7/87 *The Education (No 2) Act 1986: Further Guidance* DES.

DES, 1987, Circular 11/87 *Sex Education at School* DES.

DES, 1987 *Grant-maintained Schools* (consultation paper), DES.

DES, 1988 Circular 7/88 *Education Reform act: Local Management of Schools* DES.

DES, 1988 Circular 10/88 *Education Reform Act 1988: Grant-maintained Schools* DES.

DES, 1988 Circular 11/88 *Admission of Pupils to County and Voluntary Schools* DES.

DES, 1989 *Amendments to the Education (School Government) Regulations 1987* (consultation document) DES.

DES, 1989 Circular 1/89 *Education Reform Act 1988: Local Arrangements for the Consideration of Complaints* DES.

DES, 1989 Circular 2/89 *Charges for School Activities* DES.

DES, Circular 3/89 *The Education Reform Act 1988: Religious Education and Collective worship* DES.

DES, 1989 Circular 17/89 *The Education (School Records) Regulations 1989* DES.

DES, 1989 Circular 18/89 *The Education (Teachers) Regulations 1989* DES.

DES, 1989 Circular 20/89 *Local Authority Training Grants Scheme: Financial Year 1990–91.*

DES, 1989 Circular 22/89 *Assessments and Statements of Special Educational Needs: Procedures within the Education, Health and Social Services* DES.

DES, 1989 *National Curriculum. From Policy to Practice*, HMSO.

DES, 1989 *The National Curriculum: Temporary Exceptions for Individual Pupils* (Draft Circular) DES.

DES, 1989 *Press Release 75/89* 13 March.

DES, 1990 *Press release 141/90* 2 May.

DES, 1990 *Teachers' Pay and Conditions Document* HMSO.

DES/Secretary of State for Education & Science 1987 *Admission of Pupils to Maintained Schools* (Consultation Paper) DES.

DES/Welsh Office, 1979 *Local Authority Arrangements for the School Curriculum* HMSO.

DES/Welsh Office, 1987 *The National Curriculum 5–16, a Consultation Document* DES.

Edis F and Brabazon E, 1982 'Inequality before the law' *New Statesman* 10 Dec.

Elliott J, 1982 'How do parents choose and judge secondary schools?' in McCormick R (ed) *Calling Education into Account* Heinemann.

Elton Lord, 1989 *Discipline in Schools. Report of the committee of enquiry chaired by Lord Elton* HMSO.

Equal Opportunities Commission, 1988 *Formal Investigation Report West Glamorgan Schools* Equal Opportunities Commission.

Felstenstein, 1988 'Strategies for improving school attendance in Reid K (ed) *Combating School Absenteeism* Hodder and Stoughton.

Frankel M and Wilson D, 1985 '*I want to know what's in my file*' Campaign for Freedom of Information.

Fredman S and Morris G, 1990 'The State as Employer: Is it Unique? *Industrial Law Journal* 19: 148–50.

Freeman M D A, 1980 'Children's education and the law' *Legal Action group Bulletin* 62.

Galloway D, 1985 *Schools and Persistent Absentees* Pergamon.

Garrett R M, 1985 'Disparaties and constraints in Peruvian education' in Brock C and Lawlor H (eds) *Education in Latin America* Croom Helm .

Goacher B, *et al* 1986 *Policy and Provision for Special Educational Needs* Cassell.

Grenville M P, 1988 'Compulsory school attendance and the child's wishes' *Journal of Social Welfare Law* 4–20.

Grenville M P, 1988 'School attendance: supervision by the courts' *Family Law* 18: 488–92.

Grenville M P, 1989 'Police truancy patrols' *Education the Law* 1(2): 65–7.

Grenville M P, 1989 'Sickness and compulsory school attendance' *Education & the Law* 1(3): 113–7.

Gray J and Clough E, 1984 *Choices at 16, a Survey: Summary of Results* University of Sheffield.

Gray J, *et al* 1983 *Reconstructions of Secondary Education* Falmer.

Griffith J, 1990 'The Education Reform Act: abolishing the independent status of the universities' *Education & the Law* 2: 97–108.

Hannon V, 1982 'The Education Act 1981: New rights and duties in special education' *Journal of Social Welfare Law* 275–84.

Harris N S, 1990 'Education By Right?: breach of the duty to provide ''sufficient'' schools' *Modern Law Review* 53: 387–98.

Hill D, 1974 *Democratic Theory and Local Government* Allen & Unwin.

Hirst P H and Peters R S, *The Logic of Education* Routledge and Kegan Paul.

H.M. Government, 1982 *Initial Government Observations on the Second Report from the Education, Science and the Arts Committee, Session 1981–82* Cmnd 8551 HMSO.

HMI, 1987 *Education Observed 5: Good Behaviour and Discipline in Schools* DES.

HMI, 1988 *Secondary Schools. An appraisal by HMI*, HMSO.

HMI, 1989 *Education Observed 13* HMSO.

HMI, 1990 *Special Needs Issues* HMSO.

HMI, 1990 *Survey of Work in Physical Education in 16 Secondary Schools* DES.

HMI (Wales), 1985 *Attendance and Achievement in Secondary Schools* Welsh Office.

Hoggett B, 1987 *Parents and Children: The Law of Parental Responsibility* 3rd ed Sweet and Maxwell.

House of Commons Education, Science and the Arts Committee, 1981 *Second Report 1981–82, The Secondary School Curriculum and Examinations,* HC 116–1, HMSO.

House of Commons Education, Science and the Arts Committee, 1987 *Session 1986–87, Third report Special Educational Needs: Implementation of the Education Act 1981* vol 1 HC 201–1 HMSO.

Hullin R P, *et al* 1987 'Truancy: legal solutions' *Family Law* 17: 324–6.

Hunter J, 1991 'Which School? A study of parental choice of secondary school', *Educational Research* 33(1): 22–30.

Jeffs T, 1986 'Children's rights at school' in Franklin B (ed) *The Rights of Children* Blackwell.

Lawton D, 1980 *The Politics of the School Curriculum* Routledge and Kegan Paul.

Leonard M, 1988 *The 1988 Education Act: A Tactical Guide for Schools* Blackwell Education.

Maclure S, 1988 *Education Re-formed* Hodder and Stoughton.

Macnair M R T, 1989 'Homosexuality in schools – Section 28 Local Government Act 1988' *Education & the Law* 1: 35–9.

McDonald I, 1989 *Murder in the Playground* Manchester City Council.

McManus M, 1989 *Troublesome Behaviour in the Classroom* Routledge.

Marson P, 1980 'Parental Choice in State Education' *Journal of Social Welfare Law* 193–208.

Meredith P, 1982 'Individual challenge to expenditure cuts in the provision of schools' *Journal of Social Welfare Law* 344–51.

Meredith P, 1984 'Falling rolls and the reorganisation of schools', *Journal of Social Welfare Law* 208–21.

Meredith P, 1989 'Educational Reform', *Modern Law Review* 52: 215–31.

Meredith P, 1989 'The Education Reform Act 1988 – Grant- maintained schools' *Education and the Law* 1(3) 95–103.

Miers D R and Page A C, 1982 *Legislation,* Butterworths.

Milman D, 1986 *Education Conflict and the Law* Routledge and Kegan Paul.

Milman D, 1987 'The Education Act 1981 in the Courts' *Journal of Social Welfare Law* 208–15.

Milman D and de Gama K, 1989 'Sexual discrimination in education: one step forwards, two steps back?' *Journal of Social Welfare Law* 4–22.

Muckle J, 1988 *A Guide to the Soviet Curriculum* Croom Helm.

Orr P, 1985 'Sex bias in schools: national perspectives' in Whyte J (ed) *Girl Friendly Schooling* Methuen.

Pack D C, 1977 *Truancy and Indiscipline in Schools in Scotland. Report of the Committee Chaired by D C Pack* HMSO.

Pannick D, 1985 *Sex Discrimination Law* Oxford University Press.

Partington J and Wragg T, 1989 *Schools and Parents* Cassell.

Peters R S, 1972 *Ethics and Education* George Allen & Unwin.

Plaskow M, 1985 'A long view from the inside' in Plaskow M (ed) *Life and Death of the Schools Council* Falmer.

Plowden Lady, 1967 *Children and their Primary Schools* vol 1 HMSO.

Pogany I, 1982 'Education: the Rights of Children and Parents under the European Convention on Human Rights' *New Law Journal* 132: 344–7.

Poole K, 1987 *Education Law*, Sweet and Maxwell.

Poulter S, 1986 *English Law and Ethnic Minority Customs* Butterworths.

Poulter S, 1990 'The religious education provisions of the Education Reform Act' *Education & the Law* 2(1): 1–11.

Poyner B and Warne C, 1988 *Preventing Violence to Staff* HMSO.

Pratt J and Grimshaw R, 1985 'An aspect of welfare justice: truancy and the juvenile court' *Journal of Social Welfare Law* 257–73.

Pratt J and Grimshaw R, 1985 'Restructuring a Juvenile Justice Pre-Court Tribunal' *Journal of Social Welfare Law* 4–15.

Pratt J and Grimshaw R, 1988 'Truancy: a case to answer?' in Reid K (ed) *Combating School Absenteeism* Hodder and Stoughton.

Reid K, 1985 *Truancy and School Absenteeism* Hodder and Stoughton.

Reid K, 1986 *Disaffection from School* Methuen.

Reid K, 1988 'Combating school absenteeism: main conclusions' in Reid K (ed) *Combating School Absenteeism* Hodder and Stoughton.

Reid K, 1988 'The Education Welfare Service – some issues and suggestions' in Reid K (ed) *Combating School Absenteeism* Hodder and Stoughton.

Richardson A, 1983 *Participation* Routledge and Kegan Paul.

Rosenbaum M, 1989 'The Children's Legal Centre: evidence to the Elton Committee' in Jones N (ed) *School Management and Pupil Behaviour* Falmer.

Ruddick J and Wood T, 1990 'In search of the Holy Grail – an alternative view' *Education & the Law* 2(1): 13–16.

Rutter M, *et al* 1979 *Fifteen Thousand Hours: Secondary Schools and their Effects on Children* Open Books.

Salter B and Tapper T, 1981 *Education, Politics and the State* Grant McIntyre.

Scutter A K, 1978 'Schoolteachers' position as to corporal punishment – 1' *Solicitors' Journal* 122: 671–3.

SEAC 1989 *Recorder* No 2 (Summer) SEAC.

Smith I T and Wood Sir J, 1990 *Industrial Law* (4th edn) Butterworths.

Solity J and Raybould E, 1988 *A Teacher's Guide to Special Educational Needs. A positive response to the 1981 Education Act* Open University Press.

St John Brooks C, 1982 'Parental choice: con or compromise?' *New Society* 26 August.

Stein P, 1982 *Legal Institutions and Dispute Resolution*, Butterworths.

Sutherland M, 1988 *Theory of Education* Longman.

Swann Committee (The), 1985 *Education for All: The Report of the Committee of Inquiry into the Education of Children from Ethnic Minority Groups* Cmnd 9453 HMSO.

Tattum D P and Lane D A (eds), 1989 *Bullying in Schools* Trentham Books.

Taylor G and Sauders J B, 1976 *The Law of Education* 8th ed Butterworths.

Taylor W, 1981 'Contraction in context', in Simon B and Taylor W (eds) *Education in the Eighties* Batsford.

Taylor W H, 1990 'Multicultural education in the "white highlands" after the 1988 Education Reform Act' *New Community* 16(3): 369–78.

Taylor Committee, 1977 *A New Partnership for our Schools*, HMSO.

Troyna B, 1990 'Reform or deform? The 1988 Education Reform Act and racial equality in Britain' *New Community* 16(3): 403–16.

Tweedie J, 1986 'Rights in Social Programmes: The Case of Parental Choice of School' *Public Law* 407–36.

Wade H W R, 1980 *Constitutional Fundamentals*, Stevens.

Wedderburn Lord, 1989 *The Worker and the Law* (3rd edn) Penguin.

Welton J and Evans J, 1986 'The development and implementation of special education policy: where did the 1981 Act fit in?' *Public Administration* 64: 209–27.

West A and Varlaam A, 1991 'Choosing a secondary school', *Educational Research* 33(1): 31–41.

Whalley G.E, 1989 'A critical view of the Education Act 1981' *Education & the Law* 1(2): 47–9.

Wilson H and Herbert G W, 1978 *Parents and Children in the Inner City* Routledge and Kegan Paul.

Wingham G, 1989 'Tackling school dropouts in the Big Apple' *Social Work Today* 7 Dec.

Wolfendale S, 1983 *Parents' Participation in Children's Development and Education* Gordon and Breach.

Wringe C, 1981 *Children's Rights: A Philosophical Study*, Routledge & Kegan Paul.

Younger Committee (The), 1972 *Report of the Committee on Privacy* HMSO.

Yudof M G, *et al* 1982 *Educational Policy and the Law* (2nd ed) McCutchan.

Zander M, 1989 *The Law-Making Process*, 3rd ed, Weidenfeld and Nicolson.

INDEX

accidents at school, *see* negligence *and* pupils, care of
Acts of Parliament, as source of regulation, 6–7, 8
admission(s) to school, 64–72
  admissions policy, 66–7
  appeals and, 65–6
  'choice' in, 64–9
  discrimination in, 70–2
  governors' meeting considering, 55
  information and school prospectus, 106
  limits on, 62–3
  'open' enrolment, 67–9
  'standard number', 68–9
aggregated schools budget, *see* local management of schools
AMMA (Assistant Masters and Mistresses Association), 96
anti-discrimination, *see* discrimination
appeals, concerning
  admission to school, 65–6
  discipline of pupil, 149
  pupil record, 98
  pupil with special educational needs, 86–7
appointment of teachers, *see* Teachers as employees
articles of government, 43–4, 208
assisted places scheme, 32–3
attendance at school, 72–81
  alternative to, 74
  enforcement of, 75

'basic' curriculum, 120
Beechen Cliff School, 36
behaviour, by pupils, 141–2
Better Schools (White Paper), 45, 80, 112, 131
Blackstone, Sir William, 61

Buck, T., 66
budget share, *see* LMS
buildings, repair and maintenance of, 51–3
Burnham Committee, 179

care proceedings, 76–7
changes to schools, *see* closure of school *and* school changes
charging for education, 5, 116, 132–4
chief education officer, 19, 181
Children's Legal Centre, 140, 148
children's rights, 60–3
choice of school, *see* admissions to school
circulars (DES), definition of, 11–15
city colleges for the technology of the arts, 31–2
city technology colleges, 31–2, 55
civil courts/proceedings, 11
closure of school, 35–6
collective worship, 2, 72, 122–3
commencement order, definition of, 8
Commission for Racial Equality, 72, 124, 126, 151, 189
complaints about curriculum, 4, 116
'common law', 10
comprehensive schools, 24, 36
compulsory school age, 74
computerised data, 99
confidentiality, 54, 94–6, 106, *see also* records
confiscation by teacher, 144
contingency fund, 51
Coopers and Lybrand Report (on LMS), 52
corporal punishment, 145, 146–7
county school, definition of, 24
criminal courts, 15–16

obiter dicta, 9
Occupier's Liability Act 1957,
   169–70
'optional extras', charging for, 133
outings
   charges for, 133–4
   safety in respect of, 168–9

Pack Committee, 75
parental rights and responsibility, 3,
   35, 38, 60–87
   parents' charter', 64
   religious education and collective
      worship, 4, 121
   school attendance, 72–81
   special educational needs, 81–7
Parliamentary Commissioner for
   Administration, 15
Parliamentary sovereignty, 6
Patten, Chris, 50
peace studies, 120
Peru, 118
Peters, R.S., 140
Plaskow, M., 110–11
Plowden Report, 44, 64
political issues, see curriculum
   (school)
Poundswick dispute, 149
premises, see school premises
primary education
   definition of, 22
   duty of LEA to provide, see local
      education authority
private members' bills, 6
probationary period of teacher, 3,
   188
Professional Association of
   Teachers, 139
punishment, 142–50, see also
   confiscation; corporal
   punishment; detention;
   exclusion from school;
   expulsion from school
   authority to punish, 142–5
   sanctions, 145–50
pupils, care of, 158–74, see also
   Health and Safety at Work etc
   Act; negligence; school premises

qualifications,
   approved, 116
   the curriculum, and, 123–6

qualified teacher status, 184–8

race, see admission to school:
   discrimination in; curriculum:
   racial harassment
racial harassment, 141
ratio decidendi, 9
records
   access, 101–4
   by councillor, 103–4
   by ombudsman, 104
   effect of, 101–2
   confidentiality, and, 102–3
   libel, 102
   pupils' progress, of, 5, 116
redundancy, see teachers as
   employees
Reid, K, 76, 77
religious education, 1, 72,
   120–2
repairs, see buildings

S.A.C.R.Es (statutory advisory
   committees on religious
   education), 123, 136 n55
school(s)
   changes to, 33–6
      approval of, 34–5
      challenges in the courts, 35–6
      character of, 34
      consultation and, 34
      discontinuance of school, 35–6
      objections to, 34–5
   single sex, 10, 14, 70–1
      see also county school; local
         education authority;
         voluntary controlled school;
         voluntary aided school
school attendance order, 76
school day, 47
school premises
   approval of, 35
   disabled persons, and, 174
   liability in respect of injury caused
      by, 169–74
   standards for, 172–4
School Examinations and
   Assessment Council (SEAC),
   115, 116
Schools Council, The, 110
secondary education
   definition of, 22